TRAVEL GUIDE
Formerly Mobil Travel Guide

SOUTHERN DISCARD
GREAT LAKES

2011

ACKNOWLEDGMENTS

We gratefully acknowledge the help of our representatives for their efficient and perceptive inspections of the lodgings listed. Forbes Travel Guide is also grateful to the talented writers who contributed to this book.

Front Cover image: ©iStockphoto.com
All maps: Mapping Specialists

ISBN: 9781936010943
Manufactured in the USA
10 9 8 7 6 5 4 3 2 1

CONTENTS

STAR ATTRACTIONS

If you've been a reader of Mobil Travel Guide, you will have heard that this historic brand partnered in 2009 with another storied media name, Forbes, to create a new entity, Forbes Travel Guide. For more than 50 years, Mobil Travel Guide assisted travelers in making smart decisions about where to stay and dine when traveling. With this new partnership, our mission has not changed: We're committed to the same rigorous inspections of hotels, restaurants and spas—the most comprehensive in the industry with more than 500 standards tested at each property we visit—to help you cut through the clutter and make easy and informed decisions on where to spend your time and travel budget. Our team of anonymous inspectors are constantly on the road, sleeping in hotels, eating in restaurants and making spa appointments, evaluating those exacting standards to determine a property's rating.

What kinds of standards are we looking for when we visit a property? We're looking for more than just high-thread count sheets, pristine spa treatment rooms and white linen-topped tables. We look for service that's attentive, individualized and unforgettable. We note how long it takes to be greeted when you sit down at your table, or to be served when you order room service, or whether the hotel staff can confidently help you when you've forgotten that one essential item that will make or break your trip. Unlike any other travel ratings entity, we visit each place we rate, testing hundreds of attributes to compile our ratings, and our ratings cannot be bought or influenced. The Forbes Five Star rating is the most prestigious achievement in hospitality—while we rate more than 5,000 properties in the U.S., Canada, Hong Kong, Macau and Beijing, for 2011, we have awarded Five Star designations to only 54 hotels, 23 restaurants and 20 spas. When you travel with Forbes, you can travel with confidence, knowing that you'll get the very best experience, no matter who you are.

We understand the importance of making the most of your time. That's why the most trusted name in travel is now Forbes Travel Guide.

STAR RATED HOTELS

Whether you're looking for the ultimate in luxury or the best value for your travel budget, we have a hotel recommendation for you. To help you pinpoint properties that meet your needs, Forbes Travel Guide classifies each lodging by type according to the following characteristics:

★★★★★These exceptional properties provide a memorable experience through virtually flawless service and the finest of amenities. Staff are intuitive, engaging and passionate, and eagerly deliver service above and beyond the guests' expectations. The hotel was designed with the guest's comfort in mind, with particular attention paid to craftsmanship and quality of product. A Five-Star property is a destination unto itself.

★★★★These properties provide a distinctive setting, and a guest will find many interesting and inviting elements to enjoy throughout the property. Attention to detail is prominent throughout the property, from design concept to quality of products provided. Staff are accommodating and take pride in catering to the guest's specific needs throughout their stay.

★★★These well-appointed establishments have enhanced amenities that provide travelers with a strong sense of location, whether for style or function. They may have a distinguishing style and ambience in both the public spaces and guest rooms; or they may be more focused on functionality, providing guests with easy access to local events, meetings or tourism highlights.

Recommended: These hotels are considered clean, comfortable and reliable establishments that have expanded amenities, such as full-service restaurants.

For every property, we also provide pricing information. All prices quoted are accurate at the time of publication; however, prices cannot be guaranteed. Because rates can fluctuate, we list a pricing range rather than specific prices.

STAR RATED RESTAURANTS

Every restaurant in this book has been visited by Forbes Travel Guide's team of experts and comes highly recommended as an outstanding dining experience.

★★★★★Forbes Five-Star restaurants deliver a truly unique and distinctive dining experience. A Five-Star restaurant consistently provides exceptional food, superlative service and elegant décor. An emphasis is placed on originality and personalized, attentive and discreet service. Every detail that surrounds the experience is attended to by a warm and gracious dining room team.

★★★★These are exciting restaurants with often well-known chefs that feature creative and complex foods and emphasize various culinary techniques and a focus on seasonality. A highly-trained dining room staff provides refined personal service and attention.

★★★Three Star restaurants offer skillfully prepared food with a focus on a specific style or cuisine. The dining room staff provides warm and professional service in a comfortable atmosphere. The décor is well-coordinated with quality fixtures and decorative items, and promotes a comfortable ambience.

Recommended: These restaurants serve fresh food in a clean setting with efficient service. Value is considered in this category, as is family friendliness.

Because menu prices can fluctuate, we list a pricing range rather than specific prices. The pricing ranges are per diner, and assume that you order an appetizer or dessert, an entrée and one drink.

STAR RATED SPAS

Forbes Travel Guide's spa ratings are based on objective evalua-
tions of more than 450 attributes. About half of these criteria assess
basic expectations, such as staff courtesy, the technical proficien-
cy and skill of the employees and whether the facility is clean and
maintained properly. Several standards address issues that impact
a guest's physical comfort and convenience, as well as the staff's
ability to impart a sense of personalized service. Additional criteria
measure the spa's ability to create a completely calming ambience.

★★★★★Stepping foot in a Five Star Spa will result in an exceptional
experience with no detail overlooked. These properties wow their
guests with extraordinary design and facilities, and uncompro-
mising service. Expert staff cater to your every whim and pamper you with the most advanced treatments and skin care lines
available. These spas often offer exclusive treatments and may
emphasize local elements.

★★★★Four Star spas provide a wonderful experience in an inviting and serene environment. A sense of personalized service is
evident from the moment you check in and receive your robe and
slippers. The guest's comfort is always of utmost concern to the
well-trained staff.

★★★These spas offer well-appointed facilities with a full complement of staff to ensure that guests' needs are met. The spa
facil ties include clean and appealing treatment rooms, changing
areas and a welcoming reception desk.

TOP HOTELS, RESTAURANTS AND SPAS

HOTELS

★★★★★FIVE STAR
Four Seasons Hotel Chicago (*Chicago, Illinois*)
The Peninsula Chicago (*Chicago, Illinois*)

★★★★FOUR STAR
The Cincinnatian Hotel (*Cincinnati, Ohio*)
Elysian Hotel (*Chicago, Illinois*)
The Ritz-Carlton Chicago, A Four Seasons Hotel (*Chicago, Illinois*)
Trump International Hotel and Tower Chicago (*Chicago, Illinois*)

RESTAURANTS

★★★★★FIVE STAR
Alinea (*Chicago, Illinois*)
Charlie Trotter's (*Chicago, Illinois*)

★★★★FOUR STAR
Avenues (*Chicago, Illinois*)
Everest (*Chicago, Illinois*)
L2O (*Chicago, Illinois*)
Les Nomades (*Chicago, Illinois*)
Seasons (*Chicago, Illinois*)
Sixteen (*Chicago, Illinois*)
Tru (*Chicago, Illinois*)

SPAS

★★★★FOUR STAR
Elysian Spa & Health Club (*Chicago, Illinois*)
The Peninsula Spa by ESPA (*Chicago, Illinois*)
The Spa at Four Seasons Hotel Chicago (*Chicago, Illinois*)
The Spa at Trump (*Chicago, Illinois*)

YOUR QUESTIONS ANSWERED

WHAT ARE THE TOP CHICAGO EXPERIENCES?

If you enjoy the great outdoors, there's nothing like summer in Chicago. The season ignites three months of celebration, during which Chicagoans cram in every outdoor activity possible before they have to hibernate again for the winter. The city's many street festivals are alfresco shindigs held every weekend, celebrating everything from folk music (Chicago Folk and Roots Festival at Welles Park) to local eats at the massive Taste of Chicago. The hot weather also ushers in another only-in-Chicago experience: Lollapalooza. The three-day music extravaganza brings big-name acts such as Radiohead and hometown heroes Wilco to Grant Park and, of course, fans from all over the country follow them.

For a real taste of Chicago in the summer, head to Green City Market, the city's only sustainable market, where you can shop alongside the area's top chefs for the freshest-of-the-fresh fruit and vegetables.

A short trek from downtown to Wrigleyville is a small distance to go for a bit of history—a visit to Wrigley Field. The home of the Chicago Cubs baseball team was built in the early 1900s, and it remains one of the city's most beloved landmarks; possibly more beloved than the ill-fated Cubbies themselves, who haven't won a single World Series in 100 years and counting. Win or lose, games at Wrigley are a cherished part of Chicago summers, and it's not hard to see why: It's a thrill to sit with the loyal Cubs bleacher bums, chow down on a ballpark dog and watch Derrek Lee hit one out of the park. A huge highlight is seeing which celebrity guest will pop in to sing Take Me Out to the Ball Game—it could be anyone from Bill Murray to Vince Vaughn stepping up to the mic. Can't get tickets? Head to Wrigley anyway and watch the game from one of the watering holes surrounding the park; the neighborhood setting is half the fun.

When day turns into night, the city just gets hotter. One place in particular that heats up is the area in the Gold Coast where Division, Rush and State streets come together. Here, a mix of locals and tourists crowd the pricey restaurants, bars or clubs. Another nightlife hub that's growing in popularity is the six-corner intersection in Wicker Park where Milwaukee, North and Damen avenues meet. All sorts of party people roam the neighborhood, ducking into clubs, music venues and hotter-by-the-minute restaurants.

Ready-for-primetime comedy is a Chicago legacy. The Second City and iO Chicago have turned out some of the best jokesters around, including Tina Fey and Steve Carell. At Second City, you'll get top-notch topical sketch shows, while iO will give you laugh-out-loud improv, an art form invented in Chicago.

YOUR QUESTIONS ANSWERED

WHAT IS THERE TO SEE AT THE INDIANA DUNES?

Located 50 miles east of Chicago in Northwest Indiana, **Indiana Dunes State Park** *(1100 N. Mineral Springs Road, Indiana, 219-926- 7561; www.nps.gov/indu)* offers great hiking as well as year-round activities, from swimming and dune climbing in the summer to cross-country skiing and snowshoeing in the winter.

Your first stop should be at the recently built **Dorothy Buell Memorial Visitor Center** *(U.S. Highway 20 and Indiana Route 49, Porter, Indiana, 219-926-7561)*, where you'll receive an overview of the woodlands and beach areas, as well as directions to good picnic spots. Begin the day with a romp through the deep sands of the dunes, then settle down for a picnic lunch along the three-mile beach, West Beach, where the Chicago skyline is visible from the shore on a clear day. Hiking the huge desertlike sand dunes is the reason to come here; the largest is Mount Baldy, whose 126-foot climb is a challenge. Don't be surprised if, like the poet Carl Sandburg, who often visited the dunes, you find bliss in the park's quiet, punctuated by the calls and songs of its more than 350 bird species. There's much to do nearby, too. The historic **Chellberg Farm** *(U.S. Highway 20 and Mineral Springs Road, Porter, Indiana)* and home shows what farm life was like back in the 1880s for the Chellbergs, an immigrant Swedish family who lived in the area. For something a little more 21st century, there's always one of the nearby riverboat casinos, the most-well known of which (thanks to its ubiquitous road-side signs) is Hammond's. **Horseshoe Casino** *(777 Casino Center Drive, Hammond, Indiana, 866-711-7463; www.horseshoehammond.com)*, whose size more than doubled after a 2008 renovation.

WHERE CAN YOU SEE FRANK LLOYD WRIGHT'S ARCHITECTURE?

Oak Park, a suburb of Chicago, is best known for having the highest concentration of homes and buildings designed and built by Frank Lloyd Wright, the preeminent American architect whose streamlined style took on the once-prominent and ornate Victorian standard. Bibliophiles also head to Oak Park to see the birthplace of Ernest Hemingway and the local museum dedicated to his life and work.

If you happen to be driving there, slow down on Chicago Avenue just east of Harlem Avenue—along the street, keep an eye out for houses numbered 1019, 1027 and 1031, all of which are Wright's not-so-exciting early works. They followed the Queen Anne-type designs that were popular before Wright created the style that would make him famous.

The **Frank Lloyd Wright Home and Studio** *(951 Chicago Ave., Oak Park, Illinois, 708-848-1976; www.wrightplus.org)* is a must-see for any fan of architecture. You won't be able to peruse the museum on your own; entry is available with a 60-minute guided tour only (just be sure to reserve a ticket online beforehand since tours often sell out). The home served as Wright's workplace and residence for the first 20 years of his career. It's not his best work—he changed it frequently for practical purposes and it has little of the grace of sites he developed nearby—but the home shows off the evolution of his style as it changed to meet the needs of his growing family. In this house and the adjoining studio, Wright and his associates invented the Prairie School of architecture, designing 125 buildings along the way, including the **Unity Temple of Oak Park** *(875 W. Lake St., Oak Park, Illinois, 708-383-8873)*, where as a congregant, Wright was asked to design a replacement for the previously burned-down church. The exterior of the building is cold and uninviting, but the interior is still exciting to see and maintains a contemporary feel more than a century after its design. Using simple angles and stained wood instead of paint, Wright managed to design a church that was both "democratic," as he set out to do, and magisterial, befitting its role as a place of worship. While you're here, be sure to check out Oakpark's other great attraction.

Very different in architectural style is the **Ernest Hemingway Birthplace** *(339 N. Oak Park Ave., Oak Park, Illinois, 708-848-2222; www.ehfop.org)*, a Victorian building refurbished to its turn-of-the-century style. The home contains some mementos from Hemingway's childhood and information about his birth and life here; understandably, it downplays the writer's characterization of Oak Park as a place of "wide lawns and narrow minds." A short walk away is the **Ernest Hemingway Museum** *(200 N. Oak Park Ave., Oak Park, Illinois, 708-524-5383)*, which has photos and Hemingway artifacts, including his childhood diary and earliest writing. The museum features a short documentary on his life and covers in detail his teenage years—good grist for parsing the psyche of this complicated man.

Beyond the Wright and Hemingway homes, there is much to do in Oak Park, which takes pride in its attention to the arts. Local art galleries show off some of the best works in the Chicagoland area. Check out **Ridge Art** *(21 Harrison St., Oak Park, Illinois, 708-848-4062; www.ridgeart.com)*, which carries unusual Haitian pieces. With tree-lined streets and amiable proprietors of charming cafés and bakeries—take a final pit-stop at **Petersen's** *(1100 Chicago Ave., Oak Park, Illinois, 708-386-6130, www.petersenicecream.com)*, for some lip-smacking old-fashioned ice cream sundaes—you'll find Oak Park a nice treat after your taste of Chicago.

WELCOME TO ILLINOIS

WHERE DO YOU START IN ILLINOIS? WITH AN URBAN ADVENTURE

beneath towering skyscrapers in Chicago? Or by ambling down the charming streets of the state's touristy towns? No matter which road you follow, you'll find an ideal getaway.

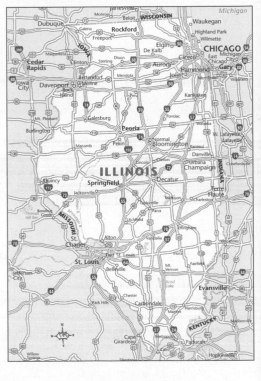

If you do start in Chicago, you'll be busy. With its famed architecture, legendary blues and jazz scenes and world-renowned museums like the Art Institute and the John G. Shedd Aquarium, Chicago is celebrated for its thriving cultural scene almost as much as its culinary classics: hot dogs and deep-dish pizzas.

When you're in Chicago, you'll want to experience the city like native Chicagoans do. That means catching a Cubs game at Wrigley Field, strolling Millennium Park, taking an architectural boat cruise on the Chicago River or twirling with the kids on Navy Pier's Ferris wheel.

If the only sights you're interested in seeing are designer labels, make Michigan Avenue your first stop. The mile-long stretch isn't named the "Magnificent Mile" for nothing. Highlighted by the seven-level Water Tower Place and big-name stores like Gucci, Chanel and Hugo Boss, the avenue is among the world's most cosmopolitan shopping districts. If you really feel like splurging, check out the high-end boutiques on Oak Street, just steps from Michigan Avenue.

Even die-hard urbanites need a break from the city. If you're starved for nature, take a breather at Utica's Starved Rock State Park, located an hour and a half southwest of Chicago. The park features sandstone canyons, gushing waterfalls and miles of hiking trails. Or stop at the 8,000-acre Pere Marquette

BEST ATTRACTIONS

ILLINOIS' BEST ATTRACTIONS

THE CAPITAL
Located near the geographical center of the state, Springfield was the home of Abraham Lincoln for a quarter of a century. Historical sites are plentiful—and interesting.

CHICAGO
The Windy City has much to offer, whether you're interested in museums, sports or shopping. Visitors are often surprised by the many beaches, too, which are sandwiched between the skyscrapers and Lake Michigan.

State Park—Illinois' largest—known for its 20-mile scenic bike trail and towering limestone cliffs.

For a more historic look at Illinois, take the family to Springfield and tip your hat to the 16th president at the Abraham Lincoln Presidential Library and Museum. Or drive toward the Illinois-Iowa border to Galena, an old lead-mining town known for its historic 19th century architecture, gorgeous vistas and boating trips down the Mississippi and Galena rivers.

CENTRAL ILLINOIS

Most visitors to Central Illinois find themselves in the capital. And really, Springfield has the most to offer. For moderate to serious history buffs, or families with children learning about our country's beginnings, you can't beat a trip to the home of Lincoln.

Of course, other areas of this region have their own strengths. Honest Abe was hardly the only famous guy from Central Illinois. You can learn the story of the Latter Day Saints at the Joseph Smith Historic Site in Nauvoo, or pay homage to Carl Sandburg in Galesburg, at the restored birthplace and cottage of this famous poet and author.

Champaign/Urbana is home to the University of Illinois, and you'll find Illinois State University in Bloomington-Normal. For lovers of the bard, the annual Illinois Shakespeare Festival is one not to miss.

WHAT TO SEE

BLOOMINGTON-NORMAL

MILLER PARK ZOO

1020 S. Morris, Bloomington, 309-434-2250; www.millerparkzoo.org

This zoo has big cats, river otters in natural settings, sea lions, a tropical rain forest and a children's zoo. Animal feeding is a daily attraction. Stroller rentals are available.

Admission: adults $5, seniors and children $3.50, children 3 and under free. Daily 9:30 a.m.-4:30 p.m.

CHAMPAIGN/URBANA

ORPHEUM CHILDREN'S SCIENCE MUSEUM

346 N. Neil St., Champaign, 217-352-5895; www.m-crossroads.org

Located in the historic Orpheum Theatre, this museum has hands-on exhibits for kids. Exhibits include Waterworks and Dino Dig, an excavation site for junior paleontologists in the outdoor courtyard.

Admission: adults $4, children $3. Tuesday- Friday 10 a.m.-4 p.m., Saturday-Sunday 1-5 p.m.

UNIVERSITY OF ILLINOIS

919 W. Illinois St., Champaign/Urbana, 217-333-4666; www.uiuc.edu

Founded in 1867, the University of Illinois has a student population of over 40,000 students. Included among 316 buildings on the main campus is the largest public university library in the United States. Also on the campus is the Krannert Art Museum, which has a collection of 9,000 works including European and American paintings and decorative arts, as well as Asian art and African art.

CHARLESTON

COLES COUNTY COURTHOUSE

651 Jackson Ave., Charleston, 217-348-0501

This courthouse sits on Charleston Square, where Lincoln practiced law in an earlier courthouse and where the Charleston Riot took place. The riot involved 300 men in armed conflict during the Civil War.

Monday-Friday 8:30 a.m.-4:30 p.m.

FOX RIDGE STATE PARK

18175 State Park Road, Charleston, 217-345-6416; www.dnr.state.il.us

This rugged area of 2,064 acres is known for its densely wooded ridges, lush valleys and scenic hiking trails. There are eight hiking trails and a 4-mile horse trail.

Daily dawn-dusk.

DECATUR

CHILDREN'S MUSEUM OF ILLINOIS

55 S. Country Club Road, Decatur, 217-423-5437; www.cmofil.com

Kids will enjoy the hands-on exhibits of arts, science and technology at this museum designed especially for children ages 3-12.

Admission: adults and children $2, children 2 and under free. Tuesday-Friday 9:30 a.m.-4:30 p.m., Saturday 10 a.m.-5 p.m., Sunday 1-5 p.m.

HIGHLIGHT

WHAT ARE THE TOP THINGS TO DO IN CENTRAL ILLINOIS?

DISCOVER WHY ILLINOIS IS THE LAND OF LINCOLN
Springfield overflows with sites honoring the 16th president of the United States. A visit here will help you uncover the man behind the tall hat.

SEE THE GREAT OUTDOORS
Parks are plentiful throughout Illinois, but Starved Rock State Park rates among the most well known and liked. Located in Utica, it offers glacial canyons, sandstone bluffs, unusual rock formations and forests.

MILLIKIN PLACE
Pine and Main streets, Decatur; www.millikin.edu
This housing development was laid out and landscaped in 1909 by Walter Burley Griffin, who designed Australia's capital, Canberra. The street features a Prairie school entrance, naturalized landscaping and houses by Marion Mahony, Griffin's wife, and Frank Lloyd Wright. Both Griffin and Mahony worked at Wright's famous Oak Park Studio. Numbers 1 and 3 Millikin Place are by Mahony; 2 Millikin Place is attributed to Wright.

ROCK SPRINGS CONSERVATION AREA AND NATURE CENTER
3939 Nearing Lane, Decatur, 217-423-7708; www.maconcountyconservation.org
This destination for nature lovers features approximately 1,320 acres, including a restored Illinois prairie, hiking and self-guided interpretive trails, a picnic area, a restored farmhouse and an asphalt bike trail. The nature center includes aquariums containing native Illinois fish and amphibians, as well as an ecocenter and a museum with hands-on educational exhibits.
Daily.

SCOVILL PARK AND ZOO
71 S. Country Club Road, Decatur, 217-421-7435; www.decatur-parks.org/zoo
The zoo has more than 500 animals, including alligators, camels and zebras—along with a carousel of "endangered species" (more than 30 colorful hand-carved animals) and a playground featuring a rock wall. For an additional fee, the Z.O. & O. Express train offers a 1-mile narrated tour through a tunnel and along Lake Decatur.
Admission: April-October, Monday-Friday 10 a.m.-5 p.m., Saturday-Sunday 10 a.m.-7 p.m.

SPECIAL EVENT

ILLINOIS SHAKESPEARE FESTIVAL

Ewing Manor, Normal, Emerson and Towanda streets, Bloomington 309-438-8974; www.thefestival.org
This annual festival includes Shakespearean performances preceded by Elizabethan-era music and entertainment. Performances began in 1978 in a cornfield and now take place in a state-of-the-art Elizabethan-style theater.
June-early August.

EUREKA
EUREKA COLLEGE
300 E. College Ave., Eureka, 309-467-6318, 888-438-7352; www.eureka.edu
One of the first coeducational colleges in the country, this school's most famous graduate is President Ronald Reagan. The grounds' Peace Garden honors his famous 1982 speech regarding the end of the Cold War.

GALESBURG
CARL SANDBURG STATE HISTORIC SITE
331 E. Third St., Galesburg, 309-342-2361; www.sandburg.org
The restored birthplace cottage of the famous poet and author is located here. Remembrance Rock, named for Sandburg's historical novel, is a granite boulder under which his ashes were placed.
Thursday-Sunday 9 a.m.-5 p.m.

LAKE STOREY RECREATION AREA
1033 S. Lake Storey Road, Galesburg, 309-345-3683; www.ci.galesburg.il.us
Centered around Lake Storey, this park offers boat rentals, as well as a 2.65 mile biking/hiking trail, an 18-hole golf course, tennis facilities, a picnic area, a playground, gardens, concessions and camping.
Daily dawn-dusk.

LERNA
LINCOLN LOG CABIN STATE HISTORIC SITE
402 S. Lincoln Highway Road, Lerna, 217-345-1845; www.lincolnlogcabin.org
This 86-acre site preserves the Thomas Lincoln Log Cabin, reconstructed on the original foundation that Abraham Lincoln's father built in 1840. A reconstructed farm surrounds the cabin. In nearby Shiloh Cemetery are the graves of Thomas Lincoln and Sarah Bush Lincoln, the president's father and stepmother. Volunteers portray those who lived in this area in 1845.
Hours vary by season.

MAHOMET
LAKE OF THE WOODS COUNTY PRESERVE
109 S. Lake of the Woods Road, Mahomet, 217-586-3360; www.ccfpd.org
This preserve offers swimming, boating rentals, fishing and golf. Be sure to

check out the lovely botanical gardens. The Early American Museum is also located here.

Daily, hours vary by season.

METAMORA

METAMORA COURTHOUSE STATE HISTORIC SITE

113 E. Partridge, Metamora, 309-367-4470; www.illinoishistory.gov

Built in 1845, this courthouse is one of two remaining courthouse structures on the old Eighth Judicial Circuit, in which Abraham Lincoln practiced law for 12 years. On the first floor is a museum containing a collection of pioneer artifacts; the second floor features the former courtroom, which is set up and furnished the way it would've been during the time period when Lincoln was practicing law.

Admission: free. March-October, Tuesday-Saturday 1-5 p.m.; November-February, Tuesday-Saturday noon-4 p.m.

NAUVOO

BAXTER'S VINEYARDS

2010 E. Parley St., Nauvoo, 217-453-2528, 800-854-1396; www.nauvoowinery.com

The family owned winery was established in 1857 and produces Old Nauvoo wines. Host tours and wine tastings are available.

January-March, Monday-Friday 9 a.m.-5 p.m., Saturday-Sunday noon-5 p.m.; April-December, Monday-Friday 9 a.m.-5 p.m., Saturday-Sunday 10 a.m.-5p.m.

JOSEPH SMITH HISTORIC SITE

865 Water St., Nauvoo, 217-453-2246; www.cofchrist.org/js

This site portrays the Latter Day Saint movement in Nauvoo during the early 1840s. Visitors can tour the Joseph Smith Homestead, an 1803 log cabin the prophet occupied after coming to Nauvoo in 1839 and the town's oldest structure, as well as the Smith's Mansion, a Federal-style frame house Smith lived in from 1843 to 1844. A 50-minute tour begins in the visitor center and includes a visit to Joseph Smith's grave.

Admission: varies by property. Hours vary by season.

OTTAWA

ILLINOIS WATERWAY VISITOR CENTER

950 N. 27th Road, Ottawa, 815-667-4054; www.byways.org

Located at the Starved Rock Lock and Dam, this site offers an excellent view across the river to Starved Rock. The history of the Illinois River from the time of the Native Americans, the French explorers, and the construction of canals to the modern Illinois Waterway is portrayed in a series of exhibits.

Admission: free. Daily dawn-dusk.

PEORIA

CORN STOCK THEATRE

Bradley Park, 1700 N. Park Road, Peoria, 800-220-1185; www.cornstocktheatre.com

Peoria's only outdoor community theater performs theater-in-the-round summer stock—dramas, comedies and musicals—under a circus-type big top. The winter season is held in the Theatre Center, also in Bradley Park.

See website for details.

PETTENGILL-MORRON MUSEUM

1212 W. Moss Ave., Peoria, 309-674-4745; www.peoriahistoricalsociety.org

An Italianate/Second Empire mansion built by Moses Pettengill, this house was purchased by Jean Morron in 1953 to replace her ancestral home, which was being destroyed to make way for a freeway. She moved a two-century accumulation of household furnishings and family heirlooms, as well as such architectural pieces as the old house's cast-iron fence, chandeliers, marble mantles and brass rails from the porch. Tours are available.

Saturday 1-3 p.m. and by appointment.

SPIRIT OF PEORIA

100 N.E. Water St., Peoria, 309-637-8000, 800-676-8988; www.spiritofpeoria.com

A replica turn-of-the-century stern-wheeler offers day and overnight cruises along the Illinois River.

See website for details.

WILDLIFE PRAIRIE STATE PARK

3826 N. Taylor Road, Peoria, 309-676-0998; www.wildlifeprairiestatepark.org

This wildlife and nature preserve features animals native to Illinois—bears, cougars, bobcats, wolves, red foxes and more—in natural habitats along wood-chipped trails. The pioneer homestead has a working farm from the late 1800s with an authentic log cabin and one-room schoolhouse.

Admission and hours vary by season.

QUINCY

JOHN WOOD MANSION

425 S. 12th St., Quincy, 217-222-1835; www.adamscohistory.org

This two-story, Greek Revival mansion was the home of the founder of Quincy and a former governor of Illinois. In about 1864, the house was cut in half and moved across a special bridge to its present location. Tours are available.

Admission: adults $3, students $1.50. April-October, Monday-Saturday 10 a.m.-2 p.m.

QUINCY MUSEUM

1601 Maine St., Quincy, 217-224-7669; www.thequincymuseum.com

Located in the Newcomb-Stillwell mansion, this museum is housed in a Richardson Romanesque-style building. Rotating exhibits and a dinosaur room are featured.

Admission: adults $4, children $2. Tuesday-Sunday 1-5 p.m.

SPRINGFIELD

ABRAHAM LINCOLN PRESIDENTIAL LIBRARY

112 N. Sixth St., Springfield, 217-558-8844, 800-610-2094; www.alplm.org

The Abraham Lincoln Presidential Library features the largest collection of books and historical materials on the state of Illinois. Visitors can also make an appointment to view the largest collection of Lincoln's personal items, including thousands of letters that both he and Mary Lincoln penned, family photos and a copy of the Gettysburg Address written by Lincoln himself.

Admission: free. Monday-Friday 9 a.m.-5 p.m.

ABRAHAM LINCOLN PRESIDENTIAL MUSEUM

212 N. Sixth St., Springfield, 217-782-5764, 800-610-2094; www.alplm.org

This presidential library offers a comprehensive look at the life of the Lincolns. The Treasures Gallery features many of the Lincolns' personal belongings, including family photos, White House china and possessions from Abraham Lincoln's childhood. Figures scattered around the museum depict life back then—the Blue Room shows Mary Lincoln being fitted for a ballgown—and make for great photo opportunities for the family. There's also a theater showing a film on the Lincoln, a kids' play area and lots more.

Admission: adults $12, seniors and students $9, military $7, children $6, children 5 and under free. Daily 9 a.m.-5 p.m.

DANA-THOMAS HOUSE STATE HISTORIC SITE

301 E. Lawrence Ave., Springfield, 217-782-6776; www.dana-thomas.org

Designed by Frank Lloyd Wright for Springfield socialite Susan Lawrence Dana, this house is the best preserved of the architect's Prairie period. The fully restored interior has more than 100 pieces of original furniture. The house was one of the largest and most elaborate of Wright's career.

Admission: adults $5, children $3, families $13. Wednesday-Sunday 9 a.m.-4 p.m.

EDWARDS PLACE

700 N. 4th St., Springfield, 217-523-2631; www.springfieldart.org

Built by Benjamin Edwards (brother of Ninian Edwards, an early Illinois governor married to Mary Todd Lincoln's older sister), this Italianate mansion was Springfield's social and political center in the years before the Civil War. Lincoln addressed the public from the front gallery. Tours begin at the top of each hour.

Admission: $3. Tuesday-Saturday 11 a.m.-2 p.m.

HENSON ROBINSON ZOO

1101 E. Lake Drive, Springfield, 217-753-6217; www.hensonrobinsonzoo.org

This 14-acre zoo is home to more than 300 animals native to Australia, Africa, Asia and North and South America. Over 90 native and exotic species are housed among naturalistic exhibits.

Admission: adults $4.50, seniors $3, children $2.75, children 2 and under free. April-October, Monday-Friday 10 a.m.-5 p.m., Saturday-Sunday 9 a.m.-6 p.m.; November-March, daily 10 a.m.-4 p.m.

LINCOLN HOME NATIONAL HISTORIC SITE

413 S. Eighth St., Springfield, 217-492-4241; www.nps.gov/liho

This 12-room, Greek Revival house is the only home Abraham Lincoln ever owned. He and Mary Lincoln purchased the house in 1844 and lived there until their February 1861 departure for Washington, D.C. It has been open to the public since 1887 and restored to its 1860 appearance.

Admission: free. Daily 8:30 a.m.-5 p.m.

LINCOLN MEMORIAL GARDEN AND NATURE CENTER

2301 E. Lake Drive, Springfield, 217-529-1111; www.lincolnmemorialgarden.org

This 100-acre garden of trees, shrubs and flowers native to Illinois is designed in a naturalistic style by landscape architect Jens Jensen. The landscape is similar to what Lincoln would have known growing up in the Midwest. There are 6 miles of trails, footbridges, a pond and wooden benches inscribed with Lincoln quotes.

Admission: free. Daily dawn-dusk.

LINCOLN TOMB STATE HISTORIC SITE

Oak Ridge Cemetery, 1441 Monument Ave., Springfield, 217-782-2717; www.Illinois.gov

Under a 117-foot granite obelisk, a belvedere—accessible via exterior staircases— offers views of a 10-foot statue of Lincoln and four heroic groupings representing Civil War armed forces. In the center of the domed burial chamber is a monumental sarcophagus. Mary Todd Lincoln and three of the four Lincoln sons are interred within the wall opposite.

Admission: free. Hours vary by season.

UTICA

MATTHIESSEN STATE PARK

Highways 71 and 178, Utica, 815-667-4868; www.dnr.state.il.us

This 1,938-acre park is particularly interesting for its geological formations, which can be explored via seven miles of hiking trails. The upper area and bluff tops are generally dry and easily hiked, but trails into the interiors of the two dells can be difficult, especially in spring and early summer. The dells feature scenic waterfalls.

Daily dawn-dusk.

STARVED ROCK STATE PARK

Highways 80 and 39, Utica, 800-868-7625; www.starvedrockstatepark.org

A local favorite for recreation and outdoor sports, Starved Rock State Park, located an hour and a half southwest of Chicago, has glacial canyons, sandstone bluffs, unusual rock formations and forests. The 2,630-acre park offers 18 canyons and 13 miles of well-marked hiking trails, fishing and boating along the Illinois River, equestrian trails, picnicking and camping. The park has a refurbished lodge with a hotel wing with 72 rooms, an indoor pool with spa and sauna, and a restaurant; 22 cabins are also available. Though it's open year-round, a prime time to visit is early spring, when waterfalls form at canyons and create a glittering natural spectacle. Another great time to visit is during the cold month of January, when the Winter Wilderness Weekend takes place. During this time, guided hikes from the Starved Rock visitor center include views of the park's spectacular ice falls and bald eagles. Cross-country skiing rentals and instruction are also available in winter.

WHERE TO STAY

BLOOMINGTON

★★★THE CHATEAU HOTEL AND CONFERENCE CENTER

1601 Jumer Drive, Bloomington, 309-662-2020, 866-690-4006; www.chateauhotel.biz

Located near Illinois State University, this hotel has an indoor pool, sauna and whirlpool. Dining is made easy with an onsite restaurant and lounge.

180 rooms. Restaurant, bar. Fitness center. Pool. Pets accepted. $61-150

SPRINGFIELD

★★★HILTON SPRINGFIELD

700 E. Adams St., Springfield, 217-789-1530; www.hilton.com

This being the only skyscraper in Springfield, rooms here have great views of the city. Its downtown location is convenient to eight Abraham Lincoln historical sites.

360 rooms. Restaurant, bar. Business center. Fitness center. Pool. $61-150

★★★PRESIDENT ABRAHAM LINCOLN HOTEL AND CONFERENCE CENTER

701 E. Adams St., Springfield, 217-544-8800, 800-228-9898; www.presidentabrahamlincolnhotel.com

Popular with business travelers, thanks to a large conference center, this hotel is also a good choice if you're in town to see all things related to Lincoln. It is the closest hotel to the Abraham Lincoln Presidential Museum and Library, and near other Lincoln sites.

316 rooms. Restaurant, bar. Business center. Fitness center. Pool. $61-150

RECOMMENDED

BLOOMINGTON

EASTLAND SUITES HOTEL AND CONFERENCE CENTER

1801 Eastland Drive, Bloomington, 309-662-0000, 800-537-8483; www.eastlandsuitesbloomington.com

Extended stay guests will enjoy oversized suites, all with fully stocked kitchens, pillow-top mattresses and balconies or patios. The conference center offers 3,200 square feet of meeting space.

111 rooms. Bar. Complimentary breakfast. Business center. Fitness center. Pool. Pets accepted. $61-150

PEORIA

HOTEL PERE MARQUETTE

501 Main St., Peoria, 309-637-6500, 800-447-1676; www.hotelperemarquette.com

This historic hotel is in the heart of Peoria's business and entertainment district. Rooms and suites feature down feather bedding and pillows.

287 rooms. Restaurant, bar. Business center. Fitness center. Pets accepted. $61-150

MARK TWAIN HOTEL

225 N.E. Adams St., Peoria, 309-676-3600, 888-325-6351; www.marktwainhotel.com

Rooms at this boutique hotel are contemporary yet cozy. Beds are topped with feather beds and down comforters. The onsite restaurant offers casual dining.

109 rooms. Restaurant, bar. Complimentary breakfast. Fitness center. Pets accepted. $61-150

UTICA

STARVED ROCK LODGE AND CONFERENCE CENTER

Highway 178 and 71, Utica, 815-667-4211, 800-868-7625; www.starvedrocklodge.com

Nestled among the forests and bluffs of Starved Rock State Park, this is the only hotel in the park. The hotel was built in the 1930s by the Civilian Conservation Corps and is listed on the National Registry of Historic Places. Its most notable feature is the largest two-sided fireplace in Illinois. Accommodations include guest rooms and deluxe and pioneer cabins.

91 rooms. Restaurant, bar. Pool. $61-150

WHERE TO EAT

RECOMMENDED
GALESBURG
LANDMARK CAFÉ AND CREPERIE

62 S. Seminary St., Galesburg, 309-343-5376; www.seminarystreet.com

For delicious crepes, try this casual café, where crepes are prepared on an open grill. Go for the Landmark crepe, stuffed with Canadian bacon, Swiss cheese, mushrooms and French mustard, and topped with a creamy chardonnay mushroom sauce.

American, French. Lunch, dinner, Saturday-Sunday brunch. Reservations recommended. Outdoor seating. Children's menu. $16-35

PACKINGHOUSE DINING COMPANY

441 Mulberry, Galesburg, 309-342-6868; www.seminarystreet.com

Housed in an authentic turn-of-the-century meat packing plant, specialties here include the prime rib and fresh-baked cinnamon rolls.

American. Lunch, dinner. Reservations recommended. Children's menu. $16-35

GENESEO
CELLAR

137 S. State St., Geneseo, 309-944-2177; www.thecellar.info

A 130-year-old building known as the Geneseo House is home to this restaurant, which is known for its steaks, chops, ribs and seafood. Try the house specialty: charcoal broiled barbeque shrimp.

American. Dinner. Closed Monday. Children's menu. Bar. $36-85

PEORIA
CARNEGIE'S 501

501 N. Main St., Peoria, 309-637-6500; www.hotelperemarquette.com

Located in the Hotel Pere Marquette, this restaurant has an extensive menu of steaks, chicken, seafood and more. But the way to go is the Five Course Dinner for Two, which includes a combination of any two appetizers, a signature salad, sorbet, two entrées, two desserts, and to top it off, two chocolate-covered strawberries.

American. Breakfast, lunch, dinner. Children's menu. Bar. $16-35

TWO25

225 N.E. Adams St., Peoria, 309-282-7777; www.two25peoria.com

Located inside the Mark Twain Hotel, Two25 offers homemade pizza, pastas and an extensive meat and potatoes menu. For starters, try the crab and artichoke gratin.

American. Lunch, dinner. Closed Sunday. $36-85.

SPRINGFIELD
MALDANER'S

222 S. Sixth St., Springfield, 217-522-4313; www.maldaners.com

This historic (since 1884) Springfield restaurant features seasonal local and regional ingredients. Large plates include Beef Wellington and a grilled pork loin with baked apple.

American. Lunch, dinner. Closed Sunday. Bar. $16-35

URBANA

TIMPONE'S

710 S. Goodwin Ave., Urbana, 217-344-7619; www.timpones-urbana.com

The menu changes daily, but items are always made of seasonal and organic ingredients. Desserts, pasta and pizza are made fresh in house. There are also several vegetarian options.

Italian, American. Lunch, dinner. Closed Sunday. Reservations recommended. Bar. $16-35

CHICAGO

No matter how old you are or what you like to do, you won't experience a dull moment in Chicago. The city has world-class museums, inviting parks and colorful neighborhoods inhabited by famously friendly Midwesterners. Add to that the sparkling, expansive Lake Michigan, and you have a magical place.

Some locals theorize that Chicago's arts and culture community owes a debt to the city's toe-freezing winters. How so? If the ground weren't frozen over for about half of the year, then artists, musicians, athletes and others wouldn't have the time to hone their skills and elevate Chicago's arts to new heights. It's just a theory, though, and with the quality work coming out of this city—from powerful plays by the Steppenwolf Theatre Company to powerhouse hits at the Friendly Confines and the Cell—we'll chalk it up to raw talent. Chicagoans are proud of their world-famous symphony orchestra, Lyric Opera and numerous and diverse dance companies. Chicago's theater community is vibrant, with more than 100 theaters. The collections at the Art Institute of Chicago, Museum of Contemporary Art and galleries in the River North area are among the best in the country. The 1996 expansion of Lake Shore Drive made it possible to create the Museum Campus. This 57-acre extension of Burnham Park provides an easier and more scenic route to the Adler Planetarium, Field Museum and Shedd Aquarium, and surrounds them with one continuous park featuring terraced gardens and broad walkways. No visit to Chicago is complete without touring Millennium Park. This downtown park area includes the Harris Theater for Music and Dance, the 50-foot-high water-spewing towers of the Crown Fountain, the Frank Gehry-designed band shell and bridge, and the Cloud Gate sculpture, which locals lovingly call "the bean."

Of course, Chicago is also famous for its architecture. A city of neat frame cottages and bulky stone mansions, it produced the Chicago School of Architecture, whose innovative style was carried on by Frank Lloyd Wright and Ludwig Mies van der Rohe.

It doesn't matter whether you're in town for a convention or for the latest outdoor music festival, you can rest easy knowing there's a hotel for you somewhere in this city. Chicago's lodging options are as diverse as they are vast. So decide what you're looking for—location? great spa? boutique hotel?—and then pick the perfect one for your stay.

Meat and potatoes rank right up there with Al Capone on the list of hardest to beat Chicago stereotypes. And that's not for lack of trying by the city's stellar culinary community. Everyone knows that some of the country's best, most innovative restaurants call Chicago home—including Charlie Trotter's, Alinea, Moto. The list goes on. Not everyone knows about the tucked-away gems in cozy neighborhoods such as Lincoln Square or Wicker Park, nor the modest but mind-bending pet projects of superstar chefs Rick Bayless, Paul Kahan and Graham Elliot. So although Chicago is proud of its "low-brow" dining history—deep-dish pizza and hot dogs are staples throughout the city—you'll never go hungry for award-winning and fine dining options. Neither will locals, who are more than happy to live in a place where dining comes in second to none.

In a place where city dwellers are slapped with ice-cold winters and jungle-humid summers, it's no surprise that there are an abundance of soothing retreats. From the head-to-toe treatments at upscale spots like the Spa at Four Seasons to quick beauty rituals (such as expert acupuncture at Ruby Room Spa), there's something for everyone—because everyone needs pampering now and again.

When it comes to shopping, surely you've heard of Chicago's Michigan Avenue. You can find the latest of pretty much everything in the mixed bag of department stores and upscale shops that line the legendary strip. Step beyond this downtown drag and you'll also happen upon unique boutiques with one-of-a-kind finds. Just be forewarned that Chicago has one the nation's highest sales tax—more than 9 percent, at press time—which doesn't seem to deter the many shoppers who flood Michigan Avenue on weekends. If you live in an area with a better tax rate, ask about having your purchases shipped to you to avoid the extra tariff.

WHAT TO SEE

ADLER PLANETARIUM
1300 S. Lake Shore Drive, Chicago (Museum Campus), 312-922-7827; www.adlerplanetarium.org

If a fear of flying took you out of contention for a career as an astronaut, then head to the Western Hemisphere's first planetarium. Interactive exhibits like Shoot for the Moon, which features Apollo 13 astronaut Jim Lovell's fully restored Gemini 12 spacecraft and some of his effects, will let you envision what your life might have been like. Stargazers should make their way to the Doane Observatory for a look through the largest public telescope in the area, but to appreciate the heavenly Chicago skyline instead, step onto the North and South terraces.

Admission: adults $10, Chicago residents $8, children 3-14 $6, Chicago residents 3-14 $5. Monday-Friday 10 a.m.-4 p.m., Saturday-Sunday 10 a.m.-4:30 p.m.; mid-June-Labor Day, daily 9:30 a.m.-6 p.m.

THE ART INSTITUTE OF CHICAGO
111 S. Michigan Ave., Chicago, 312-443-3600; www.artic.edu/aic

The Art Institute is best known for its vast stock of Impressionist works. With the spring 2009 opening of The Modern Wing, it now also houses collections of modern art, photography, and architecture and design. With this addition

WHAT ARE THE TOP THINGS TO DO IN CHICAGO?

CRUISE THE CHICAGO RIVER
Take the Chicago History Museum's Architecture River Cruise, which winds through the Chicago River and gives you a rundown of the city's most significant buildings.

EXPLORE MILLENNIUM PARK
During summer, check out the park's weekly concerts (many of them free), public art exhibitions and expos. The park is also home to the lovely, peace-inducing Lurie Garden; the interactive, wet-and-wild Crown Fountain; and everyone's favorite reflective bean-shaped sculpture, Cloud Gate.

HAVE A FERRIS BUELLER TYPE OF DAY
You've seen it in the movie, but now experience the Art Institute of Chicago in the flesh. The new Renzo Piano-designed Modern Wing, opened in 2009, is simply stunning and one of the city's best attractions. Set aside an afternoon to take in this massive museum, which boasts an impressive collection of Impressionist and post-Impressionist pieces, plus 20th century classics.

SHOP UNTIL YOU DROP ON THE MAGNIFICIENT MILE
The Magnificent Mile is a huge shopping destination on Michigan Avenue. Walk north on Michigan between the Chicago River and Oak Street, and your closet will lack for nothing. You'll find stores such as Gap, Guess, Neiman Marcus, Bloomingdale's, the Apple Store and Niketown. You'll be hard-pressed to go home empty-handed.

TAKE IN THE CITY FROM HIGH ABOVE
Head to the observation deck at the 103rd floor of the Willis Tower, formerly the Sears Tower, where you can see up to 40 miles out in either direction on a clear day. Then, hit the John Hancock Observatory and take the elevator to the 95th floor Signature Room Lounge, where you can get vistas for the cost of a slightly sugary cocktail.

of 264,000 square feet, the Art Institute is the second-largest art museum (in square feet) in the United States at approximately 1.2 million square feet. Among the museum's permanent collection of approximately a quarter million pieces (in ten curatorial departments) are iconic works such as *American*

Gothic, A Sunday on La Grande Jatte and *Nighthawks*. The Modern Wing has its own full-service entrance.

Admission: adults $18, children, seniors and students $12; children under 14 free. Free admission from 5 p.m.-8 p.m. on Thursdays. Monday-Wednesday 10:30 a.m.-5 p.m., Thursday-Friday 10:30 a.m.-8 p.m., Saturday-Sunday 10 a.m.-5 p.m.

BUDDY GUY'S LEGENDS

700 S. Wabash Ave., Chicago, 312-427-1190; www.buddyguys.com

Buddy Guy's might have new digs, but that's about all that has changed at this Chicago institution. Drop in and you'll still be rewarded with classic, electrifying Chicago blues, sometimes courtesy of Guy himself. (He's in town the month of January, and on and off the rest of the year in between touring engagements.) There's a free acoustic blues set on Fridays from 5:30-8 p.m. and Saturdays from 6-8:30 p.m.; the full-on jams, however, start around 9:30 p.m. nightly, usually for a $10-$15 cover.

Monday-Friday 11 a.m.-2 a.m., Saturday 5 p.m.-3 a.m., Sunday 6 p.m.-2 a.m.

CHICAGO CULTURAL CENTER

78 E. Washington St., Chicago, 312-744-6630; www.cityofchicago.org

While locals head to the Cultural Center for the free art exhibits, daily concerts and other performances, visitors go to gape at its magnificent Tiffany stained-glass dome, which is the biggest in the world. If you zoom your camera in on the center of the 1897 dome, which was refurbished in 2008, you might be able to make out the signs of the zodiac. After craning your neck to see the dome, make like a native and see if any of the art offerings are worth a look—or just escape the downtown crowds with a quick bite at the center's Randolph Café.

Monday-Thursday 8 a.m.-7 p.m., Friday 8 a.m.-6 p.m., Saturday 9 a.m.-6 p.m., Sunday 10 a.m.-6 p.m.

CHICAGO HISTORY MUSEUM

1601 N. Clark St., Chicago, 312-642-4600; www.chicagohs.org

As Chicago's oldest cultural institution, the Chicago History Museum predates the Great Chicago Fire of 1871. And the CHM gets better with age. A major 2006 renovation provided new galleries, which feature shows such as Chicago: Crossroads of America. The comprehensive permanent exhibit looks at the city's many neighborhoods, and its disasters and innovations. The CHM tries to go beyond stuffy historical documents with past exhibits like Chicago@40: The Band and Its City, an homage to the legendary soft-rock band, and Chic Chicago: Couture Treasures from the Chicago History Museum, a collection of dazzling gowns worn by local fashionistas, including the first couture dress designed for an uncorseted woman as well as modern designer pieces by the likes of Versace.

Admission: adults $14, seniors and students $12, children 12 and under free. Free Monday. Monday-Saturday 9:30 a.m.-4:30 p.m., Sunday noon-5 p.m.

CHICAGO TRIBUNE TOWER

435 N. Michigan Ave., Chicago, 312-222-3232, 800-874-2863; www.chicagotribune.com

When the Chicago Tribune needed a bigger space in 1922, the newspaper held a contest challenging architects to create the world's most beautiful office building for the prosperous paper. The unanimous winning entry: A distinctive 36-story Gothic skyscraper topped with dramatic floodlights from New York City architects John Mead Howells and Raymond M. Hood. To ensure the tower's grandeur, embedded into its lower elevations are fragments from well-known buildings throughout the world, including a chunk of the Great Wall of China. Although you can't tour inside the tower, which now serves as the Tribune Company's headquarters, its ground-level radio room lets the public peek at live broadcasts of WGN talk radio, and you can peruse the **Chicago Tribune Store** *(312-222-3080)* to buy an authentically Chicago trinket (like the Tribune logo mug etched with an image of the top of the tower, or a framed poster of the front page of the Chicago Tribune announcing Barack Obama's presidential victory).

Store hours: Monday-Friday 9 a.m.-5:30 p.m., Saturday 10 a.m.-4 p.m.

DUSABLE MUSEUM OF AFRICAN-AMERICAN HISTORY

740 E. 56th St., Chicago, 773-947-0600; www.dusablemuseum.org

The DuSable Museum was created in 1961 when a local art teacher cleared out her living room furniture, replaced it with a collection of African-American art and artifacts, and hung a modest sign labeled simply "African-American Museum." Since then, it's grown quite a bit. Now in a building on the eastern side of Washington Park, the museum doesn't have the resources of, say, the Field Museum, but it holds a remarkable collection of more than 13,000 paintings, photographs and other artifacts. A large part of its collection focuses on local artists and history, with one wing dedicated to Chicago's first African-American mayor, Harold Washington. The exhibit, Red, White, Blue & Black: A History of Blacks in the Armed Forces, looks at how African-American military men struggled with enemies abroad and racism back home. The museum also hosts ongoing events, such as jazz concerts, poetry readings and film screenings.

Admission: adults $3, seniors and students $2, children 6-12 $1, children under 6 free. Free Sunday. Monday-Saturday 10 a.m.-5 p.m. (closed Mondays June-January 2), Sunday noon-5 p.m.

FIELD MUSEUM OF NATURAL HISTORY

Roosevelt Road and Lake Shore Drive, Chicago (Museum Campus), 312-922-9410; www.fieldmuseum.org

Lurking in the grand Stanley Field Hall that greets visitors at this historic museum is Sue—at 42 feet long and 13 feet high at the hips, it is the most complete, best-preserved and largest Tyrannosaurus rex fossil ever discovered. Unearthed in South Dakota in 1990, Sue (named after the woman who found her) is no plastic replica (though the creature's skull is so heavy the real thing is housed upstairs while a stand-in graces the actual body), and the skeleton's placement near the entry is a reminder of the museum's commitment to displaying authentic remnants from nature's past. Spread out over 400,000 square feet, the museum also holds popular exhibits on ancient Egypt as well as artifacts and wilderness scenes from all parts of the globe. The museum's newly renovated Grainger Hall of Gems features rare jewels, gold objects and designer creations, including a collection from Tiffany & Co.

Admission: adults $15, seniors and students $12, children 3-11 $10. Daily 9 a.m.-5 p.m. Additional charge for special exhibits.

WHAT ARE THE BEST PLACES FOR FAMILY FUN IN CHICAGO?

Adler Planetarium:
A visit here is a must, if only because it is the Western Hemisphere's first planetarium. Interactive exhibits include a fully restored Gemini 12 spacecraft.

Navy Pier:
The tourist-packed pier and lakefront area offers all kinds of entertainment, including a Ferris wheel, fireworks displays, IMAX theater and much more.

GRACELAND CEMETERY

4001 N. Clark St., Chicago, 773-525-1105;
www.gracelandcemetery.org

Graceland is called "The Cemetery of Architects" for being the final resting place for such acclaimed architects as Daniel Burnham, William Le Baron Jenney, Louis Sullivan and Ludwig Mies van der Rohe. But many of early Chicago's major players have their permanent home here as well, including businessman Marshall Field and power couple Potter (the business mogul who came up with the idea of store sales and policies such as money-back guarantees for any reason) and Bertha Palmer (the socialite trumped her hubby's accomplishments; she claimed to have invented the brownie). The cemetery, which is on the National Register of Historic Places, is also known for its artistry. A popular site on the grounds is Eternal Silence, a 1909 sculpture by Lorado Taft. Also called the Statute of Death, the haunting work features a black slab of granite fronted by a hooded bronze figure that menacingly covers his mouth and chin with his long robe. While the cemetery doesn't offer tours, it provides a free map for those who want to have a go at it by themselves, and the **Chicago Architecture Foundation** (*312-922-8687; www.architecture.org*) and the **Chicago History Museum** (*312-642-4600; www.chicagohistory.com*) offer walking tours. Try planning a fall visit, when the colorful leaves make for a beautiful backdrop.
Daily dawn-dusk.

GRANT PARK

337 E. Randolph St., Chicago;
www.chicagoparkdistrict.com

Grant Park's Buckingham Fountain is known for its role in the opening credits for the TV show *Married... With Children*, but don't dismiss the beloved Chicago site as a tourist trap. Come on the hour to see one of the world's largest fountains and its elaborate 20-minute water display (daily 8 a.m.-11 p.m., the last starting at 10 p.m.), which features colored lights and music at dusk and a water jet stream at the center that shoots 150 feet high (mid-April to mid-October, weather permitting). Grant Park also hosts many popular outdoor festivals in the summer, including the Taste of Chicago, a massive annual event that offers samples from hundreds of the city's restaurants, and Blues Fest, a yearly celebration featuring preeminent blues artists. Music fans also flock to Grant Park each August for

Lollapalooza, a three-day extravaganza that's featured big-name acts such as Lady Gaga and Kings of Leon.
Daily dawn-dusk.

GREEN MILL
4802 N. Broadway, Chicago, 773-878-5552; www.greenmilljazz.com

The Mill's legend goes beyond the fact that Al Capone and his cronies used to hang out at the bar in the '20s. After a brief decline in the '70s, current owner Dave Jemilo bought it in 1986 and restored its speakeasy décor, cool-cat vibe, and '30s- and '40s-inspired jazz sounds. On any day of the week, you can find discerning jazz fiends of all stripes: middle-aged suits be-bopping their heads alongside fresh-out-of-college hipsters. If you're lucky, you'll show up on the day of the week when resident and internationally recognized jazz vanguard Patricia Barber takes the stage. The Sabertooth Quartet still jams from midnight through 4 a.m. on Saturday nights, while the Uptown Poetry Slam showcases verses on Sunday nights.
Daily noon-4 a.m.

HOLY NAME CATHEDRAL
735 N. State St., Chicago, 312-787-8040; www.holynamecathedral.org

Built in the 1870s to replace a church destroyed in the Great Chicago Fire of 1871, the cathedral's gothic architecture sits uneasily against the Magnificent Mile's modern skyline. But Holy Name Cathedral has grown up with Chicago and has been a spiritual home to the city's Roman Catholic population. It is the seat of the Roman Catholic Archdiocese of Chicago and was host to a mass by John Paul II in 1979. Open the 1,200-pound bronze doors (they open easily thanks to a finger-touch hydraulic system) and peek inside the church to see five galeros—the red, broad-brimmed hats worn by cardinals—suspended from the ceiling. A galero used to be raised to the ceiling of a cardinal's cathedral upon his death and left there until it decayed as an example that all earthly glory passes. Also check out the stained-glass windows; made in Milan, they tell a story of humankind's movement from darkness into light. The western windows are dominated by dark shades of blue and red, but lighten up until they become primarily white and gold behind the altar and crucifix. The cathedral is also a part of Chicago's macabre lore, since it was the site of a battle between Al Capone-era mobsters over turf. Bullet holes remain in a Philippians inscription, now covered by stairs.
Mass schedule: Weekdays 6 a.m., 7 a.m., 8 a.m., 12:10 p.m., 5:15 p.m.; Saturday vigil 5:15 p.m., 7:30 p.m.; Sunday 7 a.m., 8:15 a.m., 9:30 a.m., 11 a.m., 12:30 p.m., 5:15 p.m. The building is open a half hour before the first Mass of the day through 7 p.m.

HOUSE OF BLUES
329 N. Dearborn St., Chicago, 312-923-2000; www.hob.com

Never mind the name: The only blues you'll find here is usually relegated to the small Back Porch Stage and presented in the form of Guy King and Jimmy Burns. What you'll find on the main stage is a cocktail of musical acts, including the likes of Cyndi Lauper, The Killers, Peter Frampton, Roger Daltrey and Jay-Z. It doesn't hurt that the Chicago outpost of this national chain is also smack-dab in the middle of the city and housed in a building that resembles a giant turtle shell—and it's even cooler for its lush sound system. Go ahead and splurge on balcony seats—the view of the stage is unbeatable, and it's a small price to pay to make sure you don't get accidentally swept into the thick standing-room-only crowd that rushes the stage downstairs.

Show times and ticket prices vary. Check website for details.

THE HOUSE THEATRE OF CHICAGO

Chopin Theatre, 1543 W. Division St., Chicago, 773-251-2195; www.thehousetheatre.com

For a taste of the future of Chicago theater, do not miss a production by this rough-and-tumble storefront troupe. Expect lots of pop-culture references, rapid-fire delivery and action-film moves. The trilogy of plays that put this group on the map spanned several centuries and took place in the Wild West, feudal Japan and 1920s gangland Chicago.

Show times and ticket prices vary. Check website for details.

HUBBARD STREET DANCE CHICAGO

1147 W. Jackson Blvd., Chicago, 312-850-9744; www.hubbardstreetdance.com

Founded in 1977 by Lou Conte, the HSDC is arguably the city's foremost dance company, specializing in contemporary modern dance. Under the leadership of current artistic director Glenn Edgerton (following Conte's retirement in 2000 and artistic director Jim Vincent's departure in 2009), the company moved from its jazz-centric beginnings into a worldlier repertoire, and is now known for brilliantly performing works by choreographers Nacho Duato, Toru Shimazaki and Jorma Elo. HSDC established the Hubbard Street Dance Center in 2006, which houses and administers the main company, along with Hubbard Street 2 (a company of young dancers), Lou Conte Dance Studio and HSDC's educational and community programs.

Check website for details.

IO CHICAGO

3541 N. Clark St., Chicago, 773-880-0199; www.ioimprov.com

Formerly Improv Olympics (the place was forced to change its name after the International Olympic Committee cried foul), this is the place for Chicago improv. Alumni include Mike Myers, Andy Richter and Amy Poehler, and talented improvisers still cut their teeth here on a nightly basis. The iO's signature show—created by one of the founding fathers of improv comedy, the late Del Close—is the long-form improvisation "the Harold," in which an improv team creates hilarious and often-convoluted "plots" with just one audience suggestion. However, it'd be a shame to miss the various other improv and sketch comedy shows at the Cabaret Theater or the Del Close Theater. The iO opened a Los Angeles branch a few years ago, a testament to its growing success on the stage as well as in Hollywood.

Admission: $5-$20. Various show times; check website for details.

JAY PRITZKER PAVILION

Millennium Park, Chicago, 312-742-1168; www.millenniumpark.org

When the Pritzker Pavilion opened to much fanfare in 2004, there were murmurs that it would be Ravinia's undoing. A Frank Gehry-designed alfresco bandshell with mostly free programming in the heart of the city? Ravinia seemed like a distant memory. Luckily, both are coexisting just fine, although the Pritzker's dramatic look and sound are nothing to scoff about. The trellis over the lawn is laced with concert hall-quality speakers, so not an inch of the 7,000-capacity Great Lawn goes hard of hearing. (There are 4,000 permanent seats near the stage, which usually work on a first-come, first-served basis for free shows.) Though regular fare includes world music (Seu Jorge, Bajofondo Tango Club), jazz (Sonny Rollins), classical (Pinchas Zukerman) and experimental (Andrew Bird, Calexico), the Pritzker is also the summer home to the Grant Park Orchestra (www.grantparkmusicfestival.com).

June-September. Check website for details.

JOFFREY BALLET

10 E. Randolph St., Chicago, 312-739-0120; www.joffrey.com

This is one of the country's preeminent ballet companies, and it is not hard to see why. Since its founding in New York City in 1956 by Robert Joffrey and Gerald Arpino (it moved permanently to Chicago in 1995), the company has built a reputation for supporting and staging contemporary American ballet pieces and choreographers, such as Twyla Tharp and Alvin Ailey. To balance out its modern tendencies, it also leans heavily on the Ballet Russes tradition, so expect some works in that style, as well as more classic ballet pieces.

Show times and ticket prices vary. Check website for details.

JOHN HANCOCK CENTER

875 N. Michigan Ave., Chicago, 312-751-3681, 888-875-8439; www.hancock-observatory.com

It may not be the first or even the second or third tallest building in Chicago, but the world-famous Hancock, which towers over the city at 1,127 feet, still holds the record for being the world's highest residence (condos begin on the 49th floor). Zoom up to the always-packed 94th-floor observatory for a view that can extend to four states on a clear day. Then check out the city's only open-air skywalk to feel the famous Chicago wind. Don't worry about taking a plunge; though the skywalk is windowless, NASA-tested stainless-steel screens will prevent you from falling. Before you leave, be sure to skim the wall murals to read about how the city went from the ashes of the Great Chicago Fire to a booming metropolis. For a less-touristy option, visit the 95th-floor Signature Room's bar (www.signatureroom.com) to enjoy the same stunning vista of the city as you sip a cocktail.

Admission: adults $15, children 3-11 $10, children under 3 free. Daily 9 a.m.-11 p.m.

LAKE MICHIGAN

Lakefront, Chicago, 312-742-7529; www.chicagoparkdistrict.com

The city's biggest surprises are its great beaches. Locals love hitting Lake Michigan's 26 miles of free lakefront for a respite during the scorching summers. On a typical sunny Saturday, you'll see hundreds of Chicagoans soaking up the sun, playing volleyball, running in the sand, barbecuing in designated grassy areas and, of course, swimming. Although there are tons of entry points to the beach in various neighborhoods, the hub is North Avenue Beach, which has a boat-shaped beach house; a restaurant (Castaways Bar & Grill, 1603 N. Lake Shore Drive, 773-281-1200; www.stefanirestaurants.com), complete with live music from cover bands on weekends; and an outdoor gym. Fitness fiends

HIGHLIGHT

WHERE IS CHICAGO'S GREATEST ARCHITECTURE?

The Great Fire of 1871 nearly leveled in Chicago, so the city had to rebuild from scratch. It needed a new architectural vision and construction technique (wood buildings weren't so resilient the last time around), all of which set the stage for innovation. The ensuing building boom in the 1880s attracted creative architects, and that's when the city's reputation as an architectural hub started.

Almost 130 years later, Chicago maintains that reputation. The world's best architects, including Ludwig Mies van der Rohe, Frank Lloyd Wright and Frank Gehry, passed through the city and left their marks in the form of towering structures of steel, glass and concrete. The city continues to be at the forefront with architects like Renzo Piano and Frank Gehry, who left their mark on the Art Institute's Modern Wing, and Millenium Park. Here are some of the most celebrated architectural wonders:

FRANK GEHRY: PRITZKER PAVILION

Millennium Park, 55 N. Michigan Ave., Chicago; www.millenniumpark.org
Gehry's 2004 Pritzker Pavilion is a remarkable sight. The 120-foot-high outdoor bandshell shows the architect's trademark use of bright steel to make buildings look like free-form sculpture. The stainless-steel layers curl upward from the stage like shaved chocolate, and a steel criss-crossed trellis covers the venue seating and lawn below. Known for his contorted steel structures, Gehry made this one of his most accessible and functional buildings. His adjacent BP Bridge echoes the unique design.

BURNHAM & ROOT: RELIANCE BUILDING

32 N. State St., Chicago
Chicago became the birthplace of skyscrapers because of buildings like this Burnham & Root 1890 masterpiece. Its glass-covered exterior makes it a precursor to today's glass-and-steel skyscrapers. The exterior looks like it's all windows, but between them you'll see narrow piers, mullions and spandrels, all covered with cream terra cotta and Gothic ornamentation. It's a prime example of the Chicago School of architecture; it combines columns of steel to house airy façades of glass. Today, the building houses the Hotel Burnham and Atwood Café, and is often sketched by students from the nearby Art Institute.

HOLABIRD & ROOT: CHICAGO BOARD OF TRADE

141 W. Jackson Blvd., Chicago
Holabird & Root created this imposing Art Deco behemoth in 1930, an unapologetically vertical structure marking an abrupt end to LaSalle Street. Head into the two-story lobby to really see its Art Deco beginnings, with its clean lines

forming intricate yet orderly geometric designs. If you're wondering what is on top of the building, it's Ceres, the Roman goddess of agriculture—a symbol of the exchange's beginnings in the agricultural commodities business.

LOUIS SULLIVAN: SULLIVAN CENTER

1 S. State St., Chicago

The former Carson, Pirie, Scott and Company Building has changed its name to honor its architect, Louis Sullivan. The 12-story structure was constructed for the Schlesinger and Mayer Department Store between 1898 and 1904 and is considered one of Sullivan's most important. After Carson's took over the building in 1904, a 12-story south addition by Daniel Burnham was made and an eight-story south addition followed by Holabird and Root in 1961—a succession of great Chicago architects competing with and complementing each other's styles in one building. The white terra cotta façade is most remarkable for Sullivan's amazingly intricate, curvy cast-iron ornamentation. The space was just renovated to house restaurants and shops.

LUDWIG MIES VAN DER ROHE: CROWN HALL

3360 S. State St., Chicago

One of the Modernist architect's masterpieces is a literal lesson to the people who work and study inside of it, as it's the location for the Illinois Institute of Technology's College of Architecture. Mies had the foresight to accommodate the changing needs of the students. He created a 120-foot-long, 220-foot-wide and 18-foot-high clear-span building without any columns, a flexible space where temporary partitions can be changed as needed (though school officials nixed student requests to use the space for keggers). Mies, who was head of the school's architecture program in 1938, also designed nearly 20 campus structures for the Illinois Institute of Technology, the largest collection of the architect's buildings.

FRANK LLOYD WRIGHT: ROBIE HOUSE

5757 S. Woodlawn Ave., Chicago; www.gowright.org

In 1910, Frank Lloyd Wright, the grandfather of American architecture, created this home in his signature Prairie style. Named for the prairie landscape of his Midwest youth, this style is characterized by sweeping horizontal lines, dramatic overhangs, art glass windows and an open floor plan—all of which can be seen at the Robie House (entry is by guided tour only; to reserve a spot, visit www.gowright.org).

also will find that the lakefront is a great place to work out; the 18-mile trail is perfect for jogging, rollerblading or biking. If group sports are more your thing, try to pick up a game at the sand volleyball courts and tennis courts that line the trail. In the summer, the best of Chicago's local theater companies put on Theater on the Lake, at Fullerton Avenue and Lake Michigan.

LINCOLN PARK
2400 N. Stockton Drive, Chicago, 312-742-7529; www.chicagoparkdistrict.com

Lincoln Park, also the name of the neighborhood in which it is located, is the largest of Chicago's parks. On its grounds, which reach from North Avenue to Hollywood Avenue, you'll find numerous beaches and the lakefront jogging/ biking trail. It's also the home of the **Lincoln Park Zoo** (*2200 N. Cannon Drive, 312-742-2000; www.lpzoo.org*). At only 35 acres, it's not as big as its suburban Brookfield counterpart, but its park surroundings make it a scenic place to visit, plus it's free and open year-round. Check out ZooLights in the wintertime, when the zoo puts out Christmas lights in animal shapes and serves warm drinks while kids visit Santa. Just past the zoo's north border is the **Lincoln Park Conservatory** (*2391 N. Stockton Drive, 312-742-7736; www.chicagoparkdistrict.com*). The free botanical garden offers four houses within its glass-domed structure: the Palm House, Fern Room, Orchid House and Show House, which hosts annual flower shows. If you head to the south end of the park, you'll see **Green City Market** (*www.chicagogreencitymarket.org*), Chicago's only sustainable green market. The market features more than 40 vendors hawking everything from baked goods (get a slice of whatever pie is in season at Hoosier Mama Pie Co.) to produce (buy juicy peaches from Mick Klug Farms) and flowers (pick up lilies from The Flower Garden). After you gather your treats, watch the chef demos to learn how pros from noted restaurants whip up culinary masterpieces. In winter, the outdoor market sets up shop indoors at the Notebaert Nature Museum.

Lincoln Park Zoo: Admission: Free. April-May, daily 9 a.m.-5p.m.; Memorial Day-Labor Day, Monday-Friday 10 a.m.-5 p.m., Saturday-Sunday 10 a.m.-6:30 p.m.; September-October, daily 10 a.m.-5 p.m.; November-March, daily 10 a.m.-4:30 p.m. Lincoln Park Conservatory: Daily 9 a.m.-5 p.m. Green City Market: Mid-May-October, Wednesday and Saturday 7 a.m.-1 p.m.; November-late December, Wednesday and Saturday 8 a.m.-1 p.m.; January-April, days and times vary.

LYRIC OPERA
Civic Opera House, 20 N. Wacker Drive, Chicago, 312-332-2244; www.lyricopera.org

Considered one of the most classical opera houses in the country—when we say "classical," we're referring to its repertoire, Art Deco digs, resident orchestra and ornate costumes—the Lyric stages eight productions per season. In recent years, these have included Mozart's The Marriage of Figaro and Puccini's Tosca. Maybe it's a sign that Chicagoans like to stick to the basics, but the Lyric sells out to 95 percent capacity for all runs, so make sure to get your tickets early. *Show times and ticket prices vary. Check website for details.*

MICHIGAN AVENUE BRIDGE
At the Chicago River between Michigan and Wabash avenues, Chicago

Motorists drive on Michigan Avenue Bridge daily, but they're too busy cursing the traffic to stop and appreciate the striking gateway to the Magnificent Mile, which connects the North and South Sides of the city. Built in 1920 by Edward Bennett, the bridge was designed not just for better transportation but also to enhance the waterfront as part of architect Daniel Burnham's 1909 Plan of Chicago. The landmark bridge later got an esplanade in 1926 and sculptures in 1928. The southwest bridge tower houses the **McCormick Tribune Bridgehouse & Chicago River Museum** (*376 N. Michigan Ave., River North, 312-977-0227; www.bridgehousemuseum.org*). Not atmospheric enough for you? There are often street performers playing saxophones or drums on either side of the bridge, adding a fitting soundtrack to the hustle and bustle.

McCormick Tribune Bridgehouse and Chicago River Museum: adults $4, seniors and children 5-12 $3, children 5 and under. May-October, Thursday-Monday 10 a.m.-5 p.m.

MILLENNIUM PARK
Michigan Avenue near Randolph Street, Chicago; www.millenniumpark.org

Widely regarded as one of the best public works projects in the city's recent memory, Millennium Park is fast becoming synonymous with Chicago. Once an eyesore filled with railroad tracks and parking lots, it's now home to the Frank Gehry-designed Jay Pritzker Pavilion (which displays the architect's well-known style of curved steel and hosts free concerts all summer long), and Crown Fountain, which is a set of two large faces (the likenesses of 1,000 Chicagoans rotate through the display) opposite one another that spit water into a play area that kids love to splash around in when the weather is warm. In fact, today the park is one of the city's most popular attractions, especially its stainless-steel sculpture Cloud Gate, which acts as a fun-house mirror from underneath and reflects the city's skyline on the outside. Just don't ask locals about the sculpture by name (they won't have any idea what you're talking about)—everyone calls it "The Bean" because the sculpture is shaped like a kidney bean.

Daily 6 a.m.-11 p.m.

MONADNOCK BUILDING
53 W. Jackson Blvd., Chicago, 312-922-1890; www.monadnockbuilding.com

It's funny that the Monadnock Building is considered a masterpiece in the Chicago School of architecture, because it's like two very separate buildings in one: John Wellborn Root designed the northern section, the tallest commercial building to be supported primarily by brick walls; and firm Holabird & Roche designed the southern section, which uses steel-frame construction. There's also the seemingly incongruous design mix of Chicago School simplicity with Egyptian elements. Put it all together, and you have a visual representation of one building tradition's end and the beginning of another. Today in the Monadnock you'll find a mix of tenants, including old-school Frank's Barber Shop, the city's finest cup of joe at Intelligentsia and women's boutique Florodora.

MUSEUM OF CONTEMPORARY ART
220 E. Chicago Ave., Chicago, 312-280-2660; www.mcachicago.org

Housed in a rather uninspired building between Lake Michigan and the Water Tower, the MCA is home to 2,345 pieces in its permanent collection, including work by Dan Flavin and Lee Bontecou. The interior space can be daunting, with wide hallways and an unusual eyelid-shaped staircase with a fish pond at the bottom that is worth viewing on its own. But despite its size, the MCA won't take long to see (perhaps an hour or two to review the museum's first-rate contemporary experimental works) before you'll want to grab some lunch at the museum's café, operated by chef Wolfgang Puck of Spago fame. If you're around on the first Friday of the month, the museum holds a happening event where, for a $16 admission ($11 for advanced tickets), you can check out the latest exhibit, enjoy live entertainment, nibble on tasty Wolfgang Puck hors d'oeuvres and sip cocktails (you can purchase extra drink tickets). Local singles pack the joint on First Fridays, which has become a meat market for culture vultures on the prowl.

Admission: adults $12, seniors and students $7, children 12 and under free. Free Tuesday. Tuesday 10 a.m.-8 p.m., Wednesday-Sunday 10 a.m.-5 p.m. First Fridays: $16; first Friday of the month 6-10 p.m.

MUSEUM OF SCIENCE AND INDUSTRY

57th Street and Lake Shore Drive, Chicago, 773-684-1414, 800-468-6674; www.msichicago.org

Opened in 1933, the MSI is the largest science museum in the Western Hemisphere—and it needs to be. It houses a full-size 727 airplane (board the plane and buckle up for a fake San Francisco-Chicago flight, complete with banter from an automated pilot); a full-scale coal mine, one of the museum's oldest displays with a great simulated trip into the depths of the mine; a refurbished Burlington Pioneer Zephyr train with interactive exhibits; the U-505 German submarine, which was captured in 1944 and has been given a new indoor arena that brings that era of American history to life; as well as farming, Internet and fairy castle-themed collections among its 2,000 exhibits. As if that weren't enough, there's the recently renovated Henry Crown Space Center in addition to its collections highlighting the history of space exploration.

Admission: adults $15, seniors $14, children 3-11 $10. Memorial Day-Labor Day, Monday-Saturday 9:30 a.m.-5:30 p.m., Sunday 11 a.m.-5:30 p.m.; Labor Day-late May, Monday-Saturday 9:30 a.m.-4 p.m., Sunday 11 a.m.-4 p.m.

MUSIC BOX THEATRE

3733 N. Southport Ave., Chicago, 773-871-6604; www.musicboxtheatre.com

Built in 1929, the Music Box Theater was originally planned with an orchestra pit, in case "sound" films (new at the time) failed. They haven't, and neither has the Music Box. The theater has shown everything from Arabic feminist films exploring the oppression of women to Sound of Music sing-alongs. But for the last 20 years, the Music Box has been the premier Chicago spot to see independent and experimental films. Over the years, the theatre has also hosted movie premieres, such as *The Break-Up* and *(500) Days of Summer*, with the stars walking the red carpet beforehand. In 1991, the Music Box added a second, smaller theater, which sweetly tries to reproduce a small Italian garden with shabbily painted stars and clouds above and plaster side walls. You'll be quite close to the dozen or so people in the audience, but also likely to watch a great indie movie that you can name-drop at your next dinner party.

Show times vary. Check website for details.

NAVY PIER

600 E. Grand Ave., Chicago, 312-595-7437, 800-595-7437; www.navypier.com

Nearly 200 navy planes remain submerged in Lake Michigan as a result of the training once done at Navy Pier. Reborn in 1995 after years of disuse, the tourist-packed pier and lakefront area have become as emblematic of Chicago as the skyscraper. The pier contains a mall (nothing notable there) as well as a 3-D IMAX theater, a small ice-skating rink, the Chicago Shakespeare Theater, the Smith Museum of Stained Glass Windows (seriously, it's a lot better than it sounds), and the Chicago Children's Museum (head here quickly, as the museum is planning to move into its own 100,000-square-foot structure in Daley Bicentennial Plaza at 337 E. Randolph St. in the next few years). The museum has plenty of hands-on but not-so-messy exhibits for the kids, including Dinosaur Expedition, which re-creates a trip to the Sahara to dig for fossils. There is also an urban "neighborhood" for toddlers to practice driving a city bus or shopping for groceries. Adults can have fun at the outdoor beer garden or on any number of dinner cruises that leave from the docks, which offer a lakeside view of the pier's 150-foot-high Ferris wheel and the Chicago skyline beyond.

Memorial Day-Labor Day, Sunday-Thursday 10 a.m.-10 p.m., Friday-Saturday 10 a.m.-midnight; Labor Day-November, Monday-Thursday 10 a.m.-8 p.m., Friday-Saturday 10 a.m.-midnight; November-March, Monday-Thursday 10 a.m.-8 p.m., Friday-Saturday 10 a.m.-10 p.m., Sunday 10 a.m.-7 p.m.; April-Memorial Day, Sunday-Thursday 10 a.m.-8 p.m., Friday-Saturday 10 a.m.-10 p.m.

OLD CHICAGO WATER TOWER AND PUMPING STATION

806 N. Michigan Ave., Chicago, 312-742-0808

After the Great Chicago Fire of 1871 roared through the city, the Old Chicago Water Tower and Pumping Station were the only public structures left unscathed. The Water Tower now houses **City Gallery** *(Monday-Saturday 10 a.m.-6:30 p.m., Sunday 10 a.m.-5 p.m.)*, which features Chicago-themed photography exhibits. The Pumping Station is now the base of the **Chicago Water Works Visitor Center** and **the Lookingglass Theatre Company** *(312-337-0665; www.lookingglasstheatre.org)*, which was co-founded by David "Ross from Friends" Schwimmer (who also writes and directs here). Try to catch a Lookingglass production by Tony Award-winning director Mary Zimmerman. Her visually stunning shows, such as *The Arabian Nights* and *Argonautika*, set the place on fire (metaphorically speaking, of course).

THE OPRAH WINFREY SHOW

1058 W. Washington Blvd., Chicago, 312-591-9222; www.oprah.com

Oprah moved to the Windy City in 1984 to be on TV morning show AM Chicago, and the city has considered her as one of its own ever since. If you're an Oprah fan, you'll likely be on the hunt for tickets to see one of her final shows. The show's 25th season, which ends in September 2011, will be its last. Tickets have always been hard to get but here are some tips: Call the Audience Department, but have your dialing finger ready and don't let busy signals stop you. The phone lines close during the summer but reopen in early August. Also, call the reservation line during off hours, as it's most busy after a broadcast. You can also try getting last-minute tickets through the show's website—screeners are always looking for people to attend shows based on the day's topic. You must be 18 years or older to attend a taping and have a valid photo ID. If all else fails, you can simply check out **The Oprah Store** *(37 N. Carpenter St., 312-633-2100)* where you can take home O's favorite things.

THE PEGGY NOTEBAERT NATURE MUSEUM

2430 N. Cannon Drive, Chicago, 773-755-5100; www.chias.org

Be one with nature at the hands-on Notebaert. Watch more than 75 species of colorful butterflies set the Judy Istock Butterfly Haven aflutter year-round in the 2,700-square-foot greenhouse. Kids love the interactive River Works, a permanent exhibit where they can splash around while learning the mechanics of a river. For some fresh air, take a walk in the museum's gardens or watch the Lincoln Park action from the rooftop. The Notebaert also houses the Green City Market, the city's only sustainable green market, during early winter, so that you can get your fill of nature along with its bounty.

Admission: adults $9, seniors and students $7, children 3-12 $6, children under 3 free. Free Thursday. Monday-Friday 9 a.m.-4:30 p.m., Saturday-Sunday 10 a.m.-5 p.m. Green City Market: November-late December, Wednesday and Saturday 8 a.m.-1 p.m.; January-April, days and times vary.

PRAIRIE AVENUE HISTORIC DISTRICT

1800 and 1900 blocks of South Prairie Avenue, Chicago

Chicago's wealthiest denizens set up mansions in this South Side neighborhood after the Great Chicago Fire of 1871. Biz whiz Marshall Field and inventor George M. Pullman were among a select few who had Prairie Avenue addresses. Many of the houses were demolished in the 20th century, but a few remain. **The Glessner House** *(1800 S. Prairie Ave., 312-326-1480; www.glessnerhouse.org)*, built by Henry Hobson Richardson for businessman John J. Glessner, has a Romanesque Revival-style façade and is one of the last remaining Prairie Avenue mansions. Walk around inside to see more than 6,000 artifacts, including Arts and Crafts Movement furniture and rare art glass. Built in 1836, the **Clarke House Museum** *(1855 S. Indiana Ave., 312-326-1480)* is the city's oldest building and it remains standing, having survived fires and two moves. The Greek Revival structure was owned by hardware dealer Henry B. Clarke and shows what life was like for a middle-class family in Chicago before the Civil War.

Single-house admission: adults $10, seniors and students $9, children 5-12 $6, children under 5 free; combo tour admission: adults $15, seniors and students $12, children 5-12 $8, children under 5 free. Free Wednesday. Glessner tour: Wednesday-Sunday 1 p.m., 3 p.m. Clarke tour: Wednesday-Sunday noon, 2 p.m.

RICHARD J. DALEY CENTER AND PLAZA

50 W. Washington St., Chicago

Named after the city's former mayor (who was recent mayor Richard M.'s father), the building is literally rusting away—it's built from a compound that uses rust to strengthen the building's façade and give it its brown color. You won't want to go in the building, given the traffic courtrooms and civic offices inside, but outside is a plaza dominated by an untitled 50-foot sculpture by Pablo Picasso, the artist's personal gift to the city. The plaza is kept busy by farmers' markets in the warmer months and festivals in winter, including the perennial **Christkindlmarket** *(www.christkindlmarket.com)*, an alfresco German market leading up to Christmas, which is a great place to sip hot apple cider and eat potato pancakes as you admire the tall, sparkly Christmas tree in the plaza.

Farmers' Market: May-October, Thursday 7 a.m.-3 p.m. Christkindlmarket: November 27-December 24, times vary.

ROOKERY

209 S. LaSalle St., Chicago

The Rookery is the city's oldest high-rise and widely considered the master-piece of famed architects John Wellborn Root and Daniel Burnham, who housed their offices in this grand 1886 building. The structure represents a transition between the use of masonry and metal construction techniques, with the outer walls supported mostly by masonry piers and the inner frame built of steel and iron. In 1905, Frank Lloyd Wright injected some of his trademark Prairie School design into the building when he remodeled its gorgeous glass-domed, two-story lobby. He added white marble and gold-leaf trim and let more light seep through the dome, all of which make it a bright, airy space that gleams when the sun hits it.

THE SECOND CITY

1616 N. Wells St., Chicago, 312-337-3992; www.secondcity.com

It's no joke: The Second City means serious funny business. How else could the theater have remained a top tourist attraction and a requisite for local comedians honing their skills (on stage and in workshops) since it was established in 1959? The Second City's brand of political and social satire still smarts, both on the mainstage and the gutsier e.t.c. stage next door—and even on TV (on shows like *Saturday Night Live* and *The Daily Show*) and film, as evident by famous, whip-smart grads such as Bill Murray, Steve Carell and Amy Sedaris. Donny's Skybox, the cabaret theater, serves as a performance space Thursday to Saturday for students.

Admission: $12-$27 depending on show. Show times vary; check website for details.

SHEDD AQUARIUM

1200 S. Lake Shore Drive, Chicago (Museum Campus), 312-939-2438; www.sheddaquarium.org

More than 32,000 animals swim, slither or crawl around this underwater wonderland, which is one of the largest and best indoor aquariums in the world. You can't miss the Caribbean Reef, a circular 90,000-gallon habitat filled with sea turtles, moray eels, sharks, rays and plenty of colorful fish, where you can watch a diver feed the sea creatures while speaking to guests. Head over to Wild Reef, where only five inches of glass separate you from more than two dozen sharks. Don't miss the new Fantasea water show where you can see dolphins, belugas and penguins perform stunts.

Admission: adults $24.95, children 3-11 $17.95. Labor Day-Memorial Day, Monday-Friday 9 a.m.-5 p.m., Saturday-Sunday 9 a.m.-6 p.m. Memorial Day-Labor Day, daily 9 a.m.-6 p.m.

SPECIAL EVENTS

CHICAGO BEARS

Soldier Field, 1410 S. Museum Campus Drive, South Loop (Museum Campus), 847-295-6600; www.chicagobears.com

Perhaps no other team is so loved across the city as "da Bears," which call Soldier Field home. After a dry spell in the 1990s and early 2000s, the Bears made a comeback in 2007 (getting all the way to the Super Bowl before losing to the Indiana Colts) with formidable defense and a promising team of young players like Brian Urlacher, Matt Forte and Devin Hester.

CHICAGO BULLS

United Center, 1901 W. Madison St., West Loop, 312-455-4000; www.nba.com/bulls

Basically immortalized across the globe by Michael Jordan, the Bulls are no longer that dream team from the '90s: they've suffered through years of losing seasons, but the late-2000s saw a batch of rookies changing the face of the team. Games now are fast-paced affairs that, although lacking the wow factor of the Jordan years, demonstrate just as much heart and action.

CHICAGO CUBS

Wrigley Field, 1060 W. Addison St., Wrigleyville, 773-404-2827; www.cubs.mlb.com

Since 1908, when the Cubs last won the World Series, the gods of baseball seem to conspire against these "lovable losers." Going to watch the "Cubbies" is a summertime rite of passage, one in which at least fans come out winning—just being inside the ivy-festooned, historic Wrigley Field is a stirring experience. Wrigley was built in 1914, and it still boasts a manual scoreboard; it installed lights to play night games only in 1988.

CHICAGO WHITE SOX

U.S. Cellular Field, 333 W. 35th St., Bridgeport, 312-674-1000; www.whitesox.mlb.com

The pride of the South Side, the Sox are often considered the Second City's second team, at least outside the confines of the city limits. Though the Sox's 2005 World Series victory seems to be turning the tides of popularity outside of Chicago, for fervent, lifelong fans here at home, it's business as usual. That means standing behind captain Paul Konerko, heavy hitters Jake Peavy, A.J. Pierzynski and Carlos Quentin, and jovial but foul-mouthed manager Ozzie Guillen as they try to keep the momentum going. The corporate-sounding name of the Sox's home, U.S. Cellular Field, is a good indication of what the stadium looks like—modern (it was completed in 1991), massive, in the middle of a sea of concrete, and by all counts a bit impersonal, especially in comparison to Wrigley. Still, fans have made "the new Comiskey" a bit friendlier by nicknaming it "the Cell". If that isn't cute and cuddly enough for you, head to Schaller's Pump (3714 S. Halsted St., 773-376-6332), where the heart of the franchise—die-hard fans—gather for a pre-game drink.

STEPPENWOLF THEATRE COMPANY

1650 N. Halsted St., Chicago, 312-335-1650; www.steppenwolf.org

Everyone has heard of The Steppenwolf's famous co-founder, Gary Sinise, and its legendary ensemble (John Malkovich, Joan Allen, Martha Plimpton, John Mahoney, et al). But this company—which started in the basement of a suburban church, with blokes and tough guys as prime subject matter—hasn't let fame, nor a slick space in Lincoln Park, go to its head. It still produces thought-provoking work with bite, like ensemble member Tracy Letts' 2008 Pulitzer Prize- and Tony Award-winning play, *August: Osage County.*

Show times and ticket prices vary. Check website for details.

SYMPHONY CENTER

220 S. Michigan Ave., Chicago, 312-294-3000; www.cso.org

In early 2008, the Chicago Symphony Orchestra named a new director, Riccardo Muti, after its ninth one, Daniel Barenboim, left in 2006. Still, we've yet to see whether a new director signals a new direction: Muti's five-year contract starts with the 2010/2011 season, which means that until then, classical music fans will probably get more of the CSO's deep and brassy signature sound. It also doesn't hurt that the cavernous Symphony Center also serves as a concert hall for touring orchestras and organizations it runs, including the Civic Orchestra of Chicago and the Youth Symphony Orchestra.

Admission: $12-$200 depending on show. Various show times; check website for details.

THE UNIVERSITY OF CHICAGO

5801 S. Ellis Ave., Chicago, 773-702-1234; www.uchicago.edu

You don't need to have high SAT scores to gain admittance to the grounds of one of America's premier universities. The Hyde Park campus features lovely collegiate buildings, in any number of which scholars are working to increase the U. of C.'s already large number of Nobel Prize winners. It was on these grounds that Enrico Fermi first sustained a nuclear reaction, that Milton Friedman created a generation of students championing his brand of economics, and that REM sleep was first discovered. The U. of C.'s Oriental Institute, devoted to art from the Near East, holds an outstanding collection of Ancient Egypt artifacts (like the gigantic 17-foot red quartzite statue of King Tut and the Book of the Dead, a collection of spells, hymns and prayers intended to secure for the deceased safe passage to the other world). And nearby is Frank Lloyd Wright's **Robie House** *(5757 S. Woodlawn Ave.)*, a Prairie-style house with dramatic overhangs and wide horizontal lines that, despite its design 90 years ago, revolutionized American architecture and looks as modern today as it did then.

WILLIS TOWER

233 S. Wacker Drive, Chicago, 312-875-9696; www.theskydeck.com

No other building says Chicago more than the Sears, er, Willis Tower. The name may have recently changed but this iconic building is still the tallest building in America (and currently the second tallest in the world) and defines the city's skyline at 1,450 feet and 110 stories high. The Skydeck on the 103rd floor gives a view of 40 to 50 miles out on a clear day, enabling you to see Michigan, Indiana, Illinois and Wisconsin. It also offers interactive multi-language kiosks and exhibits. The recently added Skydeck Ledge features glass boxes extending four feet from the Skydeck that deliver a stomach churning view of the city 1,353 feet below. Although there are displays on the building's history to keep you busy while waiting to snag an elevator to get to the Skydeck, avoid the long, long lines by heading here before the observation deck opens, or after 5 p.m., when it tends to be less crowded.

Admission: adults $15.95, children 3-11 $11, children under 3 free. April-September, daily 9 a.m.-10 p.m.; October-March, daily 10 a.m.-8 p.m.

WRIGLEY BUILDING
400 N. Michigan Ave., Chicago, 312-923-8080; www.wrigley.com

Sitting on the north bank of the Chicago River, the Wrigley Building signals the start of the Magnificent Mile. The white terra-cotta building with its distinctive clock tower is particularly stunning when it stands in contrast against the night sky. Built to house the headquarters of William Wrigley, Jr.'s chewing gum empire, the building is actually two structures connected by ground-level and third-floor walkways. To create the building, Graham, Anderson, Probst and White used the Seville Cathedral's Giralda Tower in Spain as a template for its shape while employing French Renaissance-style ornamentation. Inside there's not much to see, because it's mostly business offices, and unfortunately, there are no free samples of Wrigley's gum or tours to be had.

WHERE TO STAY

★★★THE ALLERTON HOTEL – MICHIGAN AVENUE
701 N. Michigan Ave., Chicago, 312-440-1500, 877-701-8111; www.theallertonhotel.com

During the Roaring '20s, the Allerton was one of the first high rises to pop up on the Chicago skyline. Now a designated landmark, the Michigan Avenue hotel retains some classic elements (such as its exterior sign that reads "Tip Top Tap"— the name of the popular cocktail lounge that closed in 1961) while adding some contemporary accents. The hotel had a makeover in May 2008 and the rooms are now in tip-top shape. The sophisticated spaces are done up in traditional navy blue and white, while modern touches, such as trendy patterned throw pillows, white upholstered headboards and iPod docking stations, are sprinkled throughout. Beware of the rooms labeled "Classic"—that's code for "tiny."

443 rooms. Restaurant, bar. Fitness center. Business center. $151-250

★★★AMALFI HOTEL CHICAGO
20 W. Kinzie St., Chicago, 312-395-9000, 877-262-5341; www.amalfihotelchicago.com

When you check into the Amalfi, you first sit for a consultation with your "Experience Designer" (or concierge) to discuss your stay. Then an "Impressionist" (doorman) brings your luggage up to your contemporary "Space" (room). This River North boutique hotel may be a bit pretentious, but it has the goods to back it up. You'll sleep well on the pillow-top mattresses and Egyptian cotton linens, and enjoy the multi-head showers and Aveda bath products. An in-room CD collection, the hotel's DVD library and the gratis breakfast on every floor make it feel like home. (Then the "Comfort Stylist" (housekeeper) knocks on the door and reminds you where you are.)

215 rooms. Restaurant, bar. Complimentary breakfast. Business center. Fitness center. Pets accepted. $251-350

HIGHLIGHT

WHAT ARE THE MOST LUXURIOUS HOTELS IN CHICAGO?

ELYSIAN

This Parisian Art Deco jewel recalls a bygone era of travel with its exquisite decor, personal service, sensational restaurants and gorgeous spa.

FOUR SEASONS HOTEL CHICAGO

Comfortable guest rooms feature a contemporary spin on 1940s French design, and you can't beat the location right on the Magnificent Mile.

THE PENINSULA CHICAGO

The rooms are beyond comfortable, with pillowy soft beds and panel-controlled everything (shades, music, lighting), while the restaurants are top-notch and the spa is one of the city's best. But it's the warm, gracious service that makes a stay here special.

THE RITZ-CARLTON CHICAGO, A FOUR SEASONS HOTEL

Located atop shopping mecca Water Tower Place, the city view from the large-windowed rooms is hard to beat. A recent makeover has made the hotel more stylish than ever.

TRUMP INTERNATIONAL HOTEL AND TOWER

This stainless steel and glass hotel, which towers over the city at 92 stories, is absolutely gorgeous. Inside you'll find a lavish spa, an excellent restaurant and a swank cocktail lounge, plus rooms that feel residential with fully stocked kitchens.

★★★THE AMBASSADOR EAST HOTEL
1301 N. State Parkway, Chicago, 312-787-7200, 888-506-3471;
www.theambassadoreasthotel.com
Many celebs have checked into this Gold Coast hotel, including Vince Vaughn, Richard Gere and Frank Sinatra (who has a celebrity suite named after him). One reason for its popularity is its location. The hotel sits among residential buildings in a tony neighborhood, plus it's near the jogging trail and volleyball courts of Oak Street Beach. Another reason may be the famed Pump Room restaurant, where Old Hollywood stars flocked to its fabled Booth One, a table that only the most exclusive diners could snag. Robert Wagner and Natalie Wood toasted their wedding in that booth, as did Lauren Bacall and Humphrey

Bogart when they got hitched. Frequent guest Judy Garland even paid tribute to the hot spot in her song Chicago: "Chicago, we'll meet at the Pump Room, Ambassador East." If you meet at the Pump Room today, you'll feast on contemporary American cuisine from executive chef Nick Sutton. Hotel impresario Ian Schraeger purchased the landmark in 2010 and is planning a massive renovation, so check with the front desk before visiting.

285 rooms. Restaurant, bar. Fitness center. Business center. $151-250

★★★THE BLACKSTONE, A CHICAGO RENAISSANCE HOTEL
636 S. Michigan Ave., Chicago, 312-447-0955, 800-468-3571; www.blackstonerenaissance.com

If there's anything to that whole law of attraction business, that's reason enough to stay at The Blackstone. This 1910 Beaux-Arts hotel, listed on the National Register of Historic Places, has hosted presidents, royalty, sports icons and celebrities (including Rudolph Valentino, Joan Crawford, Spencer Tracy, Katharine Hepburn, Tennessee Williams, Truman Capote and Carl Sandburg). If you are not one to name names, though, the handsome renovation completed in the spring of 2008 will still convince you. Preserving the old-fashioned elegance and architectural integrity, Sage Hospitality Resources bought the long-dormant property, stripped it, then gave it a modern edge. The finished product features a grand gilded lobby with opulent designer details and extravagant extras like a video-generated computer art piece or the constantly changing lakefront landscape; a curated collection of more than 1,400 pieces of original art by Chicago artists is displayed on the walls. The guest rooms weren't forgotten either, tastefully adorned with black, white and red décor, rainshowers, Aveda bath amenities, Eames furniture, flat-screen TVs (and TVs integrated into the bathroom mirrors in upgraded rooms). Locals crowd the restaurant, Mercat a la Planxa, for delicious Catalan-inspired food and drinks.

332 rooms. Restaurant, bar. Business center. Fitness center. $251-350

★★★CONRAD CHICAGO
521 N. Rush St., Chicago, 312-645-1500; www.conradhotels.com

Architecture buffs will want to check into the Conrad, located in the landmark McGraw-Hill Building. Be sure to take a look at the façade's sculpted zodiac panels, which make the Art Deco structure stand out. Although it's situated above shops such as A|X Armani Exchange and Nordstrom, this Magnificent Mile hotel can help you find some quiet. You'll discover tranquility in your room by lounging on 500 thread-count Pratesi linens while watching the 42-inch plasma TV, playing the Bose entertainment system or listening to your iPod on the room's docking station. A better escape is the rooftop Terrace at Conrad. It may only be five stories up, but it's still a swanky place where you can enjoy a cocktail and tapas underneath the Chicago sky while gazing at the skyscrapers.

311 rooms. Restaurant, bar. Business center. Fitness center. Pets accepted. $251-350

★★★DANA HOTEL
660 N. State St., Chicago, 888-301-3262; www.danahotelandspa.com

Dana is relatively new to Chicago's boutique hotel scene, having opened in June 2008. To compete with the other boutique hotels, Dana offers guests some extras, including luxurious treatments at the Spa (try the hydramemory facial to treat jet-lagged skin) and tasty bites from a floating sushi bar. The rooms are filled with light wood and natural tones for a Zen vibe, and the luxe bathrooms feature Italian rain showers roomy enough for two. To unwind, dip into the stocked wine chiller in your room. Or if you want some scenery, visit the rooftop Vertigo Sky Lounge, which features a fire pit to keep you warm on those chilly Chicago nights.

216 rooms. Restaurant, bar. Fitness center. Spa. Pets accepted. $251-350

★★★THE DRAKE HOTEL CHICAGO

140 E. Walton Place, Chicago, 312-787-2200, 800-774-1500; www.thedrakehotel.com

The Drake is the hotel of choice for visiting politicians and dignitaries. Winston Churchill, Pope John Paul II and Princess Diana all roomed at the 1920 landmark hotel, ideally located at the beginning of North Michigan Avenue. But this old star could use some polish to regain its luster. While the public spaces still preserve the splendor of the past and some rooms got updated in early 2008, other guest rooms haven't yet gotten their makeovers. Avoid disappointment by asking for a newly renovated room (with gold and white linens and a flat-screen TV).

535 rooms. Restaurant, bar. Fitness center. Business center. $251-350

★★★★ELYSIAN HOTEL

11 E. Walton, Chicago, 312-646-1300, 800-500-8511; www.elysianhotels.com

If Madame Coco Chanel were alive today, she would most certainly feel at home at the Elysian. The chandeliers are inspired by her jewels, the drapes are patterned after her dress designs and the casual restaurant on the third floor, Balsan, is named after Étienne Balsan, the man who financed her first shop. Designed by Lucien Lagrange, the Parisian Art Deco jewel recalls a bygone era of travel with its old fashioned motor court, flawless service (note that the staff does not accept tips), and exquisite décor featuring white marble, velvet sofas, stacks of art books on antique tables and a sophisticated gray, white and black color palette. Guest rooms are spacious (there are only 10 per floor) with fireplaces, terraces, white marble baths and wet bars with handy refrigerator drawers. The hotel's two restaurants, the fine-dining Ria, and the more casual Balsan, are both sensational (the latter is a chic spot for cocktails and snacks). A handsome bar with wood paneling and leather seats is located on the second floor. Be sure to also visit the lavish spa, complete with Greek columns, mosaic pool and men's atelier.

188 rooms. Restaurant, bar. Fitness center. Pool. Spa. $351 and up

★★★EMBASSY SUITES CHICAGO – DOWNTOWN

600 N. State St., Chicago, 312-943-3800, 800-362-2779;
www.embassysuiteschicago.com

A less sophisticated alternative to its nearby sister inn in Streeterville, this outpost screams "hotel chain" with old-style comforters in mauves and blues and the obligatory generic framed landscapes in the bedrooms. What this place lacks in style, it makes up for in roominess. The spacious suites include a separate living room with a sofa, not to mention microwave, coffeemaker and fridge. If you don't feel like chowing down on a frozen dinner, stop off for a complimentary aperitif at the daily manager's reception (5:30-7:30 p.m.)

WHAT ARE THE BEST BOUTIQUE HOTELS IN CHICAGO?

Dana Hotel:
To compete with the other boutique hotels, Dana offers guests some extras, including luxurious all-natural treatments at the spa and tasty bites from a floating sushi bar, luxe bathrooms featuring Italian rain showers roomy enough for two and stocked wine chillers in the rooms.

The James Hotel:
This comfortable boutique hotel features rooms with full-size bars—not that you're likely to spend much time in your room considering that the bar and lounge are both hotspots, and David Burke's Primehouse is downstairs.

The Wit:
The city's newest boutique hotel is located in the Loop in a stylish glass-encased tower. While rooms are contemporary and comfortable, the main draw here is the wildly popular rooftop bar.

before heading to the hotel's Osteria Via Stato & Enoteca for some Italian eats.

367 rooms. Restaurant, bar. Complimentary breakfast. Business center. Fitness center. Pool. $151-250

★★★EMBASSY SUITES CHICAGO - DOWNTOWN/LAKEFRONT

511 N. Columbus Drive, Chicago, 312-836-5900, 888-903-8884; www.chicagoembassy.com

Traveling families can spread out here and make it a home away from home. The two-room suites have a separate living room with a sofa bed and dining table, a microwave, a coffeemaker and a fridge. After a March 2008 renovation, the bland beige-hued suites got an upgrade with two flat-panel TVs per room and local artwork on the walls to add some Chicago flavor. If sticking close to your new home makes you stir-crazy, head to the atrium lounge, order a cocktail from the nearby bar and enjoy the soothing sound of the 70-foot cascading water wall. Or you can just wait until the free daily manager's reception to tipple and munch on some appetizers. Also be sure to take advantage of the complimentary made-to-order breakfast before rounding up the kids and trekking over to nearby Navy Pier—you'll need the energy.

455 rooms. Restaurant, bar. Complimentary breakfast. Fitness center. Pool. Business center. $151-250

★★★THE FAIRMONT CHICAGO, MILLENNIUM PARK

200 N. Columbus Drive, Chicago, 312-565-8000, 866-540-4408; www.fairmont.com

The Fairmont wrapped up renovations in June 2008, and with them came a change from traditional chintzes and furniture to Mid-Century modern neutrals and large Warwick Orme floral images. Rooms are an updated retreat with flat-screen TVs and remodeled bathrooms with marble tile and rainshowers. Locals head to the new mySpa for treatments. The spa is all about the details: It uses vegan nail polish and pipes your iPod's music into the treatment room. Located in the lobby is Eno, a wine, chocolate and cheese room enclosed by a glass art wall in a bamboo pattern.

687 rooms. Restaurant, bar. Fitness center. Pets accepted. $151-250

★★★★★FOUR SEASONS HOTEL CHICAGO

120 E. Delaware Place, Chicago, 312-280-8800; www.fourseasons.com/chicagofs

With its prime Mag Mile location and attractive,

contemporary rooms, this luxe hotel is a top choice for visiting celebrities and those who appreciate the peace and quiet the polished staff practically guarantees. A recent renovation took the formerly traditional English country décor and transformed it by adding French deco style, with flowery prints replaced with rich chocolate, deep blue and shimmery silver hues, and new leather window seats in many rooms overlooking Lake Michigan and the Gold Coast. The lobby, grand ballroom, restaurants and the larger suites and apartments received updates in early 2009. Two things that haven't changed: the wonderful, personal service, and the location. It's situated just above Bloomingdale's and other stores such as Gucci, Williams-Sonoma and Michael Kors in the 900 North Michigan building.

346 rooms. Restaurant, bar. Fitness center. Pool. Spa. Business center. $351 and up

★★★HARD ROCK HOTEL
230 N. Michigan Ave., Chicago, 312-345-1000, 866-966-5166; www.hardrockhotelchicago.com

Located in the landmark Carbide and Carbon Building, the Hard Rock gives some edge to the Art Deco skyscraper. Step into the lobby, which was recently renovated for a classic vibe. Be sure to tour the hotel's display cases, which show off noted musicians' outfits, instruments and other rock 'n' roll memorabilia. But the hotel is more sleek than kitschy. Its modern silver-gray rooms offer Aveda toiletries, pillow-top beds and laptop safes, and they keep to the music theme with bathroom murals of icons such as Bowie and the Beatles. Get the rock-star treatment by staying in the Extreme Suite, a 950-foot penthouse that's on its own floor with private elevator access.

381 rooms. Restaurant, bar. Business center. Fitness center. Spa. Pets accepted. $151-250

★★★HILTON CHICAGO
720 S. Michigan Ave., Chicago, 312-922-4400; www.hilton.com

Overlooking Grant Park, Lake Michigan and Millennium Park, this South Loop hotel is all about grandeur. The sumptuous Renaissance-style Great Hall is decorated in white with towering columns and gold accents to go along with intricate ceiling work. The theme tries to carry to the guest rooms with gold-trimmed wood dressers and cabinets and gold-tinged ornate duvets, but it doesn't translate as well in a smaller space. Still, the location across from Grant Park is superb, and if you're in town for St. Patrick's Day, onsite Kitty O'Shea's is the place to be.

1,544 rooms. Restaurant, bar. Business center. Fitness center. Pool. Pets accepted. $151-250

★★★HILTON SUITES CHICAGO/MAGNIFICENT MILE
198 E. Delaware Place, Chicago, 312-664-1100; www.hilton.com

This all-suite hotel is in the heart of downtown, making it a convenient choice for business travelers and families alike. The classic navy and maroon suites come with a separate living room complete with a flat-screen TV, mini-fridge and pullout sofa. But who would want to veg on the couch when you can head to the nearby Hancock Tower and peer out from the 94th-floor observatory or—even better—zip up to the 95th-floor Signature Lounge to relax with a sidecar and a vista of downtown? Go ahead and order another round or two; your hotel is within stumbling distance anyway.

345 rooms. Restaurant. Fitness center. Pool. Business center. Pets accepted. $151-250

★★★HOTEL ALLEGRO

171 W. Randolph St., Chicago, 312-236-0123, 800-643-1500; www.allegrochicago.com

An early 2008 renovation has transformed Hotel Allegro into a stylish retreat. The blue and gray rooms have sleek geometric-patterned walls, 37-inch flat-screen TVs, zebra-print bathrobes in premier rooms and suites, Aveda toiletries and alarm clocks with iPod docking stations. Savor the soothing ambiance by indulging in an in-room spa treatment—go for the Calm Mind massage, which will fill the room with scents of lavender. If you can pry yourself out of your room, head to the gratis wine hour in the lobby. For sustenance, grab dinner at 312 Chicago for some delicious Italian eats, and then sip a pomegranate Mojito from Encore Liquid Lounge before catching a play at the Cadillac Palace Theatre next door.

483 rooms. Restaurant, bar. Business center. Fitness center. Spa. Pets accepted. $251-350

★★★HOTEL BLAKE

500 S. Dearborn St., Chicago, 312-986-1234; www.hotelblake.com

Located in a 19th century building, Hotel Blake is a nice option in Printers Row. The contemporary, spacious rooms feature high ceilings, large windows (in some rooms they are floor to ceiling) and earth tones with splashes of red. For dinner, head to the hotel's equally sophisticated Custom House Tavern, where you'll find delicious American fare and an extensive bar menu if you're just looking for a quick bite after a day of meetings. The hotel is near shopping on State Street, Grant Park and the Chicago Board of Trade.

162 rooms. Restaurant, bar. Business center. Fitness center. Spa. $151-250

★★★HOTEL BURNHAM

1 W. Washington St., Chicago, 312-782-1111, 877-294-9712; www.burnhamhotel.com

The landmark Hotel Burnham, the first precursor to modern skyscrapers, retains touches of its past life, with mosaic floors, marble ceilings and walls, and ornamental metal grills on the elevators and stairwells. The rooms, not so much: Decked out in navy and gold, they take on a nautical look, with the sunburst mirror and gold emblem on the deep-blue headboard mimicking a ship's wheel. Located across from the former Marshall Field's department store (now Macy's), the hotel is nestled in the middle of the Theater District. Before you catch a show, stop in the Atwood Café, an upscale American restaurant with an inviting jewel-tone dining room that resembles an old Parisian brasserie. Perks for pets are as swanky as those for guests: Animals get beds made of hypoallergenic fleece and cedar chips with an optional turndown service. If you left Fido at home and are feeling lonely, the hotel will lend you a goldfish to keep you company.

122 rooms. Restaurant, bar. Fitness center. Pets accepted. $151-250

★★★HOTEL INDIGO

1244 N. Dearborn St., Chicago, 312-787-4980, 866-521-6950; www.goldcoastchicagohotel.com

If you want something beyond a cookie-cutter hotel room bathed in banal beige, retreat to Hotel Indigo. The guest rooms are more like calming beach houses than typical hotel spaces. Hardwood floors, whitewashed furniture, teak benches, and navy and indigo blue dominate the rooms along with lime green accents, and vibrant wall-size photo murals of blueberries, irises and sky-blue cable-knit sweaters transform the space. Certain touches make it clear that it's not just another day at the beach: spa-style showerheads, sleek Melitta coffeemakers, Aveda toiletries and personal trainers at the fitness center.

165 rooms. Restaurant, bar. Fitness center. Spa. Business center. Pets accepted. $251-350

★★★HOTEL INTERCONTINENTAL

505 N. Michigan Ave., Chicago, 312-944-4100, 800-628-2112; www.chicago.intercontinental.com

Originally the 1929 Medinah Athletic Club, Hotel InterContinental still maintains some of its old-time glory. Its 12th floor Art Deco Junior Olympic pool is where Olympic swimmer and Tarzan actor Johnny Weissmuller frequently escaped from the jungle to do some laps. The hotel now has a state-of-the-art three-story fitness center, one of the largest hotel gyms in the city. If you don't want to be quite that healthy, swing by ENO, where you can order wine flights accompanied by artisanal cheese or luscious chocolate. The rooms in the Main Building are plain-Jane with cream duvets, maroon throw pillows, and maroon-and-gold striped curtains. If you like Old World décor, you'll appreciate the historic tower's rooms, which use the same color palette, but replace mahogany headboards with carved ones and basic bedding with fancy patterned covers.

790 rooms. Restaurant, bar. Fitness center. Pool. Business center. Pets accepted. $251-350

★★★HOTEL MONACO

225 N. Wabash Ave., Chicago, 312-960-8500, 866-610-0081; www.monaco-chicago.com

It's om sweet om at the Hotel Monaco. Although the rooms feature whimsical Art Deco-inspired décor, with thick pistachio and butter cream striped walls, they are actually Zen dens. Each room comes with a meditation station, a large window with fluffy pillows meant for reflection. You can flip on the in-room yoga program and use the provided accessories to practice your sun salutation. If that doesn't work, take a bath with Aveda products. Then slip into the pillow bed and put the Relaxation Station on the TV, which will fill the room with soothing sounds and images. The Karen Neuburger suite is a retreat with a spacious living room and plush KN towels and soft bamboo-blend sheets. But if you don't do low-key, book the Rock and Roll Suite, which rolls out the zebra-print carpet with plush red velvet couches, a jukebox, guitar and amp.

192 rooms. Restaurant, bar. Fitness center. Business center. $151-250

★★★HOTEL SAX

333 N. Dearborn St., Chicago, 312-245-0333; www.hotelsaxchicago.com

Techies will blog about the high-end game room here, which is open to all guests and includes five Xbox 360 stations with wireless controllers, five Zune MP3 players preloaded with music and movies, and two laptops with Internet access. But gossip bloggers will write about the hotel's visiting celebrities, when famous DJs hit the red-hued Crimson Lounge. It's no wonder the hotel, which sits next to the House of Blues, draws such high-profile guests. The too-hip-to-handle slate-gray guest rooms are wallpapered with damask prints super-imposed with fake shadows of candelabras, and textures abound with leather paisley headboards, suede throw pillows and chestnut furniture.

354 rooms. Bar. Business center. Fitness center. $251-350

★★★THE JAMES HOTEL
55 E. Ontario St., Chicago, 312-337-1000, 877-526-3755; www.jameshotels.com

The James attracts more stars than an awards show: Jessica Simpson, Jennifer Hudson, Jeremy Piven and Jack Johnson have all checked into the hotel. The draw could be David Burke's Primehouse, which is known for its dry-aged steaks and whimsical desserts such as cheesecake lollipops. Or it could be popular nightspot J Bar. You also can't discount the attractive rooms: Dashes of brown, red or black give the all-white, contemporary design a mod slant, and features like vinyl headboards make this one chic spot. Forget your standard mini-bar. Each room here comes outfitted with a large bar of high-end liquors.

297 rooms. Restaurant, bar. Fitness center. Business center. Pets accepted. $151-250

★★★MARRIOTT CHICAGO DOWNTOWN MAGNIFICENT MILE
540 N. Michigan Ave., Chicago, 312-836-0100, 800-228-9290; www.marriott.com

As its name implies, this Marriott is conveniently situated on the Magnificent Mile. But the harried shoppers below won't faze you when you've melted underneath the plush down comforter in your bold blue- and gold-colored room (courtesy of upgrades in spring 2006) for a nap. If you can't get any Z's, take a dip in the hotel pool, or give in and join the crowds at nearby Oak Street Beach. Those who are all work-and-no-play should head to the onsite Starbucks to get some java and free WiFi. Self-check out kiosks also will help business travelers on tight schedules.

1,198 rooms. Restaurant, bar. Business center. Fitness center. Pool. $151-250

★★★OMNI CHICAGO HOTEL
676 N. Michigan Ave., Chicago, 312-944-6664, 888-444-6664; www.omnihotels.com

If the name sounds familiar, it's because Oprah puts up many of her show's guests at this all-suite hotel. The beige and cream suites offer roomy digs and plasma TVs. Kids get milk and cookies the first night, as well as a goodie bag at check-in. Ask for a free Get Fit Kit ($50 deposit is required), which includes a mat and weights so that you can work out in your hotel room while the little ones play. Afterward, head up to one of the two rooftop decks where you can catch some sun in warm weather.

347 rooms. Restaurant, bar. Business center. Fitness center. Spa. Pool. Pets accepted. $251-350

★★★PALMER HOUSE HILTON
17 E. Monroe St., Chicago, 312-726-7500;
www.palmerhousehiltonhotel.com

Named after business mogul Potter Palmer, the historic Palmer House is one of the longest continuously running hotels in the U.S., and also the first to be equipped with electric lights and telephones in each room. A 2008 renovation aimed to return the massive hotel to its roots, and thankfully it included more than just lights and phones; a health club and spa, standard elsewhere, were finally added. The rooms are now bathed in lavender, brown and sage, shades that mimic the lobby's original terrazzo flooring and opulent Beaux-Arts ceiling, but the décor is updated with monogrammed pillows, swirly and striped linens, and ebony headboards. Executive level rooms were renovated in 2009—they have a French Empire style with flowery pastels and ornate gold mirrors—and you get your own private concierge and a buffet of goodies such as the Palmer House brownies, which is appropriate since Bertha Palmer invented the chocolate creation and the Palmer House debuted it at the 1893 World's Fair.

1,639 rooms. Restaurant, bar. Business center. Fitness center. Pool. Pets accepted. $151-250

★★★PARK HYATT CHICAGO

800 N. Michigan Ave., Chicago, 312-335-1234, 800-233-1234; www.parkchicago.hyatt.com

The luxe Park Hyatt showers guests with butlers, personal safes with laptop rechargers and storage for wardrobes (who can travel without that?). The chic décor is simple and understated with cherry wood-filled guest rooms, gold and mocha accents and leather chairs. Make sure to bathe in the oversized tub; as you soak you can slide open the wall to reveal the bedroom and views of the skyline or Lake Michigan. For more relaxation, pamper yourself at the onsite medispa Tiffani Kim Institute with a customized facial. If you're the sporty type, borrow one of the hotel's free bicycles and do some sightseeing while pedaling along Chicago's many bike paths. Afterward, complete the experience with dinner at NoMI, an excellent contemporary French-Asian restaurant overlooking Michigan Avenue.

198 rooms. Restaurant, bar. Fitness center. Spa. Pool. Business center. Pets accepted. $351 and up

★★★★★THE PENINSULA CHICAGO

108 E. Superior St., Chicago, 312-337-2888, 866-288-8889; www.chicago.peninsula.com

Stars like Ellen DeGeneres, Chris Rock and Brad Pitt and Angelina Jolie visit The Peninsula for its luxurious rooms and spa, but don't overlook it as a dining destination. The hotel is known for its highly acclaimed Shanghai Terrace and Avenues restaurants. There are also the afternoon teas, which offer exotic blends, including those made especially for The Peninsula, as well as a lavish chocolate buffet on Fridays and Saturdays. Even without the food options, The Peninsula stands out. The Peninsula Spa by ESPA offers a full menu of services and a relaxation lounge where you can doze under a comforter in a sectioned-off area and relax uninterrupted after your treatment. Luxurious guest rooms are bright with light wood and muted earth tones, and the marble bathrooms have roomy tubs where you can watch TV while you soak. A bedside control panel allows you to shut off the light and signal that you don't want to be disturbed, all without having to leave the comfort of your 300-thread-count sheets.

339 rooms. Restaurant, bar. Fitness center. Spa. Pool. Business center. Pets accepted. $351 and up

★★★★THE RITZ-CARLTON CHICAGO, A FOUR SEASONS HOTEL

160 E. Pearson St., Chicago, 312-266-1000, 800-621-6906; www.fourseasons.com/chicagorc

When you're at the Ritz, which rests atop shopping mecca Water Tower Place, the city view from the large-windowed rooms is hard to beat. The spacious guest rooms and executive suites were given a makeover in 2007, and floral-patterned duvets and dark wood furniture were replaced with crisp white linens and a soothing grey color palette. (Renovations were completed on all other suites in 2010.) If you don't want to leave, send up for the spa's in-room signature aromatherapy massage or have a customized fragranced bath drawn for you in your marble bathroom. After your treatment and soothing bath, you might want to rest your heavy head on the down pillow and bury yourself underneath the down blanket. But force yourself to grab a bite in Deca. The bar and restaurant on the 12th floor where ladies used to lunch is now a chic spot servings fizzy cocktails, oysters and bistro favorites such as duck confit.

434 rooms. Restaurant, bar. Fitness center. Spa. Pool. Business center. Pets accepted. $351 and up

★★★SHERATON CHICAGO HOTEL AND TOWERS

301 E. North Water St., Chicago, 312-464-1000, 800-325-3535; www.sheratonchicago.com

Overlooking the Chicago River, the Sheraton chain's flagship branch touts itself as the "premier convention and business hotel in the Midwest." In fact, its enormous size makes it seem more like a convention center than a luxury hotel. But the simply decorated cream and beige rooms with beds resting against wood-paneled walls are inviting, especially when you add in the calming views of the water. For a change of scenery, visit the surprisingly hip Chi Bar, where you can kick back in a cocoa-colored leather chair with a Chicago Sunset martini and forget about the conventioneers flitting around the rest of the hotel.

1,209 rooms. Restaurant, bar. Business center. Fitness center. Pool. Pets accepted. $151-250

★★★SOFITEL CHICAGO WATER TOWER

20 E. Chestnut St., Chicago, 312-324-4000; www.sofitel.com

You can't miss the stylish Sofitel—look for the triangle-shaped building near downtown. The glass and steel structure looks like it leapt out from the pages of an interior design magazine and into the Gold Coast. The rooms aren't too shabby, either. They are a tad small but airy, thanks to light wood furniture, cream walls, bedding and mirrored closet doors. The bathrooms are roomier, with separate showers and tubs. This hotel goes Francophile all the way, with Café des Architectes, a French restaurant, and Le Bar, which has floor-to-ceiling glass walls and is the perfect place for a wine flight and a cheese plate.

415 rooms. Restaurant, bar. Fitness center. Business center. Pets accepted. $251-350

★★★THE SUTTON PLACE HOTEL – CHICAGO

21 E. Bellevue Place, Chicago, 312-266-2100, 866-378-8866; www.suttonplace.com

White is the shade of choice for the linens in the rooms here, while the drapes, carpeting and wallpaper are beige, replacing the old gloomy gray that used to dominate the rooms. The only vibrant color you'll see is a smattering of purple and bold blue in a stray chair or pillow. On the bright side, you can escape to The Whiskey Bar & Grill to unwind with some authentic Mexican fare; try the shrimp tacos and wash them down with a margarita or two, which will put some color in your cheeks if your room is without.

246 rooms. Restaurant, bar. Business center. Fitness center. Pets accepted. $251-350

★★★SWISSÔTEL CHICAGO

323 E. Wacker Drive, Chicago, 312-565-0565, 800-637-9477; www.swissotelchicago.com

After renovations in April 2008, the Swissôtel Chicago—the sole stateside outpost of the Swiss hotel chain—is more appealing to business travelers. Upgrades included larger desks, ergonomic chairs, tech docking stations to use various media devices simultaneously and 37-inch split-screen plasma TVs. And the hotel recently added more meeting space. Families will be at home here, too. Kid-friendly suites have double beds to match the theme of the room (Shedd Aquarium, Field Museum or Adler Planetaerium), toys, a play area and books. Parents can hunker down within the heather gray and ivory striped walls and rest in a white bed with an oversized fabric headboard. Whether you're there for business or pleasure, be sure to take a dip in the 45-foot indoor pool. It's on the 42nd floor and offers a nice view of Lake Michigan, as well as a wall that features a beautiful tiled mural of the Chicago skyline.

661 rooms. Restaurant, bar. Business center. Fitness center. Pool. $251-350

★★★★TRUMP INTERNATIONAL HOTEL AND TOWER
401 N. Wabash Ave., Chicago, 312-588-8000, 877-458-7867;
www.trumpchicagohotel.com

The Donald put his stamp on the Chicago skyline with his stainless-steel and iridescent glass hotel, which towers over the city at 92 stories. And he continues the splendor inside the tower. The modern, slate-gray rooms have floor-to-ceiling windows that give gorgeous vistas of the city, custom-designed furniture warms up the spaces, and chefs will come to your room to cook up a meal in your state-of-the-art kitchen. The lap-of-luxury treatment doesn't end there. You can get purifying massages using ruby and diamond-infused oils at the spa. If you don't opt for the in-room chef, go to the restaurant Sixteen, which has a seasonally driven menu. Afterward, have a drink at the inviting Rebar, which offers a lovely view of the adjacent Chicago River.

339 rooms. Restaurant, bar. Business center. Fitness center. Spa. Pool. $351 and up

★★★W CHICAGO – CITY CENTER
172 W. Adams St., Chicago, 312-332-1200, 877-946-8357; www.whotels.com

Staying at the W is less about the rooms and amenities and more about the scene. Socialites and Loop workers crowd the bar for happy hour in the neo-gothic lobby, or the "Living Room," with long drapes at the entryways, and art projected on a wall set to music. The onsite Ristorante We serves Tuscan-inspired cuisine, and rooms are stylish and comfortable with pillow-top beds and eggplant comforters. The downside: if you want to visit the excellent Bliss spa, you'll have to head to the W's Lakeshore location.

368 rooms. Restaurant, bar. Business center. Fitness center. Pets accepted. $251-350

★★★W CHICAGO - LAKESHORE
644 N. Lake Shore Drive, Chicago, 312-943-9200; www.starwoodhotels.com

Business travelers who yawn at the usual tedious hotel environs will seek refuge at the W, which has a prime spot on Lake Shore Drive. After settling into your small, dimly lit but sophisticated room, which offers a mix of taupe and deep purples, head up to the hotel's eighth floor to pamper yourself with a treatment at Bliss, a cheerful spa that lives up to its name. There you can have a pedicure while you watch your own personal TV. Afterward, return to your room, crawl under the goose-down duvet and watch a DVD from the lending library. Or go to the penthouse lounge, Whiskey Sky, where you sip a cocktail and admire the Lake Michigan views. Adjacent to Whiskey Sky is Altitude, a revolving banquet room that would be an impressive spot for a business meeting.

520 rooms. Restaurant, bar. Business center. Fitness center. Pool. Spa. Pets accepted. $251-350

★★★THE WESTIN MICHIGAN AVENUE

909 N. Michigan Ave., Chicago, 312-943-7200, 800-937-8461; www.westin.com/michiganave

The Westin tries to offer a little something for everyone. Shopaholics will love the hotel for its location across from Water Tower Place. Kids will enjoy the Kids Club, whose membership comes with a drawstring bag with a world map and make-your-own postcard kit upon check-in. Parents of newborns will appreciate getting their own drawstring bag filled with first-aid items, socket covers and a nightlight. Pets sleep soundly on their own beds. Joggers will lap up the Runner's World-approved maps of local running routes. And everyone will have a restful sleep on the hotel's legendary plush mattresses. As this hotel is constantly packed, it's no suprise that it shows a little wear.

752 rooms. Restaurant, bar. Business center. Fitness center. Pets accepted. $251-350

★★★THE WIT

201 N. State St., Chicago, 312-467-0200; www.thewithotel.com

Wake-up calls from Barack Obama, Mayor Daley and Harry Caray are par for the course at The Wit (they are impersonators from The Second City improv troupe). And while they're just recordings, they give a feel for the tongue-in-cheek nature on display at this unique Loop hotel. Rooms are cheerful and contemporary, with pillow-top beds and down duvets, plus flat-screen TVs and in-room snack bars. When walking through the corridors, expect to hear birds chirping during the day and owls hooting at night (just another witty touch). You'll have to compete for a seat with the locals who crowd into ROOF, the 27th-floor rooftop lounge that offers incredible city views and cozy seating arranged around indoor fireplaces (be sure to walk out on what they call "the hangover," a portion of the roof that is suspended over the street; apparently it's a popular spot for proposals and has amazing views). If you can't get in at ROOF, head to the Phoenix Lounge, which offers a live music series. The hotel also houses its own high-definition theater, Screen, which features comfortable recliners and cushy love seats and is available for private screenings, as well as a spa and two onsite restaurants, including the popular Cibo Matto. It's all part of the fun at this refreshing hotel.

298 rooms. Restaurant, bar. Business center. Fitness center. Spa. $151-250

RECOMMENDED

FAIRFIELD INN AND SUITES CHICAGO DOWNTOWN

216 E. Ontario St., Chicago, 312-787-3777, 800-228-2800; www.fairfieldsuiteschicago.com

The Fairfield, just steps from Michigan Avenue and a half mile from Oak Street Beach, is simply decorated and modestly sized, which suits its guests just fine—the proximity to the Mag Mile is the main draw. If you are looking for incentives, check out the packages: One for anyone who loves to shop includes a $50 gift card, plus a free breakfast and valet parking.

185 rooms. Complimentary breakfast. Fitness center. Business center. $61-150

HAMPTON INN CHICAGO AND SUITES

33 W. Illinois St., Chicago, 312-832-0330, 800-426-7866; www.hamptoninnchicago.com

Business travelers and Internet junkies will be at home at Hampton Inn. Each room comes with a portable wooden laptop desk, so you can work or surf the web from the comfort of your bed. If you have to burn the midnight oil to get that big report done, the hotel offers free coffee 24 hours a day at a beverage station and you'll have a gratis hot breakfast waiting for you in the morning. Traveling for pleasure? Go for a meal at Ruth's Chris Steak House, lounge at nightspot Ballo, laze on the sundeck or check out the Frank Lloyd Wright-inspired lobby. The hotel brags that the rooms also are influenced by the architect's signature style, but really, Wright probably would have shrugged at the standard tan-and-cream-hued suites.

230 rooms. Restaurant, bar. Complimentary breakfast. Business center. Fitness center. Pool. $61-150

HOMEWOOD SUITES CHICAGO DOWNTOWN

40 E. Grand Ave., Chicago, 312-644-2222; www.homewoodsuiteschicago.com

Families will appreciate the roomy suites here, but the bedrooms have a cookie-cutter feel thanks to unimaginative tan décor. Although the living rooms are somewhat brighter with a red and gold sleeper sofa and chair, they're still generic. Yet the reason to come here is the full kitchen. It offers plenty of cupboard space, plates and accessories, a microwave, a fridge, a dishwasher and more. If you're not in the mood to cook, there's a free daily breakfast buffet and complimentary receptions Monday through Thursday from 5 to 7 p.m. featuring a light meal and drinks.

233 rooms. Complimentary breakfast. Business center. Fitness center. Pool. $61-150

HOTEL FELIX

111 W Huron St., Chicago, 312-447-3440; www.hotelfelixchicago.com

Hotel Felix sets the mark for what an eco-friendly should be—not just LEED certified but chic and charming and relaxing, proving that helping the planet does not mean you have to sacrifice luxury or comfort. The guest rooms, while on the small size, make excellent use of their space, with flatscreen televisions, drawers in the platform beds and efficient workstations. The modern rooms have a cool silver and grey color palette, comfortable beds with super-soft linens, and bathrooms stocked with natural, water-based H20 products. Best of all, the hotel is a short walk to Michigan Avenue, the River North Galleries and some of the city's liveliest nightspots, but far enough away from the hustle and bustle to be a calm oasis. After enjoying Chicago's local attractions, take advantage of the hotel's full service spa or the seasonal restaurant Elate, before making your way to the cozy, dimly lit (from an interesting glass chandelier) lounge for a nightcap in front of the fire. All in all, Hotel Felix is a natural choice for anyone looking for a great value in the heart of downtown.

225 rooms. Restaurant, bar. Fitness center. Spa. $151-250

HOTEL PALOMAR CHICAGO

505 N. State Street, Chicago, 312-755-9703, 877-731-0505; www.hotelpalomarchicago.com

Hotel Palomar Chicago is a welcome addition to the Chicago hotel scene, offering comfortable, affordable accommodations in the heart of downtown. The Kimpton Hotel features art-themed decor, an indoor rooftop pool, and a buzzing restaurant, Sable Kitchen & Bar. Guest rooms feature neutral tones with pops of color and images from the 1993 Chicago World's Fair, floor-to-ceiling windows, complimentary wireless Internet and honor bars with organic products. The hotel is just two blocks from Michigan Avenue.

261 rooms. Restaurant, bar. Business center. Fitness center. Pool. Pets accepted. $151-250

THE TREMONT CHICAGO

100 E. Chestnut St., Chicago, 312-751-1900; www.tremontchicago.com

The pale hues, dark wood and floral textiles in the small rooms aim for a romantic vibe, but they make this European-style hotel seem dated. The rooms also provide a strange juxtaposition to the hotel's restaurant, the decidedly unflowery Mike Ditka's Restaurant, owned by the legendary Bears coach. The two-floor steakhouse replaces the faux romanticism with a cigar lounge and a live Sinatra-esque singer. Odd pairings aside, the Tremont's best perk is its location; it's a half block away from Michigan Avenue, right near the Hancock Center and Water Tower Place shopping paradise.

130 rooms. Restaurant, bar. Business Center $151-250

WHERE TO EAT

★★★★★ALINEA

1723 N. Halsted St., Chicago, 312-867-0110; www.alinea-restaurant.com

Not only did Alinea's internationally respected chef Grant Achatz win the 2008 James Beard Outstanding Chef Award, he's also got a hell of a story to tell. In 2007, Achatz was diagnosed with tongue cancer, and doctors said he might lose his sense of taste forever. An aggressive treatment looks to have beaten the cancer, and Achatz's sense of taste was saved. So now he's back in the kitchen, creating some of the most wildly creative dishes in the country. Alinea, the Latin word for that funny little symbol (¶) indicating the need for a new paragraph—or a new train of thought—is at the forefront of the molecular gastronomy movement, which re-imagines familiar foods in stunningly innovative ways. Behind the restaurant's purposefully hidden entrance and up a floating glass-and-metal staircase, you'll be treated to breathtaking creations such as the black truffle explosion, featuring truffle-topped ravioli filled with truffle broth, which "explodes" in your mouth. Another dish is duck served with mango and yogurt on a pillow of juniper air. The complex meals often require equally complicated instructions from the patient waitstaff, but trust us—you won't complain.

Contemporary American. Dinner. Closed Monday-Tuesday. $86 and up

★★★ARIA

The Fairmont Chicago, 200 N. Columbus Drive, Chicago, 312-444-9494; www.ariachicago.com

Technically, Aria is located inside the Fairmont hotel, just east of tony Michigan Avenue. But the fact that the restaurant has its own entrance symbolizes how chef Brad Parsons wants his eclectic spot to separate itself from the norm. The globally influenced restaurant boasts its own tandoori oven for naan, and a hip sushi bar draws a lively crowd of saketini sippers. Those who want a globe-spanning culinary experience will have a great time in the dramatic dining room, which is filled with orchids and Tibetan artwork. The menu ranges from shrimp and chicken pad thai to a perfectly prepared New York strip steak to Hong Kong barbecue duck and lobster chow mein.

International. Breakfast, lunch, dinner. Bar. $36-85

WHICH CHICAGO RESTAURANTS HAVE THE MOST CUTTING-EDGE FOOD?

ALINEA

Some people call it sci-fi food. Chef Grant Achatz's food is indeed high-tech. The chef endlessly plays with food—the textures, the aromas, the flavors—as if he were in a chem lab, and yet it somehow manages to all feel familiar at the same time.

AVENUES

Chef Curtis Duffy offers cuisine that manages to be both simple and extravagant. He favors unusual pairings that work despite seeming contradictory, such as the grilled Wagyu steak with smoked coconut and African blue basil.

L20

Chef Laurent Gras offers a French-oriented seafood menu in which hard-to-find varieties are prepared in interesting ways, say, lobster that has been vacuum-cooked or snapper smoked over cherry wood.

MOTO

Chef Homaro Cantu of Moto keeps liquid nitrogen, helium and organic food-based inks sitting alongside pots, pans and spoons. After you order, the rice-paper menu itself is the first course (it tastes like risotto).

SCHWA

Maverick chef Michael Carlson's restaurant is bare bones—tiny room, no liquor license, the cooks also serve as the waitstaff—but the food is remarkably innovative. Carlson offers three- and nine-course menus that feature knockout dishes such as a savory beer cheese soup with a pretzel roll, and a gently-seared kona kampachi with galangal, lime and a tiny splash of maple syrup.

★★★ARUN'S
4156 N. Kedzie Ave., Chicago, 773-539-1909; www.arunsthai.com
Thai cuisine in Chicago was once consigned to BYOB storefronts, but owner Arun Sampanthavivat's gorgeous restaurant, which he opened in 1985, brought his native land's food to the level of haute cuisine. The 2,500-square-foot, bi-level dining room—its every nook and cranny filled with gorgeous Thai art

(much of it painted by the owner's brother)—is located in far-flung Albany Park. The almost museum-like surroundings complement a dining experience that brilliantly combines heat and sweetness. The constantly changing offerings are part of a 12-course tasting menu consisting of six appetizers, four entrées and two desserts, and preparations range from a beef curry in a spicy sauce to whole tamarind snapper. The personable service is always ready to accommodate any preferences or tolerance for spiciness, and a meticulous wine-pairing is available for the asking.

Thai. Dinner. Closed Monday. $86 and up

★★★ATWOOD CAFÉ

Hotel Burnham, 1 W. Washington St., Chicago, 312-368-1900; www.atwoodcafe.com

You can't get much more centrally located than the Atwood Café, which sits in the heart of the action of Chicago's Loop and provides floor-to-ceiling views of bustling State Street. And you can't get much more comfortable than the food on the Atwood Café's menu, which presents new takes on classic American standbys. The expansive bar serves as an ideal place for a drink before heading to the nearby Theater District (we told you it was centrally located) for a show.

Contemporary American. Breakfast (Monday-Saturday), lunch (Monday-Saturday), dinner, Sunday brunch. $36-85

★★★AVEC

615 W. Randolph St., Chicago, 312-377-2002; www.avecrestaurant.com

Avec means "with" in French, which fits here because you're likely to end up dining with complete strangers at one of the communal tables. You won't mind, because the restaurant's Euro-Mediterranean fare and surprisingly reasonable prices put you in such a good mood that you're happy to talk with your neighbors about the amazing food in front of you. Co-owned by chef Paul Kahan, Avec offers delicious fare prepared by chef de cuisine (and recent James Beard award winner) Koren Grieveson. Popular items include the chorizo-stuffed Medjool dates wrapped in smoked bacon and topped with a piquillo pepper-tomato sauce, and the crispy focaccia with taleggio cheese, truffle oil and fresh herbs. The menu, which is divided into large and small plates, is always changing, which means this restaurant is worth a trip every time you're in town. For example, in spring Grieveson might whip up a heavenly English pea crostini with mint oil, roasted spring onion vinaigrette and Pecorino; in fall, she might prepare the pork shoulder with chestnut-bacon dumplings and butternut squash. The small room looks almost sauna-like with its fully paneled cedar walls and ceiling, and its back display of glass wine bottles is both colorful and whimsical. Speaking of bottles, Avec offers some 130 wines from France, Italy, Spain and Portugal; we recommend buying a bottle to share with the newfound friends you'll undoubtedly meet at your table.

Contemporary American, Mediterranean. Dinner. Bar. $36-85

★★★★AVENUES

The Peninsula Chicago, 108 E. Superior St., Chicago, 312-573-6695; www.chicago.peninsula.com

Forget the plain name, and overlook the fact that the intimate Avenues is in a hotel (though the hotel is the Peninsula, one of the best in the city). You might have to tolerate a setting that's a little more staid than luxurious. Instead, try to focus on the food, as chef Curtis Duffy offers cuisine that manages to be both simple and extravagant. Duffy succeeded acclaimed toque Graham Elliot Bowles (who left to start his own eponymous River North restaurant). But Duffy, who was Grant Achatz's right-hand man at Alinea, has made Avenues all his own. He favors unusual pairings that work despite seeming contradictory: A grilled Wagyu steak comes with smoked coconut and African blue basil, and lamb is poached in tangerine oil with mint blossom. The best bet might be to take a seat at the bar in front of the open kitchen and watch Duffy work his magic.

Contemporary American. Dinner. Closed Sunday-Monday. Reservations recommended. Bar. $86 and up

★★★BISTRO CAMPAGNE

4518 N. Lincoln Ave., Chicago, 773-271-6100; www.bistrocampagne.com

We know this Lincoln Square bistro isn't exactly centrally situated, but the classic French fare and immaculate wine list make the cozy neighborhood spot well worth the trip to the North Side. Acclaimed chef Michael Altenberg is a vocal sustainable-food advocate, so he uses local, organic ingredients to create dishes like his flawless pan-seared salmon with braised lentils and succulent steak piled high with delicious fries. We can't talk about Bistro Campagne—let alone visit here—without mentioning Altenberg's steamed mussels, served in a tasty Belgian ale. The restaurant itself has a rustic feel with Prairie-style design touches and dark wood trim, while the outdoor space provides a beautiful mosaic fountain and a quaint cottage for a secluded retreat.

French. Dinner, Sunday brunch. Bar. $36-85

★★★BLACKBIRD

619 W. Randolph St., Chicago, 312-715-0708; www.blackbirdrestaurant.com

When chef Mike Sheerin took over the reigns from chef/owner Paul Kahan, no one knew quite what to expect; Kahan's food was beloved by foodies everywhere. But Sheerin has not disappointed, bringing a slight element of playfulness to Kahan's solid menu. Now, for instance, short ribs might come with sesame gnocchi and ground cherries and "fried" chicken with a smoked potato salad. Foodies love it just as much as they always have. As for the restaurant itself, it's sleek and minimalist—but it's not exactly roomy. Tables are packed tightly together, but you won't mind overhearing a few conversations for food of this caliber. The prix fixe lunch menu, which includes three courses for $22, is one of the best deals in town.

Contemporary American. Lunch (Monday-Friday), dinner. Closed Sunday. Reservations recommended. $36-85

★★★BOB SAN

1805-07 W. Division St., Chicago, 773-235-8888; www.bob-san.com

Bob San's owner Bob Bee has created a veritable sushi empire throughout Chicago, giving the city fixtures like Sai Café, Sushi Naniwa and Hachi's Kitchen. But it's Wicker Park's bustling Bob San that's earned Bee his biggest buzz. The restaurant features lively lounge music, an open wooden-beam ceiling and playful fish-shaped lighting fixtures. But the focus here is the expansive menu, which features some 45 handcrafted rolls that include classics like the spider roll with soft-shell crab, avocado and cucumber. There are also a dozen entrées for non-sushi eaters, including a teriyaki New York strip steak. The tables are packed closely together, so if you're hoping for a romantic meal, try to get one of the tables by the window, close to the bar.

Japanese. Dinner. Bar. $36-85

★★★★★CHARLIE TROTTER'S

816 W. Armitage Ave., Chicago, 773-248-6228; www.charlietrotters.com

There's not much about internationally renowned chef Charlie Trotter that hasn't already been said. Awards? He has them in spades. Books? He's written them. TV shows? He stars in a cooking series. Which brings us back to Trotter's food, and for that he uses only naturally raised meats, line-caught fish and organic produce to craft his world-famous fare. The formal waitstaff speak in hushed tones when talking about Trotter's exactingly prepared menu, which includes dishes such as chilled trout with watercress and crayfish, and Crawford Farm lamb rack with chanterelle mushrooms and fermented black garlic. Housed in an unassuming brick building in the tony Lincoln Park neighborhood, the understated restaurant—there is no art on the walls, as Trotter believes any art should be on the plate—provides a tasteful environment for what is always a remarkable evening. For those who want to see the restaurant's inner workings firsthand, Trotter's offers a table in the kitchen that comes with its own custom-prepared menu.

Contemporary American. Dinner. Closed Sunday-Monday. $86 and up

★★★CHICAGO CHOP HOUSE

60 W. Ontario St., Chicago, 312-787-7100; www.chicagochophouse.com

It's hard to capture authenticity—some places have it, while other spots feel like a couple of marketing majors drummed up a concept. The Chop House has authenticity to spare, from the classic green awnings on the Victorian façade to the 1,400 pictures of Chicago icons on the walls. Of course, old-school charm is irrelevant if the food doesn't work—but the reasonably priced steaks here are wet-aged and perfectly prepared. The menu is light on perks, so don't expect anything fancy. Just start out with the prosciutto-wrapped asparagus before going for the massive New York strip (or the 64-ounce porterhouse, if you're up to it). The award-winning wine list features more than 600 bottles, from Oregon pinot noirs to renowned French cabernets. Just be sure to leave the baseball caps and T-shirts at home; the dress code, while relatively relaxed, encourages smart attire.

Steak. Dinner. Reservations recommended. Bar. $36-85

★★★CROFTON ON WELLS

535 N. Wells St., Chicago, 312-755-1790; www.croftononwells.com

In a city that features such renowned chefs as Charlie Trotter and Grant Achatz, it's telling that Suzy Crofton's eponymous River North restaurant has survived—thrived, actually—since 1997. By leaving the foam and froth to others, Crofton has earned a truckload of awards for her elegant contemporary cuisine. Crofton's French-tinged cooking is elegant and thoughtful, without pretense. She puts as much thought into her appetizers—including the crab cake and sautée of wild mushrooms with bacon, cracked peppercorn and brioche—as she does on her farm chicken and pork tenderloin topped with her famous smoked-apple chutney. Vegetarians aren't relegated to a cursory dish at the corner of the menu—Crofton puts out a separate vegetarian menu, as well as several vegan options. Desserts include a delicious banana cream pie.

Contemporary American. Dinner. Closed Sunday. Bar. $36-85

★★★CUSTOM HOUSE TAVERN
Hotel Blake, 500 S. Dearborn St., Chicago, 312-523-0200; www.customhouse.cc

The old Custom House, a steakhouse helmed by chef Shawn McClain, has evolved into the Custom House Tavern, an upscale but comfortable urban tavern with hearty offerings. Executive chef Perry Hendrix takes a seasonal approach to urban American food with dishes such as smoked trout "rilletes" with cucumber and crème fraiche; roasted beets with Greek yogurt, lamb's lettuce and candied bacon; and gold rice risotto with ramps, wild mushrooms, sugar snap peas and pistachio. The main dining room is still elegant and refined; you can also settle into the comfortable bar lounge area where you'll find an expanded bar bites menu.

Contemporary American. Lunch (Monday-Friday), dinner. Reservations recommended. Bar. $36-85

★★★DAVID BURKE'S PRIMEHOUSE
The James Hotel, 616 N. Rush St., Chicago, 312-660-6000; www.davidburke.com

Sure, many Chicago restaurants claim to be serious about their steaks, but we're guessing not many of them go as far as David Burke's Primehouse, which boasts its own salt-tiled aging room, in which the owners dry-age their own beef. Even more impressive: David Burke owns a stud steer in Kentucky whose offspring produce the meat for his aged steaks. These are just two of the reasons this spot stands apart from the herd. The room is a veritable ode to all things bovine: The chairs are a deep brown leather and the tables are wrapped in red leather. The steaks are the main draw, from the "South Side" bone-in filet to the châteaubriand for two. There are a respectable number of non-steak options as well, including a seared Alaskan king salmon and a wonderful roasted chicken. They're equally as good, though when else will you have a chance to trace the family tree of your prime rib? Burke is also famous

---

WHAT ARE THE BEST CELEBRITY CHEF RESTAURANTS IN CHICAGO?

Frontera Grill: The always-popular spot has a festive atmosphere with colorful walls and hanging papier-mâché animals, which provides a perfect environment to enjoy Rick Bayless's housemade moles and freshly ground corn tortillas.

Table Fifty-Two: Art Smith will likely forever be known as Oprah's chef, although that's probably not such a bad thing. The menu boasts Smith's upgraded take on Southern classics.

Charlie Trotter's: The master chef's eponymous Lincoln Park restaurant is a fixture in Chicago, consistently great year after year.

for whimsical creations such as the cheesecake lollipop.

Steak. Breakfast, lunch (Monday-Friday), dinner, Saturday-Sunday brunch. Bar. $36-85

★★★★EVEREST

440 S. LaSalle St., Chicago, 312-663-8920; www.everestrestaurant.com

It takes a certain bravado to name a restaurant after the tallest mountain in the world—the damning reviews practically write themselves. Thankfully, chef Jean Joho's Everest has scaled the culinary heights and remains perched at the top of Chicago's fine-dining realm. Appropriately located on the 40th floor of the Chicago Stock Exchange, its magnificent city views (framed by floor-to-ceiling drapes) are a perfect companion for Joho's highbrow Alsatian cuisine. Served by an exceedingly polite waitstaff clad in suits, the menu includes a filet of wild sturgeon wrapped and roasted in cured ham, and venison served with wild huckleberries and braised pear. It's safe to say that a night at Everest will leave you feeling, well, on top of the world.

French. Dinner. Closed Sunday-Monday. $86 and up

★★★FRONTERA GRILL

445 N. Clark St., Chicago, 312-661-1434; www.rickbayless.com

If you can't quite spring for the upscale offerings of Topolobampo next door—or maybe you want to save your money for Rick Bayless' acclaimed margaritas (we don't blame you)—you won't feel cheated if you opt for Frontera Grill. The always-popular spot has a festive atmosphere with colorful walls and hanging papier-mâché animals, which provides a perfect environment to enjoy the famous chef's housemade moles and freshly ground corn tortillas. The menu changes monthly but you may find such mouthwatering fare as Puerco Al Chipotle, a grilled pork loin in a red-bean chipotle sauce, and Carne Asada a la Oaxaquena, a grilled Angus rib steak marinated in red chile and served with black beans and plantains. Be forewarned: The restaurant takes reservations only for a limited number of tables, which explains the lines that form well before the doors open for dinner.

Mexican. Lunch (Tuesday-Friday), dinner, Saturday brunch. Closed Sunday-Monday. Bar. $36-85

★★★GENE & GEORGETTI

500 N. Franklin St., Chicago, 312-527-3718; www.geneandgeorgetti.com

Chicago's famed stockyards officially closed in 1971, but the city's carnivorous tradition is still going strong—and perhaps no stronger than at this timeless Italian steakhouse that's resided in the shadow of the El since 1941. From the pictures of Frank Sinatra and Bob Hope on the walls to the red vinyl chairs, G&G (as it's known) is old-school through and through. The waiters have as much character as the classic environs, and they're not exactly known for their geniality, but you'll forget their brusqueness the second you dig into the juicy wet-aged New York strip or the 18-ounce filet that stands some four inches tall.

Italian, Steak. Lunch, dinner. Closed Sunday. Bar. $36-85

★★★GIBSONS

1028 N. Rush St., Chicago, 312-266-8999; www.gibsonssteakhouse.com

Pinky rings and massive steaks are the hallmark of Gibsons, a Gold Coast fixture since 1989. The walls are adorned with pictures of celebs ranging from Muhammad Ali to Clint Eastwood, but the restaurant is just as well-known as the haunt of local powerbrokers who make their deals over Gibsons' fishbowl-sized martinis and then celebrate with a gargantuan 24-ounce porterhouse. Big spenders go for the surf and turf, which features a huge Australian lobster tail served with a massive fillet. You could save room for dessert, but we're guessing you won't get too far into the famed macadamia turtle pie.

Steak. Lunch, dinner. Reservations recommended. Bar. $36-85

★★★GIRL & THE GOAT

809 W. Randolph St., Chicago, 312-492-6262; www.girlandthegoat.com

The girl is Stephanie Izard, 2008 winner of Bravo's Top Chef; the goat appears in dishes like smoked goat pizza with sautéed kale and tart cherries. The renovated manufacturing space on the West Loop's restaurant row is ultra trendy, with lofted ceilings and an industrial vibe, but Izard is definitely the focus. She reportedly did it all for the 2010 opening, including having her own Washington state wine blended and an exclusive cheese made. Real foodies may be drawn to the wood oven roasted pig face, garnished with a sunny side egg; the less adventurous can choose from a bevy of seemingly simple vegetable dishes, such as roasted cauliflower with pine nuts and mint. Wash it all down with a meticulously concocted cocktail or crafted beer—Izard edited the extensive list of drafts and bottles herself. Be forewarned: Prepare for a wait, even with a reservation.

American. Dinner. Outdoor seating. Bar. $36-85

★★★GRAHAM ELLIOT

217 W. Huron St., Chicago, 312-624-9975; www.grahamelliot.com

You'll either love or loathe the kookiness at acclaimed chef Graham Elliot Bowles' River North restaurant. The "informalized" dining room features '80s pop tunes (think Flock of Seagulls and Billy Ocean), and the snack between courses is popcorn (Parmesan-dusted and truffled popcorn, but popcorn none-theless). Clad in jeans and Chuck Taylors, servers bring Bowles' playful haute cuisine (his opening menu included a duck leg confit served with Maytag blue cheese and Budweiser beer foam, and an aged cheddar risotto, featuring Pabst-glazed onions and Cheez-It crackers) that's divided into hot and cold appetizers and land and sea entrées. He tones it down a little for his entrées, as the grilled rack of pork features a massive loin tastefully infused with root-beer barbecue sauce, while the salmon BLT served with crispy bacon and fresh tomatoes is delicious—good enough, even, to endure the overly-loud Reagan-era jams.

Contemporary American. Dinner. Closed Sunday. $36-85

★★★GREEN ZEBRA

1460 W. Chicago Ave., Chicago, 312-243-7100; www.greenzebrachicago.com

Vegetarians often feel like they get a raw deal at restaurants, with maybe a token eggplant dish tossed their way at the corner of the menu. Not so at Green Zebra, chef Shawn McClain's small-plates ode to non-carnivores. After all, even a filet fanatic would get hooked on slow-roasted shiitake mushrooms in a crispy potato with savoy cabbage, or grilled asparagus with Camembert beignets. The elegant, earth-toned décor is more upscale than granola; you're more likely to hear Joy Division than the Grateful Dead, and the service is efficient and refined. If you simply must eat meat, there are one or two non-vegetarian items on the menu—though considering the diverse and delicious plant-based options, why settle for chicken?

Contemporary vegetarian. Dinner, Sunday brunch. $16-35

★★★JAPONAIS
600 W. Chicago Ave., Chicago, 312-822-9600; www.japonaischicago.com

You'll need to cab it over to this gentrifying but not exactly glitzy part of town. But when you're enjoying Japanese-French fusion next to some of the city's most stylish foodies, you'll see why Japonais remains one of the hottest tables in town. Gently thumping lounge music and chic décor provide a perfect environment for the glammed-up crowd (Brad and Angelina dined here when she was filming Wanted) that can be found sipping on colorful drinks in the downstairs lounge and outdoor patio. If you're all about the food, you'll be just as pleased. The menu leans toward sushi but also includes a seven-spice Wagyu rib eye and Le Quack Japonais, a smoked duck served with hoisin sauce and chutney (yes, that's neither Japanese nor French, but trust us, it's delicious). If you like to play with your food, order The Rock, in which thinly sliced New York strip steak is cooked on a hot rock at your table. Whatever you order, be sure to add a side of fries, which come with a spicy sauce that's always a crowd pleaser. Cap off the night with an after-dinner drink in the downstairs lounge, where in summer months, you can sip on a patio overlooking the river.

Japanese, French. Lunch (Monday-Friday), dinner. Bar. $36-85

★★★★L2O
2300 N. Lincoln Park West, Chicago, 773-868-0002; www.l2orestaurant.com

At L2O, acclaimed chef Laurent Gras offers a French-oriented seafood menu that's as sophisticated as the restaurant's beautiful décor, with the dining room separated by partitions of stainless-steel cables. The menu is divided into Raw, Warm and Main sections, with the four-course tasting option offering one of each, plus a dessert. The generous selections range from fluke with lemon vinegar, caviar and basil seeds to black bass in shellfish bouillon with saffron and Rhode Island mussels. Even the bread service is memorable, with offerings of bacon croissants, anchovy twists and demi-baguettes served with housemade butter. To get an idea of Gras's meticulous nature, seize the opportunity to take the optional tour of the painstakingly clean kitchen—and keep an eye out for his astounding array of spices.

French, Contemporary American. Dinner. Closed Tuesday. $86 and up

★★★LA MADIA
59 W. Grand Ave., Chicago, 312-329-0400; www.dinelamadia.com

You know a place is good when restaurant owners go there to eat. The heavenly pies served at this contemporary pizzeria have a crispy and slightly chewy crust and come in such interesting combinations as triple pepperoni with truffle oil and taleggio with three-hour roasted grapes. Unfortunately, everything else on the menu here is equally delicious, making ordering tough. Chef Jonathan Fox often uses ingredients he picked up at the market that morning which might inspire a lovely pumpkin pizza with crunchy pumpkin seeds or a whole new dish that might get added to the menu for a day, or a season. Menu standbys such as the impossibly tender short rib with creamy risotto and delicate homemade ricotta gnocchi with housemade sausage are also wonderfully satisfying. The wine list is vast and the chef's suggested pairings are spot on.

American, Italian. Lunch, dinner. $36-85

★★★LANDMARK

1633 N. Halsted St., Chicago, 312-587-1600;
www.landmarkgrill.net

With its striking décor and boisterous crowd, you'd forgive the owners of Landmark (who also run nearby Perennial and Boka) if they concentrated a little less on the food. But chef Kurt Guzowski ensures the fare remains a priority at this massive Lincoln Park favorite, committing to the details on his wide-ranging menu. Appetizer options include smoked ravioli with braised pork belly, and Kobe beef sliders with truffles, foie gras and Moroccan ketchup. Entrées including a lobster club sandwich and grilled black pepper ribeye with blue cheese potato gratin. We recommend going earlier in the evening, because the place gets packed at night with a throng that's clearly not there for the food.

Contemporary American. Dinner. Closed Monday. Bar. $16-35

★★★LE COLONIAL

937 N. Rush St., Chicago, 312-255-0088;
www.lecolonialchicago.com

Chicago's Rush Street is a loud, bombastic avenue, often filled with rowdy revelers and tipsy tourists. But that's not the only reason the restrained elegance of Le Colonial stands out here. With its slowly rotating ceiling fans and potted palm trees, Le Colonial serves French-Vietnamese fare in a space that vividly evokes the feel of French colonial Southeast Asia. The authentic Vietnamese fare starts with pho, the popular beef soup with rice noodles and flavorful slivers of ginger and chilies. Then it's on to entrées like Ca Chien Saigon, a seared snapper in a sweet, spicy sauce, and Bo Bitet Tom Nuong, a grilled filet mignon with shrimp and tomato rice pilaf. Afterward, enjoy a cocktail in the sexy upstairs lounge, which is a pleasant way to savor the last drop of atmosphere before heading back out into the boisterous night.

French, Vietnamese. Lunch, dinner. Bar. $36-85

WHAT ARE THE BEST OVERALL RESTAURANTS IN CHICAGO?

Alinea:
Alinea burst onto the scene a few years back with some of the most wildly creative dishes in the country, and the complex meals here continue to blow us away.

Charlie Trotter's:
There's not much about internationally renowned chef Charlie Trotter that hasn't already been said. His exactingly prepared food is always a treat.

★★★★LES NOMADES

222 E. Ontario St., Chicago, 312-649-9010; www.lesnomades.net

From its location in a former townhouse to the fresh flowers placed throughout the restaurant, Les Nomades is nothing but low-key elegance. Despite being a mere croissant's throw from nearby Michigan Avenue, the serene spot is secluded, intimate and ideal for those seeking a romantic getaway within the city. That's not to say the French haute cuisine is an afterthought, though. From rack of lamb in a delicate mushroom soubise to roasted venison loin with sage braised root vegetables and prune confit, Les Nomades' prix fixe French fare is expertly prepared and perfectly fits the restaurant's elegant atmosphere. In keeping with the formal feel, jackets are required for men, and cell phones are strictly prohibited.

French. Dinner. Closed Sunday-Monday. $86 and up

★★★MIRAI SUSHI

2020 W. Division St., Chicago, 773-862-8500; www.miraisushi.com

Need to impress a sashimi aficionado? Head to Mirai, where the emphasis is solely on the fish. In-the-know sushi lovers flock here for the unagi trio, a roll with unagi, avocado and an unagi sauce. Chef/partner Jun Ichikawa also specializes in elegantly simple rolls, such as the tuna tuna salmon, which features poached salmon topped with tuna and drizzled with a light wasabi mayonnaise. Those who want something other than sushi won't be disappointed with offerings like the perfectly made teriyaki salmon or kani ebi korekke (shrimp and snow crab cakes). For a pre- (or post-) dinner cocktail, Mirai has a funky lounge upstairs.

Japanese. Dinner. Bar. $36-85

★★★MK

868 N. Franklin St., Chicago, 312-482-9179; www.mkchicago.com

Founder Michael Kornick is no longer preparing meals at his namesake restaurant (that falls to executive chef Erick Williams), but there's still a lot of substance beneath the style of this renowned loft-like spot with the brick walls and massive skylight. The chic lounge is a popular stop for a pre-dinner drink, while the spacious bi-level dining room provides a warm atmosphere for a classic contemporary American menu. Williams doesn't exactly reinvent the wheel, but we're not complaining: His specialties include grilled veal porterhouse in a cognac green peppercorn sauce, and bison rib eye with a cabernet sauce. The dessert menu offers standbys like crème brûlée and sorbet, but you'll be glad to step outside the box for the Cake & Shake, which features layers of buttermilk chocolate cake, chocolate mousse, bittersweet chocolate pavé, chocolate meringue buttercream and a vanilla malted milkshake.

Contemporary American. Dinner. $36-85

★★★MOTO

945 W. Fulton Market, Chicago, 312-491-0058; www.motorestaurant.com

Moto's brilliant chef Homaro Cantu has repeatedly said he wants his customers to play with their food. But sometimes, when facing the concoction the renowned chef has created, the desire is to stare in awe rather than disrupt such a lavish creation. Cantu's whimsical dinners begin with an edible menu (vegetable inks on modified food starch) and go on to feature 10 to 20 courses, which may include inverted pumpkin pie or instant risotto. Some of Cantu's more celebrated dishes have included veal breast served with rice and runner beans, and fish cooked in an insulated box at the table. As you might expect, the presentation is both outrageous and practical. The "toro, sturgeon caviar, and utensil study," for instance, features a piece of tuna dabbed with caviar, served on a custom-made utensil for which the stem has been hollowed out and filled with fresh thyme. Playful? Certainly. Sublime? Absolutely.

International. Dinner. Closed Sunday-Monday. Reservations recommended. Bar. $86 and up

★★★N9NE

440 W. Randolph St., Chicago, 312-575-9900; www.n9negroup.com

With its subtly changing light scheme and cosmo-sipping, air-kissing crowd, the slick N9NE occasionally gets criticized for being more of a scene than a restaurant. Whoever says that likely hasn't delved into the menu, which features huge, prime-aged steaks and chops, augmented with a Maine lobster tail or Alaskan crab legs for a reasonable $23. There's also a wide array of seafood options, including a miso-marinated cod with scallions and shiitake mushrooms. Bolstering the restaurant's argument is a caviar service, offering Russian caviar by the ounce. In any case, they must be doing something right, as this spot begat the N9NE/Ghost Bar in Las Vegas and Dallas.

Steak. Lunch (Monday-Friday), dinner. Closed Sunday. $36-85

★★★NACIONAL 27

325 W. Huron St., Chicago, 312-664-2727; www.nacional27.net

The "27" in the name refers to the number of Latin American countries, but it also reflects this stylish restaurant's culinary diversity. In a large, dramatic space, Nacional 27 offers Nuevo Latino dishes that blend flavors and influences from throughout Central and South America. Starters include ceviche sampling platters with shrimp, scallops, ahi tuna and salmon. The menu also offers tapas (such as miniature lamb tacos with avocado salsa and smoked chicken empanadas), a four-course party menu (for four or more guests served family style), and à la carte dishes including a delicious grilled marinated skirt steak. There's also a tapas tasting menu Monday through Friday for $27 per person. If the food itself doesn't get you dancing, the restaurant's resident DJ will get you on the floor with weekend salsa and merengue music. (Have a mojito to best bring out your dance moves.)

Latin American. Dinner. Closed Sunday. Bar. $36-85

★★★NAHA

500 N. Clark St., Chicago, 312-321-6242; www.naha-chicago.com

In-the-know Chicagoans didn't need proof that NAHA, the creation of cousins Carrie and Michael Nahabedian, offers excellent contemporary cuisine with a Mediterranean flair. But that validation came anyway in the form of a 2008 James Beard award. Carrie's meals are served in an elegant, tranquil setting and emphasize locally grown, organic fare such as wood-grilled rib eye with spring onions, macaroni gratin, blue cheese and oxtail sauce, and honey-lacquered aged moulard duck breast with huckleberries and carrots. Not everything is such highbrow fare: The Angus hamburger served on a sea-salt crusted ciabatta bun with glazed onions wins raves as well, elevating the simple hamburger above its typical reputation. You have to get it for lunch, though. Otherwise, you're stuck ordering from the fantastic dinner menu.

Contemporary American. Lunch (Monday-Friday), dinner. Closed Sunday. Reservations recommended. Bar. $36-85

★★★NOMI

Park Hyatt Chicago, 800 N. Michigan Ave., Chicago, 312-239-4030; www.nomirestaurant.com

When you first arrive at NoMI, you have to go through a glass-encased wine "cellar" and take several turns before entering the main dining room. It's almost as if they want to reward you for your efforts—and what a reward it is. The beautiful space, which offers stunning views of Michigan Avenue and the Water Tower across the street, matches executive chef Christophe David's cuisine: simple, unpretentious and elegant. Sushi makes up much of the menu, with à la carte pieces and larger plates of several rolls offered. David also presents entrées such as black truffle risotto, with a Perigord black truffle purée, soft poached egg and celery root. After your meal, the outdoor garden's gently pulsing lounge music, comfortable tables and spectacular view make a perfect environment for a relaxing after-dinner drink.

French, Asian. Breakfast, lunch (Monday-Saturday), dinner, Sunday brunch. Reservations recommended. Bar. $36-85

★★★NORTH POND

2610 N. Cannon Drive, Lincoln Park, 773-477-5845; www.northpondrestaurant.com

Talk about off the beaten path: North Pond is situated in the middle of a pastoral setting in Lincoln Park, surrounded by trees and blocks away from the neighborhood's occasionally lunkheaded bar scene. The restaurant's gorgeous Prairie-style building—originally built in 1912 as a lodge for ice-skaters—overlooks a small pond and provides a stunning view of the Chicago skyline. Almost as impeccable is chef Bruce Sherman's sustainable-minded fare, which emphasizes seasonal local items in dishes such as oil-poached Alaskan halibut with smoked caviar, and Dijon-crusted rib eye with roasted farro. Sherman puts the websites of local nonprofits on his menu, but with a meal this delicious—capped by wonderful desserts such as decadent chocolate panna cotta with bing cherries and red beet sorbet—you'll put up with a little political grandstanding.

Contemporary American. Lunch (June-September, Tuesday-Friday), Sunday brunch. Closed Monday; also closed Tuesday from January-April. $36-85

★★★ONE SIXTYBLUE

1400 W. Randolph St., Chicago, 312-850-0303; www.onesixtyblue.com

For many Chicagoans, One Sixtyblue is known only as the restaurant that features Michael Jordan as one of the owners. He's still known to occasionally drop in, which is enough to bring in a crowd hoping to shake hands with His Royal Airness. For everyone else, the contemporary American cuisine—which perfectly matches the quiet, romantic atmosphere of this converted former pickle factory—is the reason to eat here. Starters may include a housemade mozzarella with roasted red, golden and candy cane beets, baby arugula and red beet vinaigrette, while entrées might feature a grilled beef tenderloin with spring onion potato gratin. (The menu changes by season.) Even if you don't spot MJ, you'll be glad you stopped by—especially if you happen to catch one of the restaurant's many specials (namely on Wednesday nights when they serve fried chicken and champagne for only $8 each).

Contemporary American. Dinner. Closed Sunday. Bar. $36-85

★★★OTOM

951 W. Fulton Market, Chicago, 312-491-5804; www.otomrestaurant.com

The lower-priced, less-formal sister of haute cuisine standby Moto, Otom is a lively mix of minimalist elegance and playful mod, with orange plastic chairs and orange tableside flowers contrasting with the exposed brick walls. Décor aside, Otom stands out for its cuisine: Salmon ceviche on crispy wontons makes a perfect light start to the meal, and chef Thomas Elliot Bowman crafts clever fare for his entrées. You never know what you're doing to get but these have featured things like the "TV Dinner," which includes chicken-fried duck confit, carrot and edamame pie, and the popular fried beef cheek ravioli with saffron-parsnip purée. Despite its proximity to its more-famous sibling, Otom's moderate prices, unique atmosphere and excellent food make it a spot worthy of standing on its own.

Contemporary American. Dinner. Closed Sunday-Monday. $36-85

★★★PERENNIAL

1800 N. Lincoln Ave., Chicago, 312-981-7070; www.perennialchicago.com

The masterminds behind Chicago fixtures Boka and Landmark have transformed this space—formerly an unimaginative chain bar/restaurant—into a must-visit scene. With its canvas ceiling, birch trees in the center of the room, and floor-to-ceiling windows, Perennial's décor is as inviting as the perpetually smiling staff and the thoughtful cuisine prepared by chef Ryan Poli. The menu features crispy duck breast with savoy cabbage, duck confit and foie gras pithivier in a dried cherry sauce, and housemade linguini carbornara that's worth every fat gram. For dessert, be sure to order the crispy hazelnut bar with creme fraiche and chocolate caramel. The adjacent lounge provides an elegant spot for a post-dinner drink—provided you can get a seat, that is.

Contemporary American. Dinner, brunch. Bar. $36-85

★★★THE PUBLICAN

837 W. Fulton Market, Chicago, 312-733-9555; www.thepublicanrestaurant.com

At the Publican, the tastemakers behind Blackbird and Avec have turned their focus to pork, oysters and beer. The space resembles a swank German beer hall. If you want privacy, ask for one of the walnut booths, which have small salon doors. Dishes are served as soon as they are ready and are meant to be shared. The grilled chicken with frites is made especially tasty with a sprinkling of espelette pepper, a Basque spice that gives the dish a subtle heat. The frites with the sunny side egg may be tempting, but go for the addictive aioli instead. The family-style Sunday dinners are a great way to try the restaurant. One past menu featured a salad with a pancetta, basil and a poached farm egg, mussels with pork confit, whole roasted pig, and butterscotch pudding for dessert.

Gastropub. Dinner, Sunday brunch. $36-85

★★★RESTAURANT TAKASHI
1952 N. Damen Ave., Chicago, 773-772-6170; www.takashichicago.com

It seemed like the pinnacle of chef Takashi Yagihashi's career: After putting together an award-winning résumé in Chicago and Detroit, he headed to Las Vegas to lead a restaurant in the Wynn Resort. Thankfully for Chicagoans, Yagihashi returned after 18 months to helm his namesake restaurant, a minimalist spot in Bucktown that expertly blends high-end American influences and French technique with the simplicity of Japanese fare. In a small, low-key room of gray walls accented with cherry wood, the menu offers hot and cold small plates that may feature fresh hamachi, salmon, tuna and other seafood. The more substantial large plates menu offers dishes such as roasted potato/prosciutto-crusted Atlantic salmon and a roasted New York strip with fresh wasabi and miso-glazed fingerling potatoes. In a neighborhood with more than a few so-so sushi spots, Takashi simultaneously expands the palate while refining the details of Japanese cuisine. If you're in the Loop, check out the chef's noodle bar in the food court of Macy's.

Contemporary American, Japanese. Lunch (Sunday), dinner. Closed Monday. $36-85

★★★RIA
Elysian Hotel, 11 E. Walton St., Gold Coast, 312-646-1300; www.elysianhotels.com

When Peking duck recently appeared on the menu at Ria, there was no indication (written, at least) that it was served as two courses: a traditional sliced breast with crispy skin in a duck port sauce; then with the rich leg meat alongside pistachio-crusted foie gras in pear purée. At Ria, the presentation is as impressive as the food, which chef Jason McLeod (who manages both Ria and the more causal Balsan just across the hall at the Elysian hotel) takes great care to source and imaginatively prepare. The menu features several seafood courses, among other dishes. The seasonal five-course menu for $87 per person (the whole table must partcipate) is a great way to experience the restaurant. You might start with something like yellowfin tuna topped with caviar, before moving on to King crab, Alaskan halibut with sweetbreads, and milk-fed veal confit with foie gras. As for the wine, Dan Pilkey, the big-smile sommelier who's into surfing and yoga, will point you to just the right bottle. (If you're doing the tasting menu, wine pairings are an additional $45.) The pastries are heavenly and the overall experience—despite the fact that a cheese cart is wheeled over to your table before dessert—is never stuffy. The simple room shimmers with golds, greens and greys, silk wall coverings and metallic leather chairs, and has an intimate, private dining feel that's a welcome change from your typical hotel restaurant.

American. Dinner. Closed Sunday-Monday. $36 and up

★★★SCHWA
1466 N. Ashland Ave., Chicago, 773-252-1466; www.schwarestaurant.com

Maverick chef Michael Carlson is viewed as the enfant terrible of the Chicago dining world. His eccentric Schwa became the apple of Chicago foodies' eyes, but then he abruptly closed for four months and was vague about what he did in the meantime. Now, the restaurant has reopened and while its quixotic charms are still evident—tiny room, no liquor license, the cooks also serve as the waitstaff—the food is still remarkably innovative. The charismatic

Carlson—who's likely to sprinkle a few uses of "dude" during your meal—offers three- and nine-course menus that feature organic ingredients and locally grown produce. The latter option includes such knockout dishes as a savory beer cheese soup with a pretzel roll, and a gently seared kona kampachi with galangal, lime and a tiny splash of maple syrup. It's a little pricey for what it is, but the cost of the meal is offset by the restaurant's BYOB policy, which allows you to carry in your own wine for a mere $2.50-per-person corkage fee. Just be sure to call ahead to snag a table; though Carlson may be unpredictable, the restaurant's popularity is not.

Contemporary American. Dinner. Closed Sunday-Monday. $36-85

★★★★SEASONS

Four Seasons Hotel Chicago, 120 E. Delaware Place, Chicago, 312-649-2349; www.fourseasons.com

Let other restaurants try to impress you with a stark, minimalist atmosphere. Seasons, located within the Four Seasons Hotel, goes the other way and spoils you with old-school luxury. How so? For starters, there's the marble fountain, armchair seats and deep mahogany wood trim. Then there is the French-leaning prix fixe five-course menu. The fare constantly changes to reflect availability of ingredients, but past favorites have included Tasmanian sea trout filled with slow-cooked Kobe short ribs, and rack of Colorado lamb wrapped in eggplant and scented with toasted cumin. After a day of Mag Mile shopping, no other place in the Gold Coast feels quite as decadently classic.

Contemporary American, French. Dinner (Wednesday-Saturday), Sunday brunch. Reservations recommended. $86 and up

★★★SEPIA

123 N. Jefferson St., Chicago, 312-441-1920; www.sepiachicago.com

Situated inside an 1890s print shop, Sepia's décor craftily mixes the old and new, much like contemporary American dishes rooted in tradition and quality products. Pork porterhouse with buttermilk mashed potatoes, grilled chicken with savory bread pudding or short ribs braised in Belgian ale are just a few examples of what you might find on the menu. When possible, ingredients are natural and organic, and the pasta, chutneys and jams are all homemade. Liquor aficionados come here for the creative cocktails, which feature housemade syrups and bitters.

Contemporary American. Lunch (Monday-Friday), dinner. $36-85

★★★★SIXTEEN

401 N. Wabash Ave., Chicago, 312-588-8151; www.trumpchicagohotel.com

As you might expect, everything at Sixteen (on the 16th floor of Donald Trump's hotel) is larger-than-life. The hostesses dress like they're about to walk down a Paris runway. The views of the city through the floor-to-ceiling windows are dazzling (and the ceiling in one of the three dining rooms is 30 feet high). Then there's the food. Chef Frank Brunacci meticulously crafts entrées like duck breasts in a date-and-kumquat chutney with black cumin, and pork with creamed corn, warm potato salad, collard greens and grilled peaches. (The menu changes daily.) The desserts—including chestnut meringue accompanied by port-wine ice cream and port reduction—take so much effort that it's recommended you order them at the start of your meal. All of this is almost enough to take your eyes off the gargantuan chandelier, which comprises more than 19,000 Swarovski crystals, or the views, which, from the 16th floor in the city's best location, are larger than life.

Contemporary American. Breakfast, lunch, dinner, Sunday brunch. Reservations recommended. Bar. $86 and up

★★★SHANGHAI TERRACE

The Peninsula Chicago, 108 E. Superior St., Chicago, 312-573-6695; www.chicago.peninsula.com

The main draw at the intimate Shanghai Terrace isn't the generous menu, with its emphasis on meticulous dim sum creations, or the elegantly appointed dining room with black lacquer chairs and daring red trim. The best reason to come here is the outdoor deck, with its stunning view of the soaring buildings that surround The Peninsula hotel. The alfresco area provides the perfect place to enjoy the delicious dim sum sampler, which includes spicy beef gyoza and foie gras and lobster dumplings. For a more complete meal, you can't go wrong with the traditional Peking duck, which offers five courses.

Asian. Lunch, dinner. Closed Sunday. Bar. $36-85

★★★SOLA

3868 N. Lincoln Ave., Chicago, 773-327-3868; www.sola-restaurant.com

Drawing inspiration from the sun (sol), her own independence (solo) and her roots (she's so L.A., as her friends joke), chef/owner and former surfer Carol Wallack dove headfirst into Chicago's dining scene when she opened Sola in January 2006. Wallack's focus is on freshness, so she sources all her produce from local farmers and all her seafood from Hawaii. Perhaps you'll find the culmination of these ingredients brought to your table in the form of a salad of Asian greens, housemade bacon, pineapple, rosemary and black vinegar; or halibut atop a bed of soy beluga lentils and wilted watercress, dressed with a lobster butter sauce. If these inventive takes on island-style dishes aren't enough to make you feel like wearing a grass skirt in Chicago, nothing will be. Note: At press time, Sola was in works to move to a new location downtown and a new restaurant from Wallack would replace it; be sure to check their website for updates.

Contemporary American, Hawaiian. Lunch (Thursday-Friday), dinner, Saturday-Sunday brunch. $36-85

★★★SPIAGGIA

980 N. Michigan Ave., Chicago, 312-280-2750; www.spiaggiarestaurant.com

Any talk of Chicago's high-end Italian restaurants begins (and arguably ends) with the gorgeous Spiaggia. How many restaurants have their own cheese cave? Exactly. The elegant setting matches the caliber of the food: The multi-tiered restaurant, appropriately perched at the outset of the city's famed Magnificent Mile, offers a view of Lake Michigan and the city's most famous street. James Beard award-winning chef and partner Tony Mantuano offers an à la carte menu that includes hand rolled potato gnocchi with ricotta sauce and black truffles. There's also a tasting menu inspired by the island of Sicily, which includes items such as pasta sheets with wood-roasted sardines, fennel pollen and black currants, and desserts such as the espresso and marscapone cheese torte with caramel and Valrhona chocolate.

Italian. Dinner. Jacket required. $86 and up

★★★SPRING

2039 W. North Ave., Chicago, 773-395-7100; www.springrestaurant.net

Spring is Chicago restaurant star Shawn McClain's first local outpost, and some still say it's his best. The spartan dining room—the building was once a Russian bathhouse, and some of the original white tiles are still on the walls—provides a relaxing environ for McClain's celebrated seafood-oriented, Asian-inflected fare, which may include such sophisticated fare as Maine sea scallop with braised oxtail, Arctic char with toasted sesame risotto and peekytoe crab, and organic roasted chicken with black garlic and ricotta dumplings. The honeydew sorbet in a plum soup makes the perfect light capper for a remarkable meal.

Contemporary American. Dinner. Closed Monday. $36-85

★★★TABLE FIFTY-TWO

52 W. Elm St., Chicago, 312-573-4000; www.tablefifty-two.com

Art Smith will likely forever be known as Oprah's chef, although that's probably not such a bad thing. After all, it's given him the chance to open TABLE fifty-two, which provides a perfect outlet for his Southern-inflected cuisine. Each table begins the meal with piping hot, fluffy buttermilk biscuits pulled fresh from the oven. The menu boasts Smith's upgraded take on Southern classics, including fried green tomatoes with a romesco purée, pickled red bell pepper and orange crème frâiche, and cornmeal-crusted catfish with cheese grits and bacon-braised collard greens. Housed in a 19th century carriage house and featuring an open-hearth oven, Smith's restaurant is as cozy and comforting as his cuisine.

American, Southern. Dinner. Reservations recommended. $36-85

★★★TOPOLOBAMPO

445 N. Clark St., Chicago, 312-661-1434; www.rickbayless.com

You can't turn on a TV today without seeing chef Rick Bayless work his culinary magic with Mexican food—the ubiquitous chef from Chicago even won the first season of Top Chef Masters. But you don't have to just stare in awe if you make the trip to Topolobampo, the sleek, multicolored restaurant that serves Bayless' inventive cuisine with a monthly changing menu. Bayless isn't always in the kitchen (chef de cuisine Brian Enyart is the man in the toque here), but Bayless' influence is all over the menu, which uses sustainably raised veggies, meat and fish to craft stunningly imaginative Oaxacan cuisine. Favorites have included Puerco Pibil, achiote-marinated Maple Creek Farm pork served as a grill-roasted loin and a slow-cooked shoulder in banana leaves, and langosto al mojo de ajo, pan-roasted Maine lobster served with olive oil-poached garlic, giant butter beans and roasted fresh favas. It's the furthest thing from a taquería, but it's a lot more memorable.

Mexican, Southwestern. Lunch (Tuesday-Friday), dinner. Closed Sunday-Monday. Reservations recommended. $36-85

★★★★TRU

676 N. St. Clair St., Chicago, 312-202-0001; www.trurestaurant.com

If you want a stellar dining experience in a large, beautifully understated room with perfectly attuned service, make a reservation at Tru. The gorgeous surroundings include an original Andy Warhol, and the food is equally inspiring. Tru offers different ways to take advantage of executive chef Anthony Martin's work, including a three-course prix fixe and a six- or nine-course "collections" tasting menu. The offerings include a bacon-wrapped monkfish with fingerling potatoes and red wine reduction, and prime beef ribeye with grilled foie gras, chanterelle mushrooms and parsley. Practically anything at Tru will delight, but we especially recommend the caviar staircase appetizer, which serves several different types of roe on an elegant glass spiral stairway. Even the bathrooms here, with their sinks made up solely of large slanted glass panels, are a sight. Recently, the restaurant carved out room for a burger joint called M Burger, where locals and Mag Mile tourists line up for burgers, fries and shakes.

Contemporary French. Dinner. Closed Sunday. Reservations recommended. Jacket required. $86 and up

★★★WEST TOWN TAVERN

1329 W. Chicago Ave., Chicago, 312-666-6175; www.westtowntavern.com

You can get fried chicken just about anywhere, but for Susan Goss' great-grandmother's tried-and-true recipe, you have to come to the West Town Tavern. Co-owner Goss breaks out the recipe every week for the popular Fried Chicken (and Biscuit) Mondays, while serious carnivores make weekly pilgrimages here for the juicy, 10-ounce Wagyu beef creations (served on grilled focaccia with herbed mayo and grilled onions) on Burger Tuesdays. The restaurant's blond wood floors, exposed brick and warm lighting also provide a welcoming environment for the tavern's delicious contemporary American cuisine with a comfort-food touch, such as the pot roast that's braised in zinfandel, and the gently seared diver scallops served with a delicate mushroom-leek risotto.

Contemporary American. Dinner. Closed Sunday. Bar. $36-85

RECOMMENDED

BALSAN

Elysian, 11 E. Walton St., Chicago, 312-646-1300; www.elysianhotels.com

There's nothing not to love about Balsan, a place named after Étienne Balsan, who financed Coco Chanel's first hat shop, and which serves charcuterie, wood-fired pizzas and other tasty treats. Chef Jason McLeod (who also runs the Elysian hotel's fine-dining Ria just right across the hall) is passionate about discovering products from local farms and artisan purveyors, such as that perfect cheese from a small farm in Wisconsin, and turning out homemade dishes. McLeod and his team have even gone so far as to purchase land in Illinios to grow their own tomatoes to ensure they have enough for their housemade ketchup and tomato sauce. The kitchen also cures some of its own meats. A long white marble bar with an antique mirror dominates the chic eatery and large windows overlook the European-style courtyard.

American. Breakfast, brunch (Saturday-Sunday), Lunch (Monday-Friday), dinner, late-night. $36-85

BIG STAR

1531 N. Damen, Chicago, 773-235-4039; www.bigstarchicago.com

This gourmet honky tonk features tacos, whiskey and tequlia. Those tacos are from chef Paul Kahan (of Blackbird, Avec and Publican fame) and are made with things such as pork belly and spit-roasted pork shoulder. Big Star took over the former Pontiac Cafe, a beloved—if run down—spot in Wicker Park that locals flocked to in the summer for its large outdoor patio out front (which is still there and has 125 seats). A square wooden bar takes up most of the interior; a few booths line the wall (only parties of four or more can sit there). Country music blares from a record player and they only take cash (there's an ATM on the premises). But the tacos make up for any inconvenience a lack of seating or no credit card policy may cause. The pork belly tacos are the best thing on the menu: rich, delicate and packed with flavor. The pork shoulder tacos are also very nice, as are the crispy fish tacos. You can also order guacamole and salads, and the whiskey and tequila selections are very good (if you don't prefer either, the house wine should do).

Mexican. Lunch, dinner, late-night. $15 and under

BIN 36

339 N. Dearborn St., Chicago, 312-755-9463; www.bin36.com

Most restaurants serve food and enhance the experience with wine. At the cavernous Bin 36, it's the other way around. You'll see that love of the grape from the many wine flights served with dinner to the wine store on the premises that will sell you that wine you really liked with your dinner. "Wine Director" Brian Duncan—he refuses to be called a sommelier—offers some 50 wines by the glass, and about 300 bottles to choose from. Despite the hullabaloo about vino, the menu is hardly an afterthought. Chef John Caputo's contemporary American fare includes sautéed herb marinated prawns with white asparagus, saffron risotto cake and spanish chorizo, and grilled lamb with sauteed spinach, lentils, ricotta salata, mint oil and lamb jus. Bin 36 offers three different dining areas, depending on your mood: the bar, the cheese bar or at a standard table in the dining room. A sophisticated environment with options galore? We'll drink to that.

Contemporary American. Breakfast, lunch, dinner. Bar. $36-85

BONGO ROOM

1470 N. Milwaukee Ave., Chicago, 773-489-0690; 1152 S. Wabash Ave., Chicago, 312-291-0100

If you're looking for an imaginative breakfast in a playful environment, you'd better head to the Bongo Room early. Even 30 minutes before the doors open, the sidewalk outside this Wicker Park standby is packed with hungover urbanites anxiously awaiting a table. The breakfast burrito filled with guacamole and fluffy scrambled eggs is a favorite, but most come here for the outrageously sweet concoctions that mix breakfast with dessert, such as Oreo cookie pancakes or chocolate tower French toast. The spot is a little less crowded when lunchtime rolls around, when the kitchen offers inventive fare like a tasty maple-and-mustard-roasted pork loin sandwich and a delectable baby spinach, golden beet and duck confit salad. If you can't stomach the interminable brunch wait, try the South Loop location, where it's slightly—note, we said slightly—less crowded.

Contemporary American. Breakfast, lunch, Saturday-Sunday brunch. $16-35

CAFÉ ABSINTHE

1958 W. North Ave., Chicago, 773-278-4488; www.cafeabsinthechicago.com

It's telling that the entrance to this Wicker Park fave is not on teeming North Avenue but in an alley around the corner. The off-the-beaten-path entry likely keeps the tippling masses from stumbling in and disrupting the restaurant's dimly lit, romantic atmosphere. Chef Jose Garcia's seasonal, American-oriented menu changes daily, but a recent incarnation featured Australian herb-marinated lamb with sautéed watercress and rosemary jus, and horseradish-encrusted salmon with garlic mashed potatoes and cabernet butter sauce. The signature dessert is a dark chocolate lava cake infused with Grand Marnier liqueur in a prickly-pear sauce—a treat that's well worth a trip down any alley.

Contemporary American. Dinner. Closed Monday. $36-85

COALFIRE

1321 W. Grand Ave., Chicago, 312-226-2625; www.coalfirechicago.com

Chicago's reputation is changing dramatically these days: No one talks about Al Capone anymore, the Cubs are actually a good team and the city's pizza fans aren't all heading out for deep dish. Places like the unassuming, relatively new Coalfire are a big reason for this last shift. This restaurant bakes its pies in a coal-heated oven, which produces an eyebrow-singeing temperature of 800 degrees. This high heat delivers a smoky, slightly charred crust that's both crispy and chewy, while the housemade tomato sauce has the perfect amount of sweetness. The surprisingly spartan list of toppings includes prosciutto, red peppers and anchovies, but regulars swear by the simple margherita, which is made up of sauce, buffalo mozzarella, ricotta and freshly cut basil leaves.

Pizza. Lunch (Saturday-Sunday), dinner. Closed Monday. $16-35

CRUST

2056 W. Division St., Chicago, 773-235-5511; www.crustchicago.com

With its stark white-brick walls and orange plastic chairs, Crust sure doesn't seem like it's at the forefront of a revolution. Yet the spot, helmed by Bistro Campagne's Michael Altenberg, has created the Midwest's first certified organic restaurant. Using organic flour and ingredients including fresh-pulled water buffalo mozzarella, Altenberg coaxes delicious pizzas (inexplicably called "wood-oven flatbreads" on the menu) from the tile-encrusted wood-burning oven. The surprisingly small menu features only 12 options, but the possibilities include such gourmet combinations as the Carbonara—topped with roasted slab bacon, peas and an egg sunny-side up—and the Mexicali blues—with provolone, mozzarella, roasted shrimp, cilantro and pico de gallo. Even some of the beer offerings are organic, letting you get soused as sustainably as possible.

Pizza. Lunch, dinner. Closed Tuesday. $16-35

EPIC

112 W. Hubbard St., Chicago, 312-222-4940; www.epicrestaurantchicago.com

Epic is perfect for, well, an epic-sized evening on the town. The cavernous, loft-like space includes a first-floor lounge, upstairs dining room and a rooftop space, a destination in itself with a special menu. It's a great place for drinks, dinner or both. Start in the lounge downstairs with a classic cocktail; head upstairs to dine on delicious plates of spiced lamb shank or crispy half chicken; and then make your way up to the roof wtih great views of the city for an after-dinner drink. With all this cocktailing, you may think the food takes a backseat. It doesn't. Stephen Wambach, the former corporate chef for Laurent Tourondel's BLT Restaurant Group in New York, is at the helm here. Be sure to try the signature appetizer of wild boar barbajuan (a fried ravioli filled with wild boar shoulder and housemade foie gras). Pastry Chef Christine McCabe prepares such heavenly desserts as the banana split made with a pineapple cake, malted chocolate, strawberry swirl and roasted banana ice creams and a cherry truffle on top. McCabe also bakes the housemade breads: a sourdough and a seasonally inspired selection. The wine list features a varied selection, with several wines available by the glass. There's also a large artisanal beer list and classic cocktails. With so many things to eat and drink, and so many spots within Epic from which to do so, it's no wonder the restaurant has been filling up since day one.

Lunch (Monday-Friday), dinner. Bar opens at 2 p.m. $86 and up

THE GAGE

24 S. Michigan Ave., Chicago, 312-372-4243; www.thegagechicago.com

From the elk ragout poutine to the Bison tartare to the roast elk with butter poached apples and ricotta, the Gage's pub grub is anything but common. Even the good ol' fish and chips get dressed up—in newspaper. The fringe-hugging menu combined with the hopping happy hour singles scene drew Christian Bale in while he was on location in the Windy City shooting The Dark Knight. Lunchtime service can get bogged down with larger groups meeting for business. Go elsewhere for a quick bite.

Gastropub. Lunch, dinner, Saturday-Sunday brunch. Bar. $36-85

GREAT LAKE

1477 West Balmoral Ave., Chicago, 773-334-9270

It is easy to miss the unassuming storefront on a side street in Chicago's north side Andersonville neighborhood but that would be a mistake, as this intimate (read: tiny) "mom & pop" pizza shop serves up some of the city's best pizza. Due to the size and popularity of the place, and the fact that the chef/owner makes every single pizza that touches the lucky few diners' lips, the wait can be excruciatingly long. But do not let that deter you. There are three nightly pizza offerings and if the mushroom pie is on the menu, order it and you will be rewarded with an earthy, salty, cheesy slice of perfection. Capitalizing on locally sourced farm fresh ingredients, other toppings may include fresh spinach, herbs and tomatoes, as well as housemade sausage. A petit fresh green salad with choice of two dressings and scoops of locally made ice cream round out the sparse but well-edited menu. Great Lake is BYOB so put your name on the list and walk to grab a bottle of wine at nearby wine shop, In Fine Spirits.

Pizza. Dinner. Closed Sunday-Tuesday. $16-35

LE BOUCHON

1958 N. Damen Ave., Chicago, 773-862-6600; www.lebouchonofchicago.com

There's a reason this tiny storefront bistro has been packing in a crowd of regulars for more than 15 years. The food is delicious, the prices are reasonable,

the mood is convivial, and the feeling is somehow unmistakably Parisian. The menu reflects owner Jean-Claude Poilevey's French roots (he's a native of Burgundy); Le Bouchon features standbys such as a creamy housemade pâté, beef Bourguignon over mashed potatoes, and white-wine poached salmon with cucumber and tomato beurre blanc. The onion tart—a classic intermingling of crispy pastry and tangy caramelized onions—is a signature dish. The closely packed tables and noisy room aren't for everyone, but those who seek out Le Bouchon's authentic environs will likely be glad they made the effort.
French. Lunch, dinner. Closed Sunday. $16-35

PIECE
1927 W. North Ave., Chicago, 773-772-4422; www.piecechicago.com

Housed in a 5,800-square-foot former garage, Piece eschews classic deep-dish Chicago pizza in favor of a delicious thin-crust variety that was invented at the famed Sally's Apizza in New Haven, Connecticut. Piece (which is co-owned by Cheap Trick guitarist Rick Nielsen, who lent one of his five-necked guitars to the restaurant) serves huge rectangular pizzas featuring toppings that are both standard (pepperoni, onions) and not-so-standard (mashed potatoes, clams). Some of the combinations might sound strange but they somehow meld perfectly with the pizza's crunchy thin crust and tangy tomato sauce. The pizzas aren't the only reason that the massive space is always packed with a randy crowd checking out the game (and each other): Piece's onsite, hand-crafted brews won the World Beer Cup's Small Brewpub Award in 2006.
Pizza. Lunch, dinner. Bar. $16-35

PIZZERIA UNO
29 E. Ohio St., Chicago, 312-321-1000; www.unos.com

Despite the trendy thin-crust-pizza spots that have been popping up across Chicago lately, many still come to the city for chewy, gooey deep-dish pizza. There are many arguments about whose stuffed pizza is the best, but no matter who's doing the rating, Pizzeria Uno is almost always near the top. This standby—which actually served the world's first stuffed pizza, back in the 1940s—draws huge crowds, and it's not exactly spacious, so either arrive early (the restaurant doesn't take reservations) or be prepared for a long wait for a table (which will likely be cramped). But oh, how it's worth the wait: The cheese is melty, the tomato sauce is sweet but has a nice zip of garlic, and the crust is slightly crunchy. You'll quickly tune out the tourists that surround you as you dig in.
Pizza. Lunch, dinner. $16-35

PROVINCE
161 N. Jefferson, Chicago, 312-669-9900; www.provincerestaurant.com

Located just west of downtown, Province is longtime former Nacional 27's chef Randy Zweiban's first restaurant. At Nacional 27, he focused on the worldly cuisine of 27 Latin American countries. It would seem that he has gone in a completely new direction at Province—the restaurant is a farm-to-table driven American restaurant with dishes such as a smoked pork belly sandwich and the signature ten-hour braised lamb. But his Spanish and South American influences are still seen in dishes throughout the extensive menu, such as rabbit confit with salsa verde and marcona almond emulsion. The layout of the menu is confusing as the dishes are separated into six different categories but regardless of whether you choose small, big or bigger dishes, the results will be delicious. House cocktails such as the Province martini or Absent Field Hand are smartly made and are a good idea before dinner.

Contemporary American. Lunch. dinner. $36-85

THE PURPLE PIG

500 N. Michigan Ave., Chicago, 312-464-1744; www.thepurplepigchicago.com

With the motto, "Cheese, Swine & Wine" what is there not to like at this sliver of porky, cheesy goodness located on Michigan Avenue's Magnificent Mile? The chain restaurants in this part of town are generally geared toward tourists walking off the double-decker buses nearby, but the Purple Pig aims higher. Developed by veteran Chicago restaurateurs Scott Harris and Jimmy Bannos, the menu is composed of a wide-selection of delicious small plates which are meant to be shared by a crowd. Smears run the gauntlet from the esoteric pork neck bone rillette to the more familiar (but no less tasty) whipped feta. Cured meats and cheese plates make for a quick bite paired with a quartino of wine— the menu includes a nice selection—while main plates such as milk-braised pork are more substantial and filling. The place is small and gets crowded. (Bonus: The restaurant is open late night.) The outdoor area—a rarity on shop-filled Michigan Avenue—is a great spot for dining and drinks when the weather is warm.

Mediterranean. Lunch, dinner, late-night. Bar. $36-85

SABLE KITCHEN & BAR

Hotel Palomar, 505 North State Street, Chicago, 312-755-9704; www.sablechicago.com

With at least as much focus on the drinks as the food, this is one place you will not regret drinking your dinner. Many of the house-designed cocktails are prepared with locally sourced ingredients and paired with reputedly one of the largest brown liquor selections in the area. The interior is over-the-top with onyx, oxblood leather, oversized chandeliers and custom light fixtures. With all this excitement over master mixology and elaborate design, the food could be easily overlooked, but that would be a mistake. Executive Chef Heather Terhune has crafted a modern menu that pairs perfectly with the cocktails such as spicy buttermilk fried quail with blue cheese slaw and crispy pork belly B.L.T's.

Contemporary American. Breakfast, lunch, dinner. Bar $36-85

SAI CAFÉ

2010 N. Sheffield Ave., Chicago, 773-472-8080; www.saicafe.com

There are plenty of neighborhood sushi restaurants in Chicago, but few offer fish that's as fresh—and generously portioned—as this Lincoln Park standby. The menu offers several different entrées, but it's the sushi that packs people into the restaurant's three laid-back rooms. Any of the sushi creations will delight you, but the rainbow maki with tuna, yellowtail, salmon and avocado delicately wrapped around rice and a crab stick is particularly fresh and delicious.

Japanese. Dinner. $36-85

SANTORINI

800 W. Adams St., Chicago, 312-829-8820; www.santorinichicago.com

Chicago's Greektown is packed with restaurants that make a solid spanakopita and serve a decent flaming saganaki. But the rustic Santorini stands apart from the crowd with its fresh seafood, white walls with dark wood trim, and bi-level dining room featuring a large fireplace. The spot serves excellent versions of Greek standards, like melt-in-your-mouth center-cut lamb chops and juicy chicken baked with vegetables and zesty feta cheese in phyllo dough. The true don't-miss entrées here are the grilled octopus (a house specialty) and whole fish such as tender red snapper, which can be fileted tableside and served in a tangy simple sauce of olive oil and lemon juice.

Greek. Lunch, dinner. $36-85

SUSHI WABI

842 W. Randolph St., Chicago, 312-563-1224; www.sushiwabi.com

From the industrial-chic exposed ductwork to the DJ spinning tunes above the dimly lit dining room, Sushi Wabi feels as much like a club as it does one of Chicago's most popular sushi restaurants. For every hipster reveling in the loft atmosphere and cool tunes, there's a sushi aficionado delving into the restaurant's fresh fish and unique creations. The maki rolls include the tried-and-true, from an expertly crafted dragon roll brushed with eel sauce to decadent specialties like the Tarantula, which bursts with soft-shell crab, avocado, chili sauce and masago mayo. Leave room for the green-tea cheesecake, which may be the world's most delicious way to enjoy antioxidants.

Japanese. Lunch (Monday-Friday), dinner. Bar. $16-35

TRATTORIA NO. 10

10 N. Dearborn St., Chicago, 312-984-1718; www.trattoriaten.com

Given its Loop location and subterranean, Old World feel, it's surprising to learn that Trattoria No. 10 chef Douglas D'Avico is fairly progressive with his menu: He features organic and locally grown ingredients in items like handcrafted ravioli filled with asparagus tips and aged provolone topped with sun-dried tomato sauce, and butternut and acorn squash in a sweet walnut-butter sauce. Although it's big with the lunch crowd, Trattoria No. 10's low ceilings, alfresco-style murals and textured walls help the restaurant overcome its substreet-level locale and create romantic, cozy environs for dinner in a decidedly non-cozy neighborhood.

Italian. Lunch (Monday-Friday), dinner. Closed Sunday. $36-85

SPAS

★★★★ELYSIAN SPA & HEALTH CLUB

Elysian Hotel, 11 E. Walton, Chicago, 312-573-6860; www.elysianhotels.com

This beautiful Greek-inspired spa resides in the lavish Elysian hotel and features a mosiac-tiled lap pool, men's atelier and luxurious changing rooms with white stone, lacquered lockers and rich walnut wood. Unique treatments include the warm lava shell massage, the homepathic facial (there are also several age-defying facials) and the Elysian Cleanse, which combines water therapy, marine massage and a body treatment to renew the skin. The men's atelier (with flat-screen televisions) offers a traditional shave, facial treatments, manicures and pedicures and haircuts. (A monthly membership is available.) Ladies can have their hair and makeup done at the onsite salon. Fitness offerings include a pilates studios and personal trainers.

★★★★THE PENINSULA SPA BY ESPA

The Peninsula Chicago, 108 E. Superior St., Chicago, 312-573-6860; www.chicago.peninsula.com

East meets Midwest at this 15,000-square-foot spa, where down-to-earth hospitality complements a full range of Asian- and European-inspired treatments. To begin your visit, step through a giant oak door and enter the newly renovated Relaxation Lounge. The area's plush wooden beds, separated by individual curtains, set the mood for serious pampering. All treatments are exclusively designed by ESPA, an English product line focusing on high-quality, all-natural ingredients. Both mind and body get attention with the Chakra Balancing Massage, which uses smooth volcanic stones to ground and balance your energy. (Sounds wacky, feels great.) Post-treatment, swim in the spa's half-Olympic size pool; its floor-to-ceiling windows provide beautiful views and a chance to find your own moment of Zen.

★★★SPA AT THE CARLTON CLUB

The Ritz-Carlton, Chicago, 160 E. Pearson St., Chicago, 312-266-1000; www.fourseasons.com

With names like Azalea, Magnolia and Lilac, treatment rooms at this elegant spa are all about organic luxury. Start your visit with a trip to the sophisticated locker room, which features a cedar sauna and private vanity areas. From there, try the Aroma-Tonic Body Envelopment, which begins with a full-body exfoliation and finishes with a clay and papaya cream mask to soothe dull, dry skin (perfect if you're here during the harsh winter). When the weather is nice, be sure to slather on the SPF before heading to the sun deck, where terrific views of the neighboring John Hancock Center make you feel like you're on top of the world. Considering the level of service you'll find here, it's more or less true.

★★★★SPA AT FOUR SEASONS

Four Seasons Hotel Chicago, 120 E. Delaware Place, Chicago, 312-280-8800; www.fourseasons.com

This spa's plush interior makes you feel right at home—that is, if fountains and marble floors are what you're used to. White suede wall panels and sound-proofed treatment rooms add to the spa's elegant feel. Put on one of the spa's thick, silky robes and prepare for the royal treatment—literally. You can enjoy a facial massage with ruby-infused oil during the 80-minute Essence of Rubies Treatment. In gemstone therapy, rubies promote passion and well-being; in this treatment, they just make our muscles feel like jelly. Or try the Champagne Paraffin pedicure, which begins with an antioxidant-rich grape seed oil exfoliation, and ends with a glass of bubbly. (The heated massage chairs make this decadent pedicure more indulgent.) The gracious staff makes you feel even more relaxed. Extend your stay as much as possible by lounging in one of the day beds after your treatment.

★★★★THE SPA AT TRUMP

Trump International Hotel and Tower, Chicago, 401 N. Wabash Ave., Chicago, 312-588-8020; www.trumpchicagohotel.com

The Donald wants to know your intentions—your spa intentions, that is. Whether you're looking to calm, balance, purify, heal or revitalize, you'll find what you need in this 23,000-square-foot den of relaxation. In concert with the property as a whole, the spa's décor is modern and sophisticated. Smooth blond wood, dim lighting and simple orchids create a comfortable, surprisingly unpretentious atmosphere. Still, it should come as no surprise that all the amenities here are the best: extra-spacious treatment rooms, deluge mood-enhancing showers (the shower lights up while water comes at you from everywhere) and an enormous health club boasting one of the most striking views in Chicago. As for the treatments, many of them focus on—what else—jewels. The Black Pearl Rejuvenation Facial combines crushed black pearls and mineral-packed oyster shell extracts to firm and tone your skin, while the Emerald Oasis Body Treatment uses mineral salt, mint and emerald-infused oils to exfoliate. If it's true that diamonds are a girl's best friend, maybe you should opt for the Purifying Diamonds Massage instead. The precious diamond and botanical essences will have you feeling engaged in Trump-style tranquility.

WHERE TO SHOP

APARTMENT NUMBER 9

1804 N. Damen Ave., Chicago, 773-395-2999; www.apartmentnumber9.com

It's almost impossible to leave this somewhat-removed Bucktown boutique without looking dashing and polished—at least if you're a guy. The store is dedicated to styling men, and to do so, it mixes the classic with the cutting-edge. Expect to find crisp dress shirts by John Varvatos, Paul Smith and Dries van Noten mingling in the racks with Splendid Mills T-shirts and Fred Perry sweaters. Clean up your act with John Allan's grooming products or the solid selection of ties and belts that hang out in the back.

Tuesday-Friday 11 a.m.-7 p.m., Saturday 11 a.m.-6 p.m., Sunday noon-5 p.m.

ART EFFECT

934 W. Armitage, Chicago, 773-929-3600; www.shoparteffect.com

Billing itself as "the modern day general store," Art Effect offers everything from great gifts (monogrammed soaps, candles, books), clothing, jewelry, toys, stationary, travel gear—you name it and this adorable shop pretty much has it. Best of all, the selection is well edited. Bath and body items feature Illume Yuzu, Tokyo Milk, and Sara Happ. Entertaining items (or lovely hostess gifts) might include marble cheese slicers and monogrammed old-fashioned glasses. You'll also find Alexis Bittar jewelry, Ella Moss clothing, and sparkly Moyna evening bags. Everything is packaged up at the end of a spree like the pretty little gifts that they are—even if you have just been treating yourself.

Monday-Thursday 11 a.m.-7 p.m., Friday 11 a.m.-6 p.m., Saturday 10 a.m.-6 p.m., Sunday noon-5:00 p.m.

BARNEYS CO-OP

2209-11 N. Halsted St., Chicago, 773-248-0426; www.barneys.com

If you regularly worship at the altar of Phillip Lim and Marc Jacobs, then

Barneys New York's quirkier baby sister needs no introduction. Cult-brand devotees religiously come to this concrete-and-metal loftlike space in Lincoln Park to find the usual urban-chic suspects—that'd be the aforementioned (Lim constantly puts out Barneys-exclusive items), Alexander Wang and Acne jeans for ladies, and PS by Paul Smith, Prada Sport and J Brand jeans for men. The salespeople—who sport trendsetting haircuts and clothes that scream "amazing staff discounts"—are helpful and not cloying, especially around the well-stocked beauty bar, massive denim wall and tightly selected shoe collection. Those with handbag addictions should head to the gritty-girly bags by Marc Jacobs, soft leather slouches by Sissi Rossi and classic bowlers by Jas M.B., which are on display near the floor-to-ceiling windows up front.
Monday-Saturday 11 a.m.-7 p.m., Sunday noon-6 p.m.

BARNEYS NEW YORK
15 E. Oak St., Chicago, 312-587-1700; www.barneys.com

The new Barneys harkens back to a time when visiting a department store was special, where you wore your best and prepared for a full-day event. This gleaming six-story building with marble floors and geometric staircases is full of beautiful clothes, shoes, purses, fragrances and cosmetics. Clerks dressed in black are ready to point you to the latest designer items, or you can take your sweet time pouring over the racks of Prada, Marc Jacobs, Lanvin, Chloé and Theory. The shoe selection is extensive, and there are dozens of beautiful handbags downstairs. Afterward, plan to spend a few blissful, lazy hours giggling over your purchases and sipping bubbly at Fred's, the store's penthouse restaurant complete with a lakeview terrace.
Monday-Saturday 10 a.m.-7 p.m., Sunday 11 a.m.-6 p.m.

BLAKE
212 W. Chicago Ave., Chicago, 312-202-0047

A boutique with no sign, no posted hours and no website? What is this, a nightclub? Well, it's almost as exclusive—the only way to get in is by ringing a lone doorbell outside (it's a weird system, but go with it), and it's so sparse in its interior design, you may mistake it for a gallery, save for the suspended racks teeming with an immaculately assembled collection. Blake caters to no-nonsense fashionistas who appreciate French, British, Italian and Belgian designers like Dries van Noten (the boutique has the largest collection in the city), Marni, Louise Goldin, Rick Owens and Maurizio Pecoraro. Accessories are displayed neatly on white islands throughout the museum-like space, and much like a museum, the pieces—like a Chloé violet-gray snakeskin purse—are almost works of art.
Monday-Friday 10:30 a.m.-7 p.m., Saturday 10:30 a.m.-6:30 p.m.

CYNTHIA ROWLEY
810 W. Armitage Ave., Chicago, 773-528-6160; 1653 N. Damen Ave., Chicago, 773-276-9209; www.cynthiarowley.com

It's only fitting that this designer's eponymous shop is in the heart of Lincoln Park, one of Chicago's hottest boutique-studded neighborhoods. Rowley—an Illinois native who sold her first collection while still a senior at the School of the Art Institute of Chicago—rolls out dynamic dresses, separates and sweaters

HIGHLIGHT

WHERE IS THE BEST SHOPPING ON MICHIGAN AVENUE?

On the Magnificent Mile's double-wide sidewalks, wide-eyed tourists mix with fashionistas, while businessmen duck into department stores and iPod-plugged hipsters navigate around the many street performers. Start on the southernmost point of the Mag Mile, where Michigan Avenue meets the Chicago River.

Your first stop is the **The Shops at North Bridge** (*520 N. Michigan Ave.*), which is anchored by Nordstrom. As any shopaholic with a sole addiction can tell you, the four-story department store has a huge shoe selection.

Cross Michigan Avenue and head inside the Midwestern flagship of **Gap** (*555 N. Michigan Ave.*), where you can find the chain's signature dependably comfortable clothes. Cross back to the left side of Michigan, where you can get timeless denim at **Levi's** (*600 N. Michigan Ave.*) and trendy, affordable clothing at the massive **Forever 21/XXI** (*540 N. Michigan Ave.*).

At Ontario Street, boutiques such as **Cartier** (*630 N. Michigan Ave.*) and **Burberry** (*633 N. Michigan Ave.*) stand on either side of Michigan, while just down the block are jeweler **Van Cleef & Arpels** (*636 N. Michigan Ave.*), Italian fashion houses **Ermenegildo Zegna** (*645 N. Michigan Ave.*) and **Salvatore Ferragamo** (*645 N. Michigan Ave.*). Chicago-based housewares giant **Crate & Barrel** (*646 N. Michigan Ave.*) has its flagship on this block. Zip across the street to explore the colossal **Niketown** (*669 N. Michigan Ave.*) and the ultramodern cube that is the **Apple Store** (*679 N. Michigan Ave.*), where hands-on displays let you play with the latest gadgets.

The next block includes **Brooks Brothers** (*713 N. Michigan Ave.*). For an even larger selection of men's garments, stop in **Saks Fifth Avenue Men's Store** (*717 N. Michigan Ave.*); inside, you'll find everything from elegant silk ties and suits to deluxe grooming lines. For more of the same but for ladies, cross Michigan Avenue to **Saks Fifth Avenue** (*700 N. Michigan Ave.*).

On the following block north, gaze in the window at the imposing **Tiffany & Co.** (*730 N. Michigan Ave.*) before you're distracted by the goods just up the block: **Banana Republic** (*744 N. Michigan Ave.*) and **Ralph Lauren** (*750 N. Michigan Ave.*). For another kind of grandeur, go across Michigan to **Neiman Marcus** (*737 N. Michigan Ave.*); just don't forget your Neiman's credit card, AmEx or cash, as the legendary designer department store doesn't take checks or other credit cards.

On the last leg of the Mag Mile, you'll want to check out the approachable and increasingly fashionable **Water Tower Place** (*835 N. Michigan Ave.*), a shopping center that houses everything from Custo Barcelona to Neiman Marcus offshoot Cusp to kid cult favorite American Girl Place. Across the street from Water Tower is **Escada** (*840 N. Michigan Ave.*), which is the first in a series of markedly more upscale stores in the northernmost reaches of this shopping strip. North of Escada, on the east side of Michigan, you'll find sharply cut variations of the traditional white blouse at **Anne Fontaine** (*909 N. Michigan Ave.*); beautiful baubles from **Bulgari** (*909 N. Michigan Ave.*); classic-chic options from **St. John** and **J. Mendel** (*919 N. Michigan Ave.*); the ubiquitous monogrammed handbag and more at **Louis Vuitton** (*919 N. Michigan Ave.*); and the classic wool suit, fragrances and eyewear at **Chanel** (*935 N. Michigan Ave.*).

From here, cross the street and double back half a block to check out **The 900 Shops** (*900 N. Michigan Ave.*), a shopping center bookended by Bloomingdale's, and which also houses MaxMara, Gucci, L'Occitane and Lululemon Athletica.

without sacrificing girliness (achieved by using bold satins, soft leathers and sheer fabrics). Her quirky take on femininity translates into the boutique's pink-and-black motif and velvet monogrammed chairs. Head to the back for handbags and shoes, or make a beeline for Rowley's Bucktown store, which opened in late 2007 in response to that neighborhood's ever-growing shopping options.

Monday-Saturday 11 a.m.-7 p.m., Sunday noon-5 p.m.

ESKELL

1509 N. Milwaukee Ave., Chicago, 773-486-0830; www.eskell.com

Nostalgia is a beautiful thing. Just ask local designers Kelly Whitesell and Elizabeth del Castillo, the designers behind Eskell. Their penchant and passion for vintage resulted in a line that masterfully incorporates retro prints into remixes of '60s- and '70s-inspired dresses, trousers, shorts and tops, as in a recently spied pretty, gathered-at-the-waist Louise blouse in a silk print with tiny rocking horses. Eskell's frocks hang side by side with other indie lines like Lorick, Samantha Pleet and In God We Trust. There's also an excellently curated rack of affordable vintage clothes near the fitting rooms and a good selection of jewelry and purses throughout the store.

Tuesday-Saturday 11 a.m.-7 p.m., Sunday 11 a.m.-5 p.m.

GAMMA PLAYER

2035 W. Division St., Chicago, 773-235-0755; www.gammaplayer.com

Legendary techno DJ Jeff Mills and his wife, Yoko Uozumi, opened this razor-sharp boutique in spring 2007. The clothing is unpredictably edgy and decidedly high fashion, so shop with an open mind and an even more open wallet. Women, check out the risky designs by Tatsuya Shida, Jean Pierre Braganza, Veil, Reality Studio and Firma. You might see a shape-shifting, spider-web-inspired vest by the latter. Guys get equal double-take-nabbing pieces from brands such as Obscur, Julius and Odeur. If you happen to catch Mills at the store, stick around—you may just get a sample of his taste in tunes. After all, a shop that's named after one of his forward-thinking techno tracks has got to have hot music by design.

Tuesday-Saturday 11 a.m.-7 p.m., Sunday noon-6 p.m.

IKRAM

873 N. Rush St., Chicago, 312-587-1000; www.ikram.com

In 2001, Ikram Goldman took what she learned from being a salesperson for 10 years at the venerated Ultimo (a Chicago fixture for nearly 20 years before it recently closed its doors) and opened up her own store. It must have been one heck of an education in designer fashion, because to this day, Ikram remains a favorite among Chicago and national élite. (First Lady Michelle Obama is a fan.) Inside the contemporary-European-styled store, bathed in a gentle cream-and-gold palette, you'll run into an eye-popping collection of designers like Alexander McQueen, Jean Paul Gaultier and Junya Watanabe. To the right of the store, near a well-edited and carefully assembled vintage collection, is the shoe selection, which almost solely consists of sharp-looking Azzedine Alaïa and Jimmy Choo pumps.

Monday-Saturday 10 a.m.-6 p.m. and by appointment.

HIGHLIGHT

WHERE IS THE BEST SHOPPING ON OAK STREET?

Michigan Avenue is all well and good for High Street fashions, but for high fashion, there's nothing like Oak Street. Start your walk of this beautiful boutique road at Michigan Avenue and Oak. On the south side of the street, make a stop at **Tod's** (121 E. Oak St., 312-943-0070) for gorgeously handcrafted leather handbags, shoes and accessories.

As expected, there's no shortage of gems and jewelry on Oak Street, so cross to the south side of the street again for a look inside **Trabert & Hoeffer** (111 E. Oak St., 312-787-1654)—if the gemstones inside don't make your heart skip a beat, then not to worry. **Graff Diamonds** (103 E. Oak St., 312-604-1000), **Lester Lampert** (57 E. Oak St., 312-944-6888) and **David Yurman** (40 E. Oak St., 312-787-7779) are all just down the road.

Young girls will want to pop into **Juicy Couture** (101 E. Oak St., 312-280-1637; www. juicycouture.com). Otherwise, back to mid-Oak: Make a stop at **Kate Spade** (56 E. Oak St., 312-654-8853) for ladylike touches, such as beautifully embossed thank-you cards or Martha's Vineyard-worthy wallets, then nip across Oak Street where shoe lovers can indulge in **Jimmy Choo's** (63 E. Oak St., 312-255-1170) elegant, sexy heels. Lovers of everything streamlined and understated must stop in at **Jil Sander's** (48 E. Oak St., 312-335-0006) museum-like digs, and makeup mavens would do well to stock up on **M.A.C.** (40 E. Oak St., 312-951-7310) cosmetics, which often collaborates with high-end designers (Liberty of London, Ungaro) on limited-edition makeup lines. Make sure you stop in at **Loro Piana** (45 E. Oak St., 312-664-6644) for luxurious knitwear.

Next, pay a visit to three formidable houses of style: **Vera Wang** (34 E. Oak St., 312-787-4696), which specializes in wedding gowns (and is by appointment only); **Prada** (30 E. Oak St., 312-951-1113), an ode to all things artistic; and **Hermès** (25 E. Oak St., 312-787-8175) which was in a smaller space down the street before it moved into the old Barneys space. The store is Chicago's only outpost of the prestigious French couture house. Wind down your walking tour at **Barneys New York** (15 E. Oak St., 312-587-1700), which only a year ago moved into its gleaming new digs and now includes an outpost of the beloved eatery Fred's. Finally, if you're still not shopped out, there's a new **Marc Jacobs** (11 E. Walton St.) just down the block, which has a great selection of the designer's pieces for men, women and children.

DETOUR: WALTON STREET One street south, parallel to Oak Street, you'll find heaven for North Shore teens and college students. Here, you'll find West Coast-style purveyor **Samantha** (64 E. Walton St., 312-951-5383), snowboarding outfitter **Burton** (56 E. Walton St., 312-202-7900), the culty **AG Adriano Goldschmied Jeans** (48 E. Walton St., 312-787-7680), basics giant **American Apparel** (46 E. Walton St., 312-255-8360), trendy **Urban Outfitters** (935 N. Rush St., 312-640-1919) and **Diesel** (923 N. Rush St., 312-255-0157).

DETOUR: RUSH STREET Starting at Chicago Avenue and walking north, you'll find luxury-clothing den Ikram; stylist fave **Intermix** (40 E. Delaware Place, 312-640-2922); Australian boots-maker **Ugg** (909 N. Rush St., 312-255-1280); athletic gear at **Adidas Originals** (923 N. Rush St., 312-932-0651); and travel accessories at **Flight 001** (1133 N. State St., 312-944-1001).

LORI'S DESIGNER SHOES

824 W. Armitage Ave., Chicago. 773-281-5655; www.lorisshoes.com

Don't even think of setting foot here on a Saturday or the first day of a major sale (often twice a year, at the end of summer and fall). The no-frills store—sales racks organized by shoe size line the perimeter of the space—has a large selection of mid-range footwear, from traditional brands like Calvin Klein, Franco Sarto and Charles David to funkier lines like Jeffrey Campbell and Jessica Bennett, for less than you'd find them anywhere else (sometimes up to 50 percent off). Don't expect much attention from the sales staff, either; the no-return policy on sales items is strictly enforced.

Monday-Thursday 11 a.m.-7 p.m., Friday 11 a.m.-6 p.m., Saturday 10 a.m.-6 p.m., Sunday noon-5 p.m.

MACY'S

111 N. State St., Chicago, 312-781-1000; www.visitmacyschicago.com

When Federated Department Stores (the owner of Macy's) decided that it was not going to retain Marshall Field's name and image after it bought the legendary Chicago department store in 2005, the announcement launched high-pitched outcries from locals. Despite all the commotion—and the wishes of disgruntled Field's loyalists who vowed never to set foot in Macy's—this State Street building is worth a visit regardless of who sells what inside. Opened for business in 1907 by Marshall Field & Company, the State Street store is pure nostalgia, with its soaring atrium, a gorgeous Tiffany stained-glass ceiling and the historic "great clocks," which are still suspended on the corner of State and Washington and State and Randolph streets. Not much has changed inside, either—Macy's kept Field's favorites like the Merz Apothecary boutique on the ground floor and the exclusive 70-year-old 28 Shop on the third, which features a wide swath of designers, from Yves Saint Laurent to Marc Jacobs, as well as private elevator access and valet. You can still sit around the fountain in the historic Walnut Room restaurant, although a trip to the new food court next door is also definitely worth a visit. The upscale food court, Seven on State, features gourmet food stations from Rick Bayless (of Frontera Grill) and Marcus Samuelsson (Marc Burger).

Monday-Saturday 10 a.m.-8 p.m., Sunday 11 a.m.-6 p.m.

P.45

1643 N. Damen Ave., Chicago, 773-862-4523; www.p45.com

The "p" in p.45 might just stand for "pioneer." When Bucktown was an up-and-coming neighborhood mainly populated by artists and musicians in the '90s, this upscale store was among the first fashion boutiques to open. To this day, it offers simple and chic sleeveless tops, skirts, dresses and jewelry. Find 3.1 Phillip Lim and Laila Azhar on the roster of designers here, all of whom have one thing in common: understated cool elegance.

Monday-Saturday 11 a.m.-7 p.m., Sunday noon-5 p.m. Open Thursday until 8 p.m. in November and December.

PAGODA RED

1714 N. Damen Ave., Chicago, 773-235-1188; www.pagodared.com

You probably won't have the space to carry a pair of original Qing-era courtyard doors home with you, but there are so many gorgeous pieces of furniture and artifacts at this large Asian home décor showroom you're bound to come home with something. Many of the items—like a simple stool we recently saw replicated in a Crate & Barrel catalog or framed Chinese drawings depicting sexy, saucy vignettes—hold up surprisingly well to the test of time and taste. The pretty, Zen entrance alone is a free lesson in feng shui, if too many options (or airline weight restrictions) leave you empty-handed.

Monday-Saturday 10 a.m.-6 p.m., Sunday noon-5 p.m.

ROBIN RICHMAN

2108 N. Damen Ave., Chicago, 773-278-6150; www.robinrichman.com

Richman opened her eponymous boutique in 1998 to showcase her own hand-knit sweaters. A little over a decade later, her boutique buzzes with a creative vibe, thanks to an in-house workshop. Richman sells small quantities of limited-production wares by emerging designers under the belief that items should be one-of-a-kind. To that end, you will find dip-dyed pieces by Marc le Bihan, jewelry made from leather and metals by Tuscan designer Riccardo Goti, and handmade wooden heels by Marsèll.

Tuesday-Saturday 11 a.m.-6 p.m., Sunday noon-5 p.m.

SOFIA VINTAGE

72 E. Oak St., Chicago, 312-640-0878; www.sofiavintage.com

Owned by two sisters with two completely different styles (one prefers a 70s boho-chic look, while the other is more traditional and conservative), Sofia Vintage is not what you would expect to see on tony Oak Street (home to Tod's, Prada, Jimmy Choo, etc., etc.). But the relative newcomer is most certainly a welcome addition. The shop offers men's and women's vintage clothing and accessories from the 1920s through the 1980s, which the two sisters find by scouring second-hand shops across the country (and sometimes even alter to make them more chic). Named after actress Sophia Lauren for her class and grace, the selection here may include Valentino and Lanvin dresses, Chanel handbags and Gucci ties. After you have scoured the perfect vintage bag or tie, browse all the other shops on Oak Street for that perfectly pulled together look. The owners may have different styles, but the store is classy all around.

Monday–Saturday 11 a.m.–7 p.m., Sunday 12 p.m. –5 p.m.

SPROUT HOME

745 N. Damen Ave., Chicago, 312-226-5950; www.sprouthome.com

You know that feeling you get when you wish you could just move into the most pretty store you know? Slap a bed in the middle of this housewares emporium and nursery, and you're home. The poured-concrete floor and wood accents give Sprout a sleek look, while the neat shelves contain playful accessories for home and garden: lampshades made of laminated Japanese silk, glazed terracotta bird feeders (with a ladder inside) and ultra-modern dinner chairs you'd never guess were made from recycled plastic. Take a stroll in the nursery, where urban gardeners get their pick of rare plants (passion flowers, anyone?), herbs and ornamental trees.

Winter: Monday-Friday 10 a.m.-8 p.m., Saturday-Sunday 10 a.m.-7 p.m.

Spring/Summer: Monday-Friday 9 a.m.-8 p.m., Saturday-Sunday 9 a.m.-7 p.m.

VOSGES HAUT-CHOCOLAT

951 W. Armitage St., Chicago, 773-296-9866; www.vosgeschocolate.com

It's curious how a space so cozy and homey could whisk you to so many exotic locales. But that's just what happens inside this pretty, purple-hued chocolate-shop-cum-retail boutique. Owner and chocolatier Katrina Markoff—a Chicagoan trained at Le Cordon Bleu—has made waves across the nation with her surprising combinations, such as smoked bacon and milk chocolate (Mo's Bacon Bar); Mexican chiles, Ceylon cinnamon and dark chocolate (Red Fire Bar); and ginger, wasabi, sesame seeds and dark chocolate (Black Pearl Bar). Indulge in any of her signature truffles, or opt for gourmet ice cream from the dessert bar in the back. There are also Vosges locations in the Shops at North Bridge and O'Hare's Terminal 1.

Monday-Wednesday 10 a.m.-8 p.m., Thursday-Saturday 10 a.m.-9 p.m., Sunday 11 a.m.-6 p.m.

CHICAGOLAND

There are great reasons to venture beyond the city limits of Chicago. For one, the suburbs offer an alternative to the faster pace of the Windy City without necessarily forsaking the great things about Chicago. Oak Park on the West Side drips with culture and architecture (Ernest Hemingway was born here; Frank Lloyd Wright spent the first 20 years of his career here and plenty of his structures remain), while just north of the city, Evanston boasts amazing Lake Michigan views, Northwestern University and acclaimed restaurants.

The western suburb Brookfield has the respected Brookfield Zoo, while Glencoe, on the North Shore, hosts the breathtaking Chicago Botanic Gardens. The Fox River Valley offers quaint downtowns, like Geneva and St. Charles, to stroll through and lose yourself in for an afternoon.

WHAT TO SEE

ARLINGTON HEIGHTS

ARLINGTON PARK

2200 W. Euclid Ave., Arlington Heights, 847-385-7500; www.arlingtonpark.com

With horse names like "Smack Daddy," "Heckofanacttofollow" and "Pass the Brandy," you don't need to be a gambler to enjoy thoroughbred racing in this six-story grandstand racetrack. Located in Chicago's northwest suburb, Arlington Heights, and only a 45 minute train ride outside the city, Arlington Park generates a diverse crowd of onlookers, from tranquil families soaking up a summer day to betters caught in the adrenaline rush of the race. With more than 50,000 seats and stables for over 2,000 horses, the dirt oval turf first made its appearance in 1927, thanks to founder Harry D. "Curly" Brown. The park received national attention in 1981 when the winner of the Arlington Million purse race, legendary "John Henry," had a thrilling come-from-behind win over 40-1 long-shot "The Bart." The statue, Against All Odds, located in the paddock, reveals the horse and his jockey, Bill Shoemaker, edging out "The Bart" by a nose. Stop by the paddock shortly before a race to see the horses being groomed

See website for race schedules.

HIGHLIGHT

WHAT ARE THE TOP THINGS TO DO IN CHICAGOLAND?

ENJOY MUSIC UNDER THE STARS
Grab a blanket, a picnic basket and a bottle of wine and head to Highland Park. The seasonal Ravinia Festival is the summer home for the Chicago Symphony Orchestra and also showcases an outstanding repertoire of diverse acts.

REMEMBER
Skokie's Illinois Holocaust Museum and Education Center is the largest of its kind in the Midwest. This sprawling museum dedicated to preserving the memory of all those lost contains the personal accounts and artifacts of Skokie residents.

SEE A SPIRITUAL WONDER
The Baha'i House of Worship is the spiritual center of the Baha'i faith in the United States, and one of only seven Baha'i temples in the world. The remarkable nine-sided structure, located in Wilmette, symbolizes unity.

STOP AND SMELL THE FLOWERS
The Chicago Botanic Garden is actually in Glencoe. Over 385 acres offer 23 display gardens, along with small lakes, a prairie area and a woodland.

AURORA
BLACKBERRY FARM
100 S. Barnes Road, Aurora, 630-892-1550; www.foxvalleyparkdistrict.org

This rural spot has a 1840s through the 1920s living history museum and working farm. Exhibits include a children's animal farm, discovery barn and train. There are also craft demonstrations, wagon and pony rides, and a farm play area.
Hours vary by season.

PARAMOUNT THEATRE
23 E. Galena Blvd., Aurora, 630-896-6666; www.paramountarts.com

This theater was built in 1931 to compete with the opulent movie palaces of the area. It has been restored to its original appearance and stages a variety of productions throughout the year.
Tours: Tuesday-Friday. Reservations required. Show times vary; check website for details.

SCHINGOETHE CENTER FOR NATIVE AMERICAN CULTURES
347 S. Gladstone Ave., Aurora, 630-892-6431; www.aurora.edu/museum

At Aurora University, this private collection contains thousands of Native American artifacts, including jewelry, textiles, pottery and baskets.

Admission: adults $3, seniors and students $2, children $1, families $7. Tuesday, 10 a.m.-7 p.m., Wednesday-Friday 10 a.m.-4 p.m., Sunday 1-4 p.m. (during the academic year).

SCITECH HANDS-ON MUSEUM
18 W. Benton, Aurora, 630-859-3434; www.scitech.mus.il.us

Housed in a historic post office building, this interactive center provides more than 150 hands-on learning exhibits using motion, light, sound and science principles.

Admission: adults and children $8, seniors $7, children 3 and under free. Tuesday-Friday 10 a.m.-3 p.m., Saturday 10 a.m.-5 p.m., Sunday noon-5 p.m.

BROOKFIELD
BROOKFIELD ZOO
3300 Golf Road, Brookfield, 708-688-8000, 800-201-0784; www.brookfieldzoo.com

West-suburban Brookfield Zoo has the pioneering Midwestern spirit. It was the first zoo in the U.S. to have a mostly cageless facility—instead it uses natural barriers such as moats—and it was the first to exhibit giant pandas. The zoo also created Tropic World, the first indoor simulated rainforest in North America, where you see monkeys amid the treetops as waterfalls cascade nearby and fake thunderstorms growl overhead. If you're not a landlubber, check out the daily indoor dolphin shows, which star bottlenose dolphins doing Flipper-like feats. Set on 216 acres, the zoo is Chicagoland's largest and is home to more than 2,000 animals, including lions and tigers and binturongs.

Admission: adults $13.50, seniors and children 3-11 $9.50. Free October-December, Tuesday and Thursday. Mid-May-Labor Day, Monday-Friday 9:30 a.m.-6 p.m., Sunday 9:30 a.m.-7:30 p.m.; Labor Day-mid-October and April-mid-May, Monday-Friday 10 a.m.-5 p.m., Saturday-Sunday 10 a.m.-6 p.m.; mid-October-March, daily 10 a.m.-5 p.m.

BUFFALO GROVE
LONG GROVE CONFECTIONARY COMPANY
333 Lexington Drive, Buffalo Grove, 800-373-3102, 888-459-3100; www.longgrove.com

Take a tour of this family-owned confectionery, which produces more than 300 sweet treats. Learn how the chocolates are made, sample the products and then purchase discounted goodies from the factory store.

Store: Monday-Saturday 9:30 a.m.-5:30 p.m., Sunday 11 a.m.-4 p.m. Tours: $2. Tuesday-Thursday 10 a.m.-noon; reservations are required.

EVANSTON
CHARLES GATES DAWES HOUSE
225 Greenwood St., Evanston, 847-475-3410; www.evanstonhistorycenter.org

A tour is required to see this 28-room house of General Charles G. Dawes, Nobel Peace Prize winner (1926) and vice president under Calvin Coolidge.

Admission: $10. Thursday-Saturday 1-3 p.m.

GROSSE POINT LIGHTHOUSE
Sheridan Road and Central Street, Evanston, 847-328-6961; www.grossepointlighthouse.net

This lighthouse was constructed after a Lake Michigan wreck near Evanston claimed 300 lives. Guided tours of the keeper's quarters, a museum and tower are offered. Children under age 8 are not permitted on tours.

Tours: adults $6, children $3. June-September, Saturday-Sunday 2-4 p.m.

LADD ARBORETUM
2024 McCormick Blvd., Evanston, 847-448-8256; www.laddarboretum.org

This arboretum has jogging and biking trails, canoeing, fishing, bird-watching and camping. An International Friendship Garden represents the 23 countries with a Rotary chapter.

Daily dawn-dusk.

MITCHELL MUSEUM OF THE AMERICAN INDIAN
3001 Central Park, Evanston, 847-475-1030; www.mitchellmuseum.org

This collection of more than 3,000 items of Native American art and artifacts includes baskets, pottery, jewelry, Navajo rugs, beadwork and stoneware. An ongoing exhibit covers the art, culture, costumes and tools of tribes from the five major regions of the United States and Canada.

Admission: adults $10, seniors, teachers, students and children $2.50, families $10. Tuesday-Wednesday, Friday-Saturday 10 a.m.-5 p.m., Thursday 10 a.m.-8 p.m., Sunday noon-4 p.m.

NORTHWESTERN UNIVERSITY
633 Clark St., Evanston, 847-491-3741; www.northwestern.edu

Founded in 1851, this private university consistently ranks as one of the top in the nation. The Dearborn Observatory, built in 1888, has free public viewings. Other places of interest include the Shakespeare Garden, Theatre and Interpretation Center, Mary and Leigh Block Museum of Art and the Pick-Staiger Concert Hall. Guided walking tours (847-491-7271 for reservations) of the lakefront campus leave 1801 Hinman Avenue.

GENEVA
GARFIELD FARM AND INN MUSEUM
Route 38, Geneva, 630-584-8485; www.garfieldfarm.org

This 281-acre living history farm includes an 1846 brick tavern, an 1842 hay barn and an 1849 horse barn, as well as gardens and prairie.

Tours: adults $3, children $2. June-September, Wednesday and Sunday 1-4 p.m.

WHEELER PARK
822 N. First St., Geneva, 630-232-4542

This 57-acre park features flower and nature gardens, hiking, tennis, ball fields, access to a riverside bicycle trail, picnicking and miniature golf. The Geneva Historical Society Museum is located in the park.

Daily dawn-dusk.

GLENCOE
CHICAGO BOTANIC GARDEN
1000 Lake Cook Road, Glencoe, 847-835-5440; www.chicago-botanic.org

Despite its name, the Chicago Botanic Garden is north of Chicago in Glencoe.

SPECIAL EVENT

CIVIL WAR LIVING HISTORY DAYS

Grove National Historic Landmark, Glenview, 1421 Glenview Road, 847-299-6096; www.glenview.il.us
Head to Glenview for a realistic battle reenactment with a hospital tent, camps of the period and participants in authentic clothing and uniforms. Exhibits, lectures and house tours are highlighted.
Last weekend in July.

Never the same on any two visits given the various blooms of its flowers, the garden is spread over 385 acres with 23 display gardens, along with small lakes, a prairie area and a woodland. Be sure to visit the Japanese Garden's three islands, where you can follow the curvy paths and find some Zen underneath the pruned trees. The garden also has a great café and offers a nice respite for those seeking a relaxing walk after several days of touring the city.
Admission: free. Early-September-June, daily 8 a.m.-dusk; mid-June-early-September, daily 7 a.m.-9 p.m.

GLENVIEW
GROVE NATIONAL HISTORIC LANDMARK
1421 N. Milwaukee Ave., Glenview, 847-299-6096; www.thegroveglenview.org
This 123-acre nature preserve is an outdoor history museum. On the grounds is the restored 1856 Kennicott House; the Interpretative Center, a nature center museum; and a house designed by George G. Elmslie, who studied under and worked with Louis Sullivan. Miles of hiking trails lead through mature oak forest and past wetland pools.
Admission: free. Monday-Friday 8 a.m.-4:30 p.m., Saturday-Sunday 9 a.m.-5 p.m.

HIGHLAND PARK
FRANCIS STUPEY LOG CABIN
326 Central Ave., Highland Park; www.highlandparkhistory.com
This 1847 cabin is the oldest structure in town. It was moved to Laurel Park in the 1960s.
Admission: free. May-October, Saturday-Sunday 2-4 p.m. and by appointment.

RAVINIA FESTIVAL
Ravinia Park, Green Bay Road, Highland Park, 847-266-5100; www.ravinia.org
This seasonal festival is one of the few things worth a trip into the suburbs if you're a strapped-for-time visitor. What began as the summer home for the Chicago Symphony Orchestra—still at the heart of Ravinia's programming—now showcases an outstanding repertoire of diverse acts. (Case in point: the 2010 season featured Sheryl Crow, Vince Gill, Sting, Carrie Underwood, Counting Crows and Nelly Furtado). But the music and the immaculate acoustics can hardly speak for the overall landscape. The expansive, tightly manicured lawn is the stuff of a Pottery Barn garden catalog, as are the picnics that patrons bring in (some replete with antique candelabras and free-flowing

wine). The pricier seats of the 3,200-seat Ravinia Pavilion aren't shabby, either. Smaller acts (like chamber music groups and youth concerts) take place at the Martin Theatre and Bennett-Gordon Hall.

Season runs June-September. Check website for details.

JOLIET

BILLIE LIMACHER BICENTENNIAL PARK

201 W. Jefferson St., Joliet, 815-724-3760; www.bicentennialpark.org

Joliet Drama Guild and other productions perform here. See outdoor concerts in the band shell during summer on Thursday evenings.

CHALLENGE PARK XTREME

2903 Schweitzer Road, Joliet, 815-726-2800; www.challengepark.com

This 150-acre complex contains a skate park, miles of mountain biking trails and 25-paintball fields.

Hours vary by season.

CHICAGOLAND SPEEDWAY

500 Speedway Blvd., Joliet, 815-727-7223; www.chicagolandspeedway.com

This 75,000-seat track hosts NASCAR events each summer. Come on the Friday before a race for qualifying/practice day, when the admission fee is cheaper and good seats are easier to come by.

June-September. Check website for details.

RIALTO SQUARE THEATRE

102 N. Chicago St., Joliet, 815-726-7171; www.rialtosquare.com

This performing arts center, designed by the Rapp brothers in 1926, is considered one of the most elaborate and beautiful of old 1920s movie palaces.

Tours: $5. Tuesday 1:30 p.m.; also by appointment.

LISLE

MORTON ARBORETUM

4100 Highway 53, Lisle, 630-968-0074; www.mortonarb.org

The Morton Arboretum was founded in 1923 by Joy Morton of the Morton salt family. This facility is renowned for its lush collection of trees and plants from around the world. On the grounds are a children's garden, a maze garden, walking trails and 9 miles of paved biking trails, and a café and restaurant.

Admission: adults $11, seniors $10, children $8, children 2 and under free. Daily 7 a.m.-dusk.

DAVID ADLER MUSIC AND ARTS CENTER

1700 N. Milwaukee Ave., Libertyville, 847-367-0707; www.adlercenter.org

This once summer residence of the distinguished neoclassical architect David Adler is now an art and music center. There are folk concerts and children's events.

See website for details.

LAMBS FARM

14245 W. Rockland Road, Libertyville, 847-362-4636; www.lambsfarm.org

The farm has grown from a small pet store to a nonprofit residential and vocational community that benefits adults with developmental disabilities. It

includes a children's farmyard, animal nursery, miniature golf and a thrift shop, as well as the Country Inn Restaurant.
Daily 10 a.m.-5 p.m.

MCHENRY
MORAINE HILLS STATE PARK
1510 S. River Road, McHenry, 815-385-1624; www.dnr.state.il.us
About half of this 2,200-acre park consists of lakes and wetlands. McHenry Dam, on the Fox River, in on the park's western border. Recreational activities include biking and hiking, boating and fishing, cross-country skiing and picnicking.
Daily dawn-dusk.

NAPERVILLE
DUPAGE CHILDREN'S MUSEUM
301 N. Washington St., Naperville, 630-637-8000; www.dupagechildrensmuseum.org
This museum has three floors of kid-friendly, hands-on exhibits. "Museum play" takes place throughout the museum every day.
Admission: adults and children $8.50, seniors $7.50. Monday 9 a.m.-1 p.m., Tuesday-Thursday 9 a.m.-5 p.m., Friday 9 a.m.-8 p.m., Saturday 9 a.m.-5 p.m., Sunday noon-5 p.m.

NAPER SETTLEMENT
523 S. Webster St., Naperville, 630-420-6010; www.napersettlement.org
A 13-acre living history museum, this site has 25 buildings in a village setting that depict a 19th-century northern Illinois town. Costumed guides lead tours.
Admission and hours vary by season.

NORTHBROOK
RIVER TRAIL NATURE CENTER
3120 Milwaukee Ave., Northbrook, 847-824-8360, 800-870-3666; www.fpdcc.com
Outdoor enthusiasts will appreciate this 300-acre nature preserve. The self-guided trails make for a nice hike.
Admission: free. March-October, daily 8 a.m.-5 p.m.; October-February, daily 8 a.m.-4 p.m.

OAK BROOK
SUNDAY POLO
Oak Brook Sports Core, 700 Oak Brook Road, Oak Brook, 630-368-6428; www.oakbrookpolo.net
To see a polo match in summer, head to these grounds. Games take place every Sunday.
July-mid-September, Sunday 1-3 p.m.

FULLERSBURG WOODS NATURE EDUCATION CENTER
3609 Spring Road, Oak Brook, 630-850-8110; www.dupageforest.com
This center has wildlife in a natural setting, a vistor center and theater, a native marsh ecology exhibit and four nature trails.
Admission: free. Daily 9 a.m.-5 p.m.

GRAUE MILL AND MUSEUM
3800 York Road, Oak Brook, 630-655-2090; www.grauemill.org
A restored mill built in 1852, this is the only operating waterwheel gristmill

in northern Illinois. It is also an authenticated station of the Underground Railroad; an exhibit is dedicated to this story and the issue of slavery.

Admission: $3.50 adults, $3 seniors, children $1.50, children 3 and under free. Mid-April-mid-November, Tuesday-Sunday 10 a.m.-4:30 p.m.

OAK PARK

ERNEST HEMINGWAY MUSEUM

Oak Park Arts Center, 200 N. Oak Park Ave., Oak Park, 708-848-2222; www.ehfop.org

A restored 1890s Victorian home, this museum includes rare photos, artifacts and letters from the author, including Hemingway's childhood diary and the famous letter from nurse Agnes von Kurowsky—later depicted in *A Farewell to Arms*—ending their engagement. Walking tours of Hemingway sites, including his birthplace, begin at the museum.

Admission: adults $8, seniors and students $6, children 5 and under free. Sunday-Friday 1-5 p.m., Saturday 10 a.m.-5 p.m.

FRANK LLOYD WRIGHT HOME AND STUDIO

951 Chicago Ave., Oak Park, 708-848-1976; www.wrightplus.org

Wright built this house in 1889, when he was 22 years old. He remodeled the inside on an average of every 18 months, testing his new design ideas while creating the Prairie school of architecture in the process. This is a National Trust for Historic Preservation property.

Daily 11 a.m.-4 p.m.

PLEASANT HOME (JOHN FARSON HOUSE)

217 S. Home Ave., Oak Park, 708-383-2654; www.pleasanthome.org

This opulent 30-room mansion, designed by prominent Prairie Style architect George W. Maher in 1897, is National Historic Landmark. It is considered one of the earliest and most prominent examples of Prairie School Architecture in the nation, and is operated as a living museum.

Tours: adults $5, students $3, children 5 and under free. March-November, Thursday-Sunday 12:30 p.m., 1:30 p.m., 2:30 p.m.; December-February, Thursday- Sunday 12:30 p.m., 1:30 p.m.

UNITY TEMPLE

875 Lake St., Oak Park, 708-383-8873; www.unitytemple.org

Home to a congregation of the Unitarian Universalist Church, this national landmark was designed by Frank Lloyd Wright in 1906. The church was his first Monolithic concrete structure and his first public building. In 2009, the National Trust for Historic Preservation named it one of the 11 Most Endangered Historic Places in America.

Admission: adults $9, seniors and students $7, children 5 and under free. Monday-Friday 10:30 a.m.-4:30 p.m., Saturday 10 a.m.-2 p.m.; Sunday 1-4 p.m.

SKOKIE

ILLINOIS HOLOCAUST MUSEUM AND EDUCATION CENTER

9603 Wood Drive, Skokie, 847-967-4800; www.ilholocaustmuseum.org

Opened in April 2009, the Illinois Holocaust Museum and Education Center is the largest one of its kind in the Midwest. The museum was originally housed in a small Skokie storefront in 1981, but with the large number of Holocaust survivors living in Skokie after World War II and the personal accounts and artifacts they willingly provided to the museum, more space was needed— 65,000 square feet to be exact. Today, the sprawling museum is both somber and hopeful. In the Zev and Shifra Karkomi permanent exhibition, you can trace the Holocaust from pre-war Germany all the way to post-war life in Skokie. The walls of the Room of Remembrance are inscribed with names of some of the victims who died during the Holocaust, homage to the six million Jews who lost their lives. In addition to several interactive exhibits, artifacts like ghetto work permits, work camp uniforms and discarded luggage are also on view. Adopting the slogan "Remember the Past, Transform the Future," the museum is dedicated to preserving the memory of all those lost, while teaching younger generations about the need to prevent future genocides by fighting hatred and intolerance all over the world.

Admission: adults $12, seniors and students $8, children $6. Monday-Wednesday, Friday 10 a.m.-5 p.m., Thursday 10 a.m.-8 p.m. Saturday-Sunday 11 a.m.-4 p.m.

ST. CHARLES
FOX RIVER TRAIL
St. Charles, 630-897-0516; www.foxvalleyparkdistrict.org

Located among hills and historic old towns, The Fox River winds a lazy path, making it ideal for recreational canoeing. Several outfitters offer canoe rentals, and there are at least four entry points. If you have a bike, the well-maintained Fox River Trail runs parallel to the river extending as far north as Crystal Lake and as far south as Aurora.

Daily dawn-dusk.

POTTAWATOMIE PARK
North Ave., St. Charles, 630-584-1028; www.st-charlesparks.org

This 92-acre park has a mile of frontage on the Fox River. The St. Charles Belle II and Fox River Queen paddle wheel boats offer afternoon sightseeing trips river. Boats depart from the park and follow the river trail of the Pottawatomie.

Daily dawn-dusk.

VERNON HILLS
CUNEO MANSION AND GARDENS
1350 N. Milwaukee Ave., Vernon Hills, 847-362-3042; www.cuneomansion.org

This Venetian-style mansion features a Great Hall with arcade balconies, a chapel with stained glass and a fresco ceiling and a collection of master paintings. The grounds include fountains, gardens, sculptures and a conservatory. Docent-guided tours are required.

Tours: adults $10, seniors and students $9. Friday-Sunday 11:30 a.m., 1 p.m., 2:30 p.m. Gardens: Friday-Sunday 11 a.m.-3 p.m.

WHEATON
CANTIGNY
1S151 Winfield Road, Wheaton, 630-668-5161; www.cantigny.org

This is the 500-acre estate of the late Robert R. McCormick, editor and publisher of the *Chicago Tribune*. The grounds include lavish gardens, a golf course and picnicking areas, as well as the country estate where McCormick lived, which now serves as a museum. A second museum is dedicated to the famed 1st Infantry Division of the U.S. Army, which can be easily spotted from the large tanks sitting right outside.

Admission: free. Museums: Tuesday-Sunday 10 a.m.-4 p.m. Gardens and grounds: November-April, daily 9 a.m.-dusk; May-October, daily 7 a.m.-dusk; closed January.

MARION E. WADE CENTER
351 E. Lincoln, Wheaton, 630-752-5908; www.wheaton.edu

Housed here is a collection of books and papers of seven British authors: Owen Barfield, G. K. Chesterton, C.S. Lewis, George MacDonald, Dorothy L. Sayers, J. R. R. Tolkien and Charles Williams.

Monday-Friday 9 a.m.-4 p.m., Saturday 9 a.m.-noon.

WHEATON COLLEGE
501 College Ave., Wheaton, 630-752-5000; www.wheaton.edu

This Christian liberal arts school, established in 1860, is home to the Billy Graham Center Museum, which features exhibits on the history of evangelism in America.

WILMETTE
BAHA'I HOUSE OF WORSHIP
112 Linden Ave., Wilmette, 847-853-2300; www.bahai.us

The spiritual center of the Baha'i faith in the United States, this remarkable nine-sided structure symbolizes unity and invites prayer to God. The temple overlooks Lake Michigan and is surrounded by nine gardens and fountains. Exhibits and slide programs are in the visitor center on the lower level.

Admission: free. Daily 6 a.m.-10 p.m.

GILLSON PARK
Sheridan Road and Michigan Avenue, Wilmette, 847-256-9656; www.wilmettepark.org

Enjoy a day at the beach at this 60-acre park, home to Wilmette Beach, which has 1,000 feet of sandy shoreline. Lifeguards are on site and there's also a beach house. Other activities include sailing and catamaran rentals.

Daily dawn-dusk.

WHERE TO STAY

DEERFIELD
★★★HYATT DEERFIELD
1750 Lake Cook Road, Deerfield, 847-945-3400, 800-633-7313; www.deerfield.hyatt.com

This Hyatt offers comfortable rooms and a central location near many Chicagoland attractions, downtown and the airport. A 24-hour gym makes getting in a workout easy. Business travelers will appreciate the spacious work area in each room. The onsite Starbucks is a nice convenience as well.

301 rooms. Restaurant, bar. Business center. Fitness center. Pool. $61-150

EVANSTON

★★★HILTON ORRINGTON/EVANSTON

1710 Orrington Ave., Evanston, 847-866-8700, 800-434-6835; www.hotelorrington.com

Located across from Northwestern University, this elegant hotel combines historic character with modern touches, like pillow-top beds with high thread-count linens and feather duvets. The hotel features amenities such as an onsite fitness center and access to the Evanston Athletic Club and Henry Crown Sports Pavilion/Norris Aquatics Center.

269 rooms. Restaurant, bar. Business center. Fitness center. Pets accepted. $61-150

GENEVA

★★★HERRINGTON INN

15 S. River Lane, Geneva, 630-208-7433, 800-216-2466; www.herringtoninn.com

Located in an old creamery building on the Fox River, the Herrington dates back to 1835. Each guest room in this lovingly restored limestone building has a fireplace, terrace, private bar and oversized whirlpool bath with heated marble floor. Turndown service includes milk and cookies.

61 rooms. Restaurant, bar. Complimentary breakfast. Business center. Fitness center. Spa. $251-350

LAKE FOREST

★★★DEER PATH INN

255 E. Illinois Road, Lake Forest, 847-234-2280, 800-788-9480; www.dpihotel.com

Patterned after a 1453 manor house in England, this half-timbered mansion has the look of a stately residence and the feel of a weekend estate. It was built in the 1920s by architect William C. Jones, who was instrumental in the design of the Chicago World's Fair. Each room, named after a National Trust property in England, is individually decorated and furnished, and many have views of the well-manicured English garden.

55 rooms. Restaurant, bar. Business center. $151-250

LINCOLNSHIRE

★★★MARRIOTT LINCOLNSHIRE RESORT

10 Marriott Drive, Lincolnshire, 847-634-0100, 800-228-9290; www.marriott.com

This hotel has an award-winning theater-in-the-round, seasonal outdoor sports facilities, half a dozen bars and restaurants, and an open lobby with wood beams and a roaring fire. Although the hotel hosts many business meetings and conferences, families looking for a little R&R find it a fun getaway.

383 rooms. Restaurant, bar. Business center. Fitness center. Pool. Golf. Tennis. $61-150

LISLE

★★★HYATT LISLE

1400 Corporetum Drive, Lisle, 630-852-1234; www.lisle.hyatt.com

Suites—with upgraded linens and plush beds and pillows—offer city or Morton Arboretum views. Venture out for a round of golf at one of three courses within an eight-mile radius of this hotel.

316 rooms. Restaurant, bar. Business center. Fitness center. Pool. $151-250

★★★WYNDHAM LISLE/NAPERVILLE

3000 Warrenville Road, Lisle, 630-505-1000, 800-996-3426;
www.wyndhamlislehotel.com

This suburban hotel offers spacious rooms and a large fitness center, which includes two racquetball courts. Guests can also appreciate breathing in clean air—rooms feature Clean Air technology and bedding is hypo-allergenic.

242 rooms. Restaurant, bar. Business center. Fitness center. Pool. $61-150

NORTHBROOK

★★★RENAISSANCE CHICAGO NORTH SHORE HOTEL

933 Skokie Blvd., Northbrook, 847-498-6500, 888-236-2427; www.marriott.com

Ten stories of rooms and facilities with a fun chess theme make up the Renaissance Chicago North Shore Hotel. Restaurants include Ruth's Chris Steak House and the American bistro, Rooks Corner.

385 rooms. Restaurant, bar. Business center. Fitness center. Pool. $61-150

OAK BROOK

★★★MARRIOTT OAK BROOK HILLS RESORT

3500 Midwest Road, Oak Brook, 630-850-5555, 800-228-9290; www.marriott.com

Those who prefer activity to camping out in their room will enjoy this hotel. The sprawling resort has indoor and outdoor pools, a fitness center and spa, volleyball and basketball courts and seasonal cross-country skiing. The 18-hole Willow Crest Golf Club, considered one of the Midwest's finest courses, is also on the property.

386 rooms. Restaurant, bar. Business center. Fitness center. Pool. Golf. Tennis. $61-150

OAK BROOK TERRACE

★★★HILTON SUITES OAKBROOK TERRACE

10 Drury Lane, Oakbrook Terrace, 630-941-0100, 800-445-8667; www.hilton.com

Adjacent to the Drury Lane Theater, this hotel is near the Oak Brook Center Mall. Each two-room suite features a sleeping room with a king or two double beds and a separate living room with a work desk and pull-out couch.

211 rooms. Restaurant, bar. Business center. Fitness center. Pool. $61-150

OAK LAWN

★★★HILTON OAK LAWN

9333 S. Cicero Ave., Oak Lawn, 708-425-7800; www.oaklawn.hilton.com

Located just four miles from Midway airport, this Hilton is designed for business travelers who will appreciate the courtesy shuttle that goes back and forth from the airport. The hotel is approximately 15 miles from downtown Chicago.

184 rooms. Restaurant, bar. Business center. Fitness center. Pool. $61-150

ROSEMONT

★★★HYATT ROSEMONT

6350 N. River Road, Rosemont, 847-518-1234, 800-233-1234; www. rosemont.hyatt.com

A short drive away from O'Hare airport, this contemporary, small hotel caters to business travelers. Rooms have spacious work areas and a complimentary airport shuttle is available 24 hours a day.

206 rooms. Restaurant. Business center. Fitness center. $151-250

★★★WESTIN O'HARE

6100 N. River Road, Rosemont, 847-698-6000; www.westin.com

This hotel is just minutes from O'Hare International Airport and provides free shuttle service. Rooms have the signature Westin bedding and baths, as well as large work desks. If you want to get some in some exercise from the privacy of your own room, ask for a workout room, which has all kinds of exercise equipment, including a treadmill. A café serves Starbucks coffee in the morning, while a casual restaurant is available for lunch and dinner.

525 rooms. Restaurant, bar. Business center. Fitness center. Pool. Pets accepted. $151-250

SCHAUMBURG

★★★HYATT REGENCY WOODFIELD - SCHAUMBURG

1800 E. Golf Road, Schaumburg, 847-605-1234; www.woodfield.hyatt.com

This hotel has Frank Lloyd Wright-inspired public spaces and spacious guest suites, and is loaded with amenities, including two pools and a health club. Allergy sufferers can breathe easy in the hypo-allergenic rooms. The onsite Fresh 1800 Restaurant offers contemporary American cuisine with a French flair.

470 rooms. Restaurant, bar. Business center. Fitness center. Pool. $151-250

ST. CHARLES

★★★HOTEL BAKER

100 W. Main St., St. Charles, 630-584-2100, 800-284-0110; www.hotelbaker.com

Built in 1928, this hotel has traditionally decorated rooms with marble-accented bathrooms and Egyptian cotton linens. The onsite restaurant has an extensive wine list and a piano lounge.

53 rooms. Restaurant, bar. Complimentary breakfast. Fitness center. $151-250

WHERE TO EAT

ARLINGTON HEIGHTS

★★★LE TITI DE PARIS

1015 W. Dundee Road, Arlington Heights, 847-506-0222; www.letitideparis.com

Chefs Susan and Michael Maddox's innovative cuisine has earned them much praise. But this local favorite is equally well known for their excellent wine list featuring more than 800 selections. Often reserved for romantic occasions, service is professional but not fussy. Be sure to save room for one of the creatively presented desserts.

French. Lunch, dinner. Closed Monday. Reservations recommended. Outdoor seating. Bar. $36-85

EVANSTON

★★★OCEANIQUE

505 Main St., Evanston, 847-864-3435; www.oceanique.com

As the name suggests, the focus of this restaurant is seafood. Dishes include a bouillabaisse of squid, salmon and shrimp in a saffron-scented broth.

French, American. Dinner. Closed Sunday. Reservations recommended. Outdoor seating. $36-85

HIGHLAND PARK

★★★CARLOS'
429 Temple Ave., Highland Park, 847-432-0770; www.carlos-restaurant.com

Owned by husband-and-wife team Carlos and Debbie Nieto, this elegant and intimate restaurant is known for its stellar haute cuisine served in classic French style: Entrées arrive topped with silver domes. The wine list has more than 3,500 international selections.

French. Dinner. Closed Tuesday. Reservations recommended. Jacket required. Bar. $36-85

HIGHWOOD

★★★FROGGY'S FRENCH CAFE
306 Green Bay Road, Highwood, 847-433-7080; www.froggyscatering.com

This cheerful bistro offers country French cuisine at reasonable prices, with specialties like onion soup, grilled duck breast and rabbit casserole. The wine list features a number of red and white burgundies, Bordeaux and champagnes, while decadent cakes and carry-out items can be purchased from the adjacent bakery.

French. Lunch, dinner. Closed Sunday. Bar. $16-35

★★★GABRIEL'S
310 Green Bay Road, Highwood, 847-433-0031; www.egabriels.com

Chef/owner Gabriel Viti turns out complex French-Italian dishes at this popular restaurant. Dishes range from grilled veal porterhouse with pommes frites to roasted Maine lobster with baby bok choy and ginger butter sauce. Seasonal specials and a tasting menu are also available.

French, Italian. Dinner. Closed Sunday-Monday. Reservations recommended. Outdoor seating. Bar. $36-85

LAKE FOREST

★★★THE ENGLISH ROOM
Deer Path Inn, 255 E. Illinois St., Lake Forest, 847-234-2280; www.dpihotel.com

Set inside the historic Deer Path Inn, a popular destination for weekend getaways and fine dining since 1929, the English Room is an elegant dining room with a traditional dinner menu that includes options like lobster bisque, roasted rack of lamb and Dover sole. The Sunday champagne brunch is especially good.

International. Breakfast, lunch, dinner, Sunday brunch. Reservations recommended. Outdoor seating. Bar. $36-85

LAKEMOOR

★★★LE VICHYSSOIS
220 W. Highway 120, Lakemoor, 815-385-8221; www.levichyssois.com

Situated across from a lake, this French country inn is a lovely spot for French cuisine. The menu includes a smaller bistro menu or the larger main menu. Either can be pared with selections from the wine list. Le Vichyssois is also an art gallery, so most of the oil paintings lining the walls are for sale.

French. Dinner. Closed Monday-Tuesday. Reservations recommended. $36-85

LOCKPORT
★★★TALLGRASS

1006 S. State, Lockport, 815-838-5566; www.tallgrassrestaurant.com

Master chef Robert Burcenski offers a well-balanced, contemporary menu. Diners can choose from three or five courses, including entrées such as sautéed veal sweetbreads and roasted capon waterzoii.

French. Dinner. Closed Monday-Tuesday. Reservations recommended. Bar. $36-85

NORTHBROOK
★★★PRAIRIE GRASS CAFÉ

601 Skokie Blvd., Northbrook, 847-205-4433; www.prairiegrasscafe.com

Award-winning chef Sarah Stegner teamed up with former colleague George Bumbaris to open this American café, a perfect spot when you need a meal that's both comforting and well prepared (there's now a second location downtown as well). Go for a juicy burger with a side of Greek fries topped with oregano and feta cheese and drizzled with red wine vinegar, or try the fish and chips with potato wedges and apple slaw. Hardwood floors, exposed brick walls and colorful oil paintings provide a setting for the satisfying fare. Desserts are prepared by the best pastry chef Stegner could find—her mother.

American. Lunch, dinner, Saturday-Sunday brunch. Reservations recommended. Children's menu. Bar. $36-85

ROSEMONT
★★★MORTON'S, THE STEAKHOUSE

9525 W. Bryn Mawr Ave., Rosemont, 847-678-5155; www.mortons.com

What better place to go for one of the juicy steaks at Morton's than in the city where the steakhouse chain originated (back in 1978). With a selection of steaks as well as fresh fish, lobster and chicken entrées, Morton's rarely disappoints. The $5 items at happy hour can't be beat.

Steak. Dinner. Reservations recommended. Bar. $36-85

★★★NICK'S FISHMARKET

10275 W. Higgins Road, Rosemont, 847-298-8200; www.nicksfishmarketchicago.com

This location of the Hawaiian-born seafood restaurant features three enormous aquariums in its comfortable dining room. Classic seafood dishes and simply grilled steaks make up the approachable menu.

Seafood. Dinner. Reservations recommended. Children's menu. Bar. $36-85

WESTERN SPRINGS
★★★VIE

4471 Lawn Ave., Western Springs, 708-246-2082; www.vierestaurant.com

This culinary oasis stands out for its seasonal contemporary American food. Entrees include such delights as the pork combination, which includes a wood-grilled loin and slow-roasted belly with roasted fennel and plum preserves. Or just try to resist the sweet potato homefries with warm prosciutto vinaigrette, Wisconsin cheese curds and milk gravy. Chef Paul Virant supports many local farms and his food proves that excellent dining isn't relegated to the big city.

Contemporary American. Dinner. Closed Sunday. $36-85

WHEELING
★★★TRAMONTO'S STEAK & SEAFOOD
Westin Chicago North Shore, 601 N. Milwaukee Ave., Wheeling, 847-777-6575, 800-837-8461; www.westinnorthshore.com

Chicago chef Rick Tramonto and pastry chef Gale Gand are the culinary duo behind this contemporary steakhouse. Cozy banquettes or white linen-topped tables fill the dining room while an impressive wine wall displays more than 1,000 bottles from around the world. The menu aptly spotlights grilled steak and seafood from skirt steak with caramelized onions to butter-poached whole Maine lobster. Steakhouse classics, such as creamy Caesar salad, creamed spinach and garlic whipped potatoes accompany the entrées.

Steak, seafood. Breakfast, lunch, dinner. Bar. $36-85

RECOMMENDED

DES PLAINES
CAFÉ LA CAVE
2777 Mannheim Road, Des Plaines, 847-827-7818; www.cafelacaverestaurant.com

Steak Diane, steak au poivre and Dijon rack of lamb are among the signature entrees at this longtime local favorite. Gluten-free entrees are denoted on the menu.

Steak. Dinner. Bar. $16-35

EVANSTON
PETE MILLER'S STEAKHOUSE
1557 Sherman Ave., Evanston, 847-328-0399; www.petemillers.com

Pete put his name on quite a few of his menu items: the shrimp cocktail, the calamari, the chopped salad, the prime burger and the aged signature cut. One question: Who is Aunt Franci, and what's in her secret marinade?

Steak. Lunch, dinner. Reservations recommended. Children's menu. Bar. $16-35

PENSIERO
Margarita European Inn, 1566 Oak Ave., Evanston, 847-475-7779; www.va-p.com

The name of this Evanston institution translates to "restorative thought." It's easy to sit and restore over dishes like broiled Lake Superior whitefish and housemade fresh tagliatelle pasta.

Italian. Dinner, Sunday brunch. Outdoor seating. Bar. $16-35

LAKE FOREST
SOUTH GATE CAFÉ
655 Forest Ave., Lake Forest, 847-234-8800; www.southgatecafe.com

Look for the barn symbol here for menu items that are organic and locally or regionally sourced, like the pork sandwich and buttermilk fried Amish chicken. The main floor bakery bakes bread daily.

American. Lunch, dinner. Reservations recommended. Outdoor seating. Children's menu. Bar. $16-35

LOMBARD

GREEK ISLANDS

300 E. 22nd St., Lombard, 630-932-4545; www.greekislands.net

The menu at this longtime restaurant includes a wide variety of Greek special-ties including mousaka and lamb with roasted potatoes. Of course, it wouldn't be a Greek meal without the flaming saganaki cheese.

Greek. Lunch, dinner. Outdoor seating. Bar. $16-35

OAK PARK

MARION STREET CHEESE MARKET

100 S. Marion St., Oak Park, 708-848-0871; www.marionstreetcheesemarket.com

A small plates menu changes with the season at the café of this cheese shop. Wine, beer and cheese flights make shopping even more palatable.

American. Lunch, dinner, Saturday-Sunday brunch. Bar. $16-35

WINBERIE'S

151 N. Oak Park Ave., Oak Park, 708-386-2600; www.winberies.com

This bistro chain features prix-fixe dinners every Tuesday through Sunday, with options like crab cakes and chicken puttanesca. House specialties include grilled Berkshire pork tenderloin, grilled shrimp dijonaisse and London broil.

American. Lunch, dinner Sunday brunch. $16-35

NAPERVILLE

MESÓN SABIKA

1025 Aurora Ave., Naperville, 630-983-3000; www.mesonsabika.com

Located in the beautiful 1847 Willoway Mansion, this Spanish restaurant offers tapas selections and entrees. Try one of their paellas such as the Valenciana, which is a mixture of chicken, shrimp, mussels and clams. Sit back and enjoy your meal with a glass of sangria (red, white, Cava, pomegranate and more) or a flight of wine.

Spanish, tapas. Lunch, dinner, Sunday brunch. Outdoor seating. Children's menu. Bar. $16-35

ROSEMONT

CARLUCCI

6111 N. River Road, Rosemont, 847-518-0990; www.carluccirosemont.com

The menu at this popular restaurant is influenced by Tuscany's cucina moderna. Pizzas are baked in a wood-burning oven, and there's a wide variety of pasta and steak dishes, as well as delicious antipasti.

Italian. Lunch, dinner. Reservations recommended. Bar. $16-35

WHERE TO SHOP

AURORA

CHICAGO PREMIUM OUTLETS

1650 Premium Outlets Blvd., Aurora, 630-585-2200; www.premiumoutlets.com/chicago

Locals flock to this outlet mall for its more than 120 stores, including staples like Gap and Nike, as well as upscale brands like Burberry and Giorgio Armani. A food court provides quick dining options.

Monday-Saturday 10 a.m.-9 p.m., Sunday 10 a.m.-6 p.m.

OAK BROOK
OAKBROOK CENTER
100 Oakbrook Center, Oak Brook, 630-573-0700; www.oakbrookcenter.com

This giant open-air shopping center (the largest in the country) has six major department stores and more than 160 shops and restaurants, all linked by gardens and fountains.
Monday-Saturday, 10 a.m.-9 p.m., Sunday 11 a.m.-6 p.m.

SCHAUMBERG
WOODFIELD SHOPPING CENTER
5 Woodfield Mall, Schaumburg, 847-330-1537; www.shopwoodfield.com

This popular suburban mall has nearly 300 restaurants and specialty shops, as well as five department stores, including Nordstrom, Macy's and Lord & Taylor.
Monday-Saturday, 10 a.m.-9 p.m., Sunday 11 a.m.-6 p.m.

SKOKIE
WESTFIELD OLD ORCHARD
34 Old Orchard Center, Skokie, 847-673-6800; www.westfield.com/oldorchard

This large outdoor mall includes a variety of popular stores including Forever 21, The Limited, Zara, Anthropologie and L.L. Bean. The mall is also anchored by Bloomingdale's, Macy's, Lord & Taylor and Nordstrom.
Monday-Saturday 10 a.m.-9 p.m., Sunday 11 a.m.-6 p.m.

NORTHERN ILLINOIS

The pace slows in Northern Illinois. Although Rockford is the state's second largest city, most people leave the urban bustle to Chicagoans. You'll likely find a hike in Rock Cut State Park more satisfying, too.

A regional standout is the quiet town of Galena. Set on terraces cut by the old Fever River, Galena was once a major crossroads for French exploration of the New World. The grand mansions standing today were built on lead and steamboat fortunes and 90 percent of the town's buildings are listed on the National Register of Historic Places. It's easy to lose an afternoon here.

WHAT TO SEE

FREEPORT
FREEPORT ARTS MUSEUM
121 N. Harlem Ave., Freeport, 815-235-9755; www.freeportartscenter.org

This art museum's collection includes Asian and Native American art, European paintings and sculptures, and Egyptian, Greek and Roman antiquities, along with contemporary exhibits.
Admission: free. Tuesday-Friday 10 a.m.-5 p.m., Saturday noon-5 p.m.

SILVER CREEK AND STEPHENSON RAILROAD
2954 S. Walnut St., Freeport, 815-232-2306, www.thefreeportshow.com

Trips are offered here on a 1912, 36-ton steam locomotive with three antique

HIGHLIGHT

WHAT ARE THE TOP THINGS TO DO IN NORTHERN ILLINOIS?

PARK IT

The parks in Northern Illinois all offer something a little different. At White Pines Park in Mt. Morris, you'll find the state's northernmost large stand of virgin white pine. You can see Lorado Taft's 48-foot-tall Eternal Indian sculpture in Oregon's Lowden State Park (that's a city in Illinois, not the state). Visitors flock to Buffalo Rock State Park in Ottawa for the Effigy Tumuli "earth art," five huge figures—a snake, turtle, catfish, frog and water strider—that were designed and formed to recall similar earth sculptures done by pre-Columbian Native Americans.

SPEND A QUIET WEEKEND IN GALENA

Stroll through charming historic Galena. Check out the shops along Main Street and the historical buildings and homes including the Ulysses S. Grant home historic site. Grab a bite to eat at the Irish Cottage Boutique Hotel and spend the next day golfing at Eagle Ridge Resort and Spa.

---

cabooses and a flat car. An onsite museum preserves Freeport's heritage.
Admission: adults $6, children $3. June-October. Check website for details.

STEPHENSON COUNTY HISTORICAL SOCIETY MUSEUM

1440 S. Carroll Ave., Freeport, 815-232-8419; www.stephcohs.org

Located in the 1857 Oscar Taylor house, this museum features 19th-century furnishings and exhibits.
Admission: adults $4, children $2, children 5 and under free. Wednesday-Sunday noon-4 p.m.

GALENA

BELVEDERE MANSION AND GARDENS

1008 Park Ave., Galena, 815-777-0747; www.belvederemansionandgardens.com

This Italianate/Steamboat Gothic mansion built in 1857 has been restored and furnished with antiques, including pieces used on set of the film *Gone with the Wind*. Guided tours are available.
Admission: adults $12, children $6. May-October, Sunday-Friday 11 a.m.-4 p.m., Saturday 11 a.m.-5 p.m.

DOWLING HOUSE

220 N. Diagonal St., Galena, 815-777-1250; www.belvederemansionandgardens.com

A restored stone house, the oldest in Galena, this house is authentically furnished as a trading post with primitive living quarters. Guided tours are available.

Daily.

GRACE EPISCOPAL CHURCH

309 Hill St., Galena, 817-777-2590; www.gracegalena.org

A Gothic Revival church built in 1848, this building was later remodeled by William LeBaron Jenney, father of the skyscraper.

Sunday services 10:30 a.m., Wednesday 7:30 a.m.

ULYSSES S. GRANT HOME STATE HISTORIC SITE

500 Bouthillier St., Galena, 815-777-3310; www.granthome.com

This Italianate house was given to General Grant on his return from the Civil War in 1865. It features original furnishings and Grant family items.

Admission: adults $4, children $2. April-October, Wednesday-Sunday 9 a.m.-4:45 p.m.; November-March, Wednesday-Sunday 9 a.m.-4 p.m.

GRAND DETOUR

JOHN DEERE HISTORIC SITE

8334 S. Clinton St., Grand Detour, 815-652-4551; www.deere.com

See where John Deere—inventor of the first commercial steel plow— lived and worked, and where the first self-scouring steel plow was made (in 1837). The site has a reconstructed blacksmith shop, restored house and gardens, and more.

Admission: $5, children 11 and under free. May-October, Wednesday-Sunday 9 a.m.-5 p.m.

MT. MORRIS

WHITE PINES FOREST STATE PARK

6712 W. Pines Road, Mt. Morris, 815-946-3717; www.dnr.state.il.us

On 385 acres, the White Pines Park contains the northernmost large stand of virgin white pine in Illinois. Recreation activities include fishing, hiking, cross-country skiing and picnicking. The park includes dining facilities and camping.

Daily dawn-dusk.

OREGON

CASTLE ROCK STATE PARK

1365 W. Castle Road, Oregon, 815-732-7329; www.dnr.state.il.us

This park located on 2,000 acres offers fishing, boating, hiking, skiing trails and tobogganing.

Daily dawn-dusk.

THE ETERNAL INDIAN

Lowden State Park, 1411 N. River Road, Oregon, 815-732-6828; www.dnr.state.il.us

Rising 48 feet above brush-covered bluffs, this monumental work by Lorado Taft was constructed in 1911 of poured Portland cement. The statue is usually referred to as Black Hawk.

Daily dawn-dusk.

OTTAWA

BUFFALO ROCK STATE PARK

1300 N. 27th Road, Ottawa, 815-433-2224; www.dnr.state.il.us

These 243 acres are part of the Illinois and Michigan Canal State Trail. Visitors can check out the two American bison that live at this park and wander along the Woodland Trail to take in the wildlife. Most visitors want to see the Effigy Tumuli, "earth art," the largest earth sculptures since Mount Rushmore. Fashioned with the use of earthmoving equipment, the five enormous figures—a snake, turtle, catfish, frog and water strider were deliberately designed and formed to recall similar earth sculptures done by pre-Columbian Native Americans as ceremonial or burial mounds called tumuli. (At press time, the Effigy Tumuli was closed. Call ahead before visiting to check if it has reopened.)

Daily dawn-dusk.

WILLIAM REDDICK MANSION

100 W. Lafayette St., Ottawa, 815-433-6100; www.reddickmansion.com

This Italianate, antebellum mansion (built between 1856 and 1857) has 22 rooms, ornate walnut woodwork and ornamental plasterwork. Period rooms contain many original furnishings.

Admission: free. Monday, Wednesday-Friday 11 a.m.-3 p.m., Saturday noon-3 p.m., Sunday noon-2 p.m.

ROCKFORD

ANDERSON JAPANESE GARDENS

318 Spring Creek Road, Rockford, 815-229-9390; www.andersongardens.org

This serene spot features formal 9-acre gardens with a waterfall, ponds and bridges. There's also a traditional tea house.

Admission: adults $7, seniors $6, students $5, children 4 and under free. May-October, Monday-Friday dawn-dusk, Saturday 9 a.m.-4 p.m., Sunday 10 a.m.-4 p.m.; November-April, Tuesday-Saturday 11 a.m.-3 p.m., Sunday 10 a.m.-2 p.m.

BURPEE MUSEUM OF NATURAL HISTORY

737 N. Main St., Rockford, 815-965-3433; www.burpee.org

This science museum features natural history exhibits and maintains a permanent collection of over 70,000 paleontology, geology, biology and anthropology specimens. A complete T-Rex-like skeleton, called Jane, is believed to be either a young specimen of the dinosaur or a smaller relative.

Admission: adults and children $7, children 3 and under free. Daily 10 a.m.-5 p.m.

DISCOVERY CENTER MUSEUM

Riverfront Museum Park, 711 N. Main St., Rockford, 815-963-6769; www.discoverycentermuseum.org

This hands-on learning museum has more than 120 exhibits illustrating scientific and perceptual principles. Visitors can leave their shadow hanging on a wall, create a bubble window, see a planetarium show, learn how a house is built, star in a TV show or visit a carboniferous coal forest. The adjacent Rock River Discovery Park features a weather station, earth and water exhibits.

Admission: $7, children 2 and under free. Daily 10 a.m.-5 p.m.

ROCK CUT STATE PARK

7318 Harlem Road, Rockford, 815-885-3311; www.rockcutpark.com

This 3,092-acre park has two artificial lakes with swimming beaches, boating, horseback trails, cross-country skiing and more.

Daily dawn-dusk.

ROCKFORD ART MUSEUM

Riverfront Museum Park, 711 N. Main St., Rockford; www.rockfordartmuseum.org

Three galleries house a collection of over 1,500 pieces. The museum focuses on modern and contemporary American art, American masters from 1830-1940, photography, contemporary glass and outsider art.

Admission: adults $7, seniors and students $3, children 12 and under free. Monday-Saturday 10 a.m.-5 p.m., Sunday noon-5 p.m.

WHERE TO STAY

GALENA

★★★EAGLE RIDGE RESORT AND SPA

444 Eagle Ridge Drive, Galena, 815-777-2444, 800-892-2269; www.eagleridge.com

Located in the Galena Territories, a 6,800-acre recreational planned community adjacent to the river town of Galena, this resort has golf courses, horseback riding, hiking, and bike and boat rentals. Villas and three- to eight-bedroom homes are available.

80 rooms. Restaurant, bar. Business center. Fitness center. Pool. Spa. Pets accepted. Golf. Tennis. $151-250

RECOMMENDED

THE IRISH COTTAGE BOUTIQUE HOTEL

9853 Highway 20 West, Galena, 815-776-0707, 866-284-7474;
www.theirishcottageboutiquehotel.com

This hotel, nestled on 20 acres, oozes Irish charm. The décor of the lobby, library and pub feature rich oaks and mahoganies, stained glass and tile, all handcrafted in Ireland and reassembled in Galena. Each room is named for a county in Ireland, and has complementing artwork by Irish artist Roisin O'Shea.

75 rooms. Restaurant, bar. Complimentary breakfast. Fitness center. Pool. Spa. $151-250

WHERE TO EAT

RECOMMENDED
GALENA

LOG CABIN STEAKHOUSE

201 N. Main St., Galena, 815-777-0393; www.logcabingalena.com

This steakhouse has been serving Galena since 1937. Steaks are hand-cut daily, and the seafood selections include jumbo frog legs.

American, Greek. Lunch, dinner. Children's menu. Bar. $16-35

WOODLANDS RESTAURANT

Eagle Ridge Resort & Spa, 444 Territory Drive, Galena, 815-777-5050, 800-998-6338;
www.eagleridge.com

This hotel restaurant offers lake views and a menu consisting of solid steak and seafood dishes. There's also an extensive wine list. The Sunday brunch is popular.

American. Breakfast, lunch, dinner, Sunday brunch. Reservations recommended. $16-35

ROCKFORD

THUNDER BAY GRILLE

7652 Potawatomi Trail, Rockford, 815-397-4800; www.thunderbaygrille.com

Dip some French bread into this restaurant's signature seafood fondue, which contains shrimp and crawfish sautéed with sherried Mornay sauce, mushrooms and scallions. The menu here features an extensive array of seafood and steak specialities.

American. Lunch, dinner, Sunday brunch. Reservations recommended. Outdoor seating. Children's menu. Bar. $16-35

WELCOME TO INDIANA

INDIANA HAS A LITTLE SOMETHING FOR EVERYONE.

If sports are your game, Indiana's your place. Through such legendary teams as the Super Bowl–champion Indianapolis Colts, Notre Dame's Fighting Irish and the Indiana University Hoosiers, Indiana's fabled sports legacy continues to grow. But if you're looking for the ultimate Indiana sporting experience, watch IndyCar drivers clock 200 laps around the Indianapolis Motor Speedway's famous oval during the Indianapolis 500.

Prefer shopping to speedways? Experience first-rate stores in Indianapolis' Wholesale District; exotic dining and arts on Mass Ave; and trendy boutiques, clubs and alfresco dining in Broad Ripple Village. Buy the kids a sundae at the old-fashioned soda fountain in the Fountain Square District or stroll along the capital's family-friendly Canal and White River State Park District.

Prefer trails to pavement? With 25 state parks, 23 fish and wildlife areas, nine reservoirs, 13 state forests and over 200 nature preserves, Indiana is hardly short on places to scuff the dirt. Hike the marked trails and comb the beaches of the Indiana Dunes National Lakeshore, then rough it on the 27-mile Adventure Hiking Trail in the Harrison-Crawford State Forest.

For an idyllic getaway, the charming resort towns in Southern Indiana are your best bet, whether you're taking a family vacation or sneaking off for a romantic weekend. Browse charming craft and antique shops in the historic artist colony of Nashville, and sip and swirl your way through the Uplands Wine Trail's nine wineries nearby. If you're in need of a getaway, the historic resort hotels in French Lick let you rejuvenate amid mineral springs, lush gardens, golf courses, spas and gorgeous surroundings.

Craving a quirkier adventure? Check out wares from hundreds of vendors at Shipshewana's outdoor flea market (May through October) or see which Big Top biggies made it into Peru, Indiana's Circus Hall of Fame.

BEST ATTRACTIONS

INDIANA'S BEST ATTRACTIONS

INDIANAPOLIS
The capital is also the largest city, and has much to offer visitors seeking sporting events, nightlife or culture.

THE REGION
While northwest Indiana is largely industrial, the preserved and protected Indiana sand dunes are worth at least a day trip.

SOUTHERN INDIANA
This hilly region differs geographically from the rest of the state, and is a must-do for mountain bikers, hikers and other lovers of the great outdoors.

CENTRAL INDIANA

Central Indiana is perhaps best known for Indianapolis. But surrounding the capital and in between miles of farmland are cities with long histories.

Among the cities to the east are Muncie and Richmond. Quakers established Richmond, a city on the Whitewater River that is one of Indiana's leading industrial communities. Muncie was once the home of the Munsee tribe of the Delaware Indians. The town became a farming center during the first half of the 19th century, but with the construction of railroads and the discovery of natural gas, it became an industrial city as well.

Ball Corporation, which produces the classic Ball jars, has its international headquarters in Muncie. The five Ball brothers took an active part in the city's life and contributed substantially to Ball State University. Muncie became famous in the 1930s as the subject of Robert and Helen Lynd's sociological studies of a "typical" small city: Middletown and Middletown in Transition.

West of Indianapolis are, most notably, Lafayette and Greencastle. Lafayette, a farming community on the east bank of the Wabash River, was named for the Marquis de Lafayette, who served as a general under George Washington in the

Revolutionary War. On the west bank of the river in West Lafayette is Purdue University. Established as an agricultural college in 1869, Purdue is known for its engineering school.

Greencastle is located within 15 miles of two manmade lakes—Raccoon Lake Reservoir and Cataract Lake. It's also the home of DePauw University, a small liberal arts school.

Kokomo lies in north Central Indiana. This lively manufacturing center is where Elwood Haynes invented the first clutch-driven automobile with an electric ignition. Since then, Kokomo manufacturers have invented several more useful items, from the first pneumatic rubber tire to canned tomato juice.

WHAT TO SEE

BATTLE GROUND
TIPPECANOE BATTLEFIELD MUSEUM AND PARK
200 Battleground Ave., Battle Ground, 765-567-2147; www.tcha.mus.in.us

This is the site of the 1811 battle in which soldiers and local militia led by General William H. Harrison, territorial governor of Indiana, defeated a confederation of Native Americans. The museum's displays detail the history and events of the Battle of Tippecanoe. The park includes a nature center and is the beginning of the Wabash Heritage Trail.

Museum admission: adults $4, seniors and active military $3, children $1. Daily 10 a.m.-5 p.m. Closed Wednesday.

WOLF PARK
4004 E. 800 N., Battle Ground, 765-567-2265; www.wolfpark.org

This education-research facility is home to several packs of wolves, a small herd of bison, coyotes and foxes. Wolves can be seen close at hand as they eat and socialize. Guided tours are available. Check out "Howl Nights" on Friday and Saturday during the spring, summer and fall and Saturday during the winter for a demonstration and lecture, which includes the opportunity to howl with the wolves.

Admission: varies by day. May-November, Tuesday-Sunday 1-5 p.m.; December-April, Saturday 7:30 p.m.

KOKOMO
ELWOOD HAYNES MUSEUM
1915 S. Webster St., Kokomo, 765-456-7500; www.kokomo-in.org

This museum was the home of Elwood Haynes, creator of one of the earliest American automobiles. Featured are memorabilia, 1905 and 1924 Haynes cars and the Haynes Stellite alloy used in spaceships. Tours are available.

Admission: free. Hours vary by season.

SEIBERLING MANSION
1200 W. Sycamore St., Kokomo, 765-452-4314; www.howardcountymuseum.org

This late Victorian mansion is home to the Howard County Historical Museum. It houses exhibits of historical and educational interest, county history and manufacturing artifacts.

Admission: adults $4, children $1. Tuesday-Sunday 1-4 p.m. Closed January.

HIGHLIGHTS

WHAT ARE THE TOP THING TO DO IN CENTRAL INDIANA?

HEAD OUTDOORS

Parks abound in Central Indiana. Get up close with wolf packs at Wolf Park in Battle Ground, and then head to nearby Tippecanoe Battlefield Museum and Park for details about the famous 1811 battle. Hayes Regional Arboretum in Richmond has 355 acres of native Indiana offerings.

LAFAYETTE
PURDUE UNIVERSITY
504 Northwestern Ave., West Lafayette, 765-494-4636; www.purdue.edu

Founded in 1869, this Big Ten conference member has nearly 40,000 under-graduate, graduate and professional students and offers more than 200 major areas of study on its 2,552-acre campus.

PERU
INTERNATIONAL CIRCUS HALL OF FAME AND MUSEUM
3076 Circus Lane, Peru, 800-771-0241; www.circushof.com

See professional circus stars daily during "Big Top Season" in July, or visit the museum from May through October to see circus greats, including colorful wagons, posters, costumes and a miniature circus.

Hours vary by season.

RICHMOND
HAYES REGIONAL ARBORETUM
801 Elks Road, Richmond, 765-962-3745; www.hayesarboretum.org

Explore Indiana's great outdoors at this 355-acre site featuring trees, shrubs and vines native to this region. The park includes a 40-acre beech-maple forest. An auto tour navigates 3 miles of the site for those not inclined to walk. There is a Fern garden, a spring house, 5 ½ miles of hiking trails, a bird sanctuary, a nature center with exhibits and a gift shop.

March-October, Tuesday-Saturday 9 a.m.-5p.m.

INDIANA FOOTBALL HALL OF FAME
815 N. A St., Richmond, 765-966-5700; www.indiana-football.org

A must-stop for Hoosier fans (or any avid football fan), this museum includes photos, plaques and memorabilia of more than 300 inductees. Indiana high schools, colleges and universities are represented.

Tuesday-Friday 10 a.m.-4 p.m.

WHERE TO STAY

RECOMMENDED
GREENCASTLE

THE INN AT DEPAW AND EVENT CENTER
2 W. Seminary St., Greencastle, 800-225-8655; www.innatdepaw.com
Located on the campus of DePauw University in Greencastle, this country
inn is a full-service hotel with warmth and charm. Pillow-top beds are
made with imported Egyptian linens, and rooms have flat-screen TVs and
DVD players.
54 rooms. Restaurant, bar. Business center. Fitness center. $61-150

WEST LAFAYETTE

UNIVERSITY PLAZA HOTEL
3001 Northwestern Ave., West Lafayette, 765-463-5511, 800-777-9808;
www.universityplazahotelwestlafayette.com
This hotel is just a mile from the Purdue University campus and adjacent
to the Purdue Research Park, and features over 13,000 square feet of
meeting and event space. Rooms are spacious, especially the 560-square-feet
two-room suites.
189 rooms. Restaurant, bar. Business center. Fitness center. Pool. $61-150

WHERE TO EAT

RECOMMENDED
RICHMOND

OLDE RICHMOND INN
138 S. Fifth St., Richmond, 765-962-2247; www.oldrichmondinn.com
This restaurant offers old-fashioned dining in a former circa 1892 home.
Seating options include small intimate rooms.
American. Lunch, dinner. Outdoor seating. Bar. $16-35

INDIANAPOLIS

Indianapolis was an area of rolling woodland, with scattered Native American
villages and only two white settler families, when it was selected as the new
Indiana state capital on June 7, 1820. The city was laid out in the wheel pattern of
Washington, D.C. It remains the capital today, and is the state's largest city.

The annual Indy 500, a 500-mile automobile race at the Indianapolis Motor
Speedway, has brought international fame to the city. But Indianapolis is also
home to the National Collegiate Athletic Association, and has been called
the nation's amateur sports capital. To date, the city has hosted more than 400
national and international amateur sporting events.

In the middle of Indianapolis is Circle Centre Mall, the largest mall in the
area that connects to the Indianapolis Artsgarden, which has concerts, botanical
displays and other cultural events. The major sports venues are downtown: Lucas
Oil Stadium; home to the Indianapolis Colts; Conseco Fieldhouse, home of the

HIGHLIGHTS

WHAT ARE THE TOP THINGS TO DO IN INDIANAPOLIS?

BE A KID AT THE CHILDREN'S MUSEUM OF INDIANAPOLIS

More than a million guests flock each year to this 472,900 square-foot facility, which houses 11 major galleries and maintains a collection of more than 110,000 artifacts — the largest collection of any youth museum in the world.

WATCH FAST CARS AT THE INDY 500

You don't have to be a race fan to get caught up in the excitement of this 500-mile IndyCar race, held annually the Sunday of Memorial Day weekend at the Indianapolis Motor Speedway.

Indiana Pacers; and Victory Field, where the Indianapolis Indians play. Victory Field is consistently voted one of the top ballparks in minor-league baseball.

But it's not all about sports in this city. Not to be overlooked are the city's many fine museums. The Children's Museum of Indianapolis is world renowned, and the Indianapolis Museum of Art recently opened 100 Acres, a top-notch museum art park. The Indiana War Memorial Plaza Historic District also has several offerings, including a memorial to those who died during the sinking of the *USS Indianapolis* in World War II.

WHAT TO SEE

100 ACRES: THE VIRGINIA B. FAIRBANKS ART & NATURE PARK

4000 Michigan Road, Indianapolis, 317-923-1331; www.imamuseum.org/100acres

Next to the Indianapolis Museum of Art, this 100-acre art park features woodlands, wetlands, meadows and a 35-acre lake. Spend the day strolling the grounds and enjoying what nature has to offer. The park also features exhibitions and discussions to help individuals strengthen their knowledge of art and nature. Feel free to bring along your dog; just make sure he's on a leash.

Admission: free. Daily, dawn-dusk.

CHILDREN'S MUSEUM OF INDIANAPOLIS

3000 N. Meridian St., Indianapolis, 317-334-3322; www.childrensmuseum.org

The largest of its kind, this outstanding children's museum has exhibits covering the physical and natural sciences, world cultures, space, history and exploration. The most popular permanent exhibits include Take Me There: Egypt, about modern Egyptian life; Fireworks of Glass, featuring the largest permanent sculpture of blown glass by renowned artist Dale Chihuly; and

Dinosphere: Now You're in Their World, a world-class collection of dinosaur fossils in settings reflecting the Cretaceous Period.

Admission: adults $15.50, seniors $14.50, children $10.50. March-August, daily 10 a.m.-5 p.m.; September-February, Tuesday-Sunday 10 a.m.-5 p.m.

CITY MARKET

222 E. Market St., Indianapolis, 317-634-9266; www.indycm.com

This renovated marketplace was constructed in 1886. Shops in the building and two adjacent areas sell smoked meats, dairy products, specialty baked goods, fruits and ethnic foods. Live music is featured on Wednesday and Friday in the summer.

Monday-Friday 7 a.m.-3 p.m., Saturday 9 a.m.-3 p.m.

COLONEL ELI LILLY CIVIL WAR MUSEUM

1 Monument Circle, Indianapolis, 317-232-7615; www.in.gov/iwm

At this museum underneath the Soldiers and Sailors Monument on down-town's Monument Circle, displays describe Hoosier involvement in the Civil War. Exhibits include photos, letters and diaries of Indiana soldiers. The museum is part of the Indiana War Memorial Plaza Historic District.

Admission: free. Wednesday-Sunday 10:30 a.m.-5:30 p.m.

EASLEY WINERY

205 N. College Ave., Indianapolis, 317-636-4516; www.easleywine.com

Visit for a wine tasting, and also peruse the outdoor garden and gift shop. Tours are available.

Monday-Saturday 9 a.m.-6 p.m., Sunday noon-4 p.m.

EITELJORG MUSEUM

White River State Park, 500 W. Washington St., Indianapolis, 317-636-9378; www.eiteljorg.org

Head to the Eiteljorg Museum to take in Western and Native American art and other cultural items such as masks and pottery. Permanent collections include art of the American West, The Gund Collection and a Native American collec-tion. Enjoy a bite to eat at the Sky City Café before you head out for the day.

Admission: adults $8, seniors $7, students and children $5, children 4 and under free. Monday-Saturday 10 a.m.-5 p.m., Sunday noon-5 p.m.

INDIANAPOLIS MOTOR SPEEDWAY AND HALL OF FAME MUSEUM

4790 W. 16th St., Indianapolis, 317-484-6747; www.indianapolismotorspeedway.com

The world's largest spectator sporting facility, the Indianapolis Motor Speedway is the site of the famous Indianapolis 500 Mile Race, better known as the Indy 500, the Brickyard 400 NASCAR race and the Red Bull Indianapolis GP motorcycle race. Many innovations in modern cars have been tested at races here. Grandstands, paddocks and bleachers line the 2 ½-mile oval track, and the speedway grounds and Hall of Fame Museum are designated as a National Historic Landmark. The museum displays approximately 75 cars, including a 1957 SSI Corvette and the Marmon "Wasp," which, with Ray Harroun behind the wheel, won the first Indy 500 in 1911.

Museum admission: adults $5, children 6-15 $3, children 6 and under free. March-October, daily 9 a.m.-5 p.m.; November-February, 10 a.m.-4 p.m.

SPECIAL EVENT

LITTLE 500

Anderson Speedway, 1311 Pendleton Ave., Anderson, 765-642-0206
This Sprint car race is held annually the day before the Indianapolis 500 and takes place on the quarter-mile Anderson Speedway.
Saturday before Memorial Day.

INDIANA STATE MUSEUM

650 W. Washington St., Indianapolis, 317-232-1637; www.indianamuseum.org
The Indiana State Museum is Indiana's museum of science and culture. Permanent exhibits tell the state's story using various artifacts including prehistoric fossils and items from contemporary pop culture. Recent exhibits have included Titanic: The Artifact Exhibition, which features more than 240 artifacts from the *Titanic* (they were found in the ocean). It is also home to an IMAX theater.
Admission: adults $7, seniors $6.50, children $4. Tuesday-Saturday, 9 a.m.-5 p.m., Sunday 11 a.m.-5 p.m.

INDIANAPOLIS MUSEUM OF ART

4000 Michigan Road, Indianapolis, 317-920-2659; www.ima-art.org
Art lovers will want to pay a visit to this 125-year-old museum, one of the 10 largest encyclopedic art museums in the United States. It features significant collections of African, American, Asian, European and contemporary art, as well as a newly established collection of design arts. The IMA collections span 5,000 years of history from across the world's continents and feature more than 54,000 works of art, including paintings, sculpture, furniture and design objects, prints, drawings and photographs, as well as textiles and costumes. Tours are available.
Admission: free. Tuesday-Wednesday, Saturday 11 a.m.-5 p.m., Thursday-Friday 11 a.m.-9 p.m., Sunday noon-5 p.m.

INDIANA WAR MEMORIAL MUSEUM

1 Monument Circle, Indianapolis, 317-232-7615; www.in.gov/iwm
Part of the Indiana War Memorial Plaza Historic District, this large three-story building is inspired by neo-classical design. It features a Shrine Room, which symbolizes peace and unity and made of materials from all over the world in honor of those who fought in the Great War, as well as a listing of all those who fought in World War I. Also listed are those killed or missing in action during World War II, the Korean War and the Vietnam War.
Admission: free. Wednesday-Sunday 9 a.m.-5 p.m.

INDIANAPOLIS ZOO

1200 W. Washington St., Indianapolis, 317-630-2001; www.indyzoo.com
This zoo includes the state's largest aquarium, an enclosed whale and dolphin

pavilion, and more than 3,000 animals from around the world. Also on the grounds are rides and attractions, such as the White River Junction Train Ride, Kōmbo family coaster and 4-D ride film adventure. The zoo's 3.3-acre White River Gardens has over 1,000 plant varieties as well as special exhibits. Stroller and locker rentals are available.

Admission: adults $14.50, seniors and children2-12 $9.50, children 1 and under free. Labor Day-October, Monday-Thursday 9 a.m.-4 p.m., Friday-Sunday 9 a.m.-5 p.m.; November-December 2, daily 9 a.m.-4 p.m.; December 3-30, daily noon-9 p.m.

MADAME WALKER THEATRE CENTER

617 Indiana Ave., Indianapolis, 317-236-2099; www.walkertheatre.com

The Walker Theatre, erected and embellished in an African and Egyptian motif, was built in 1927 as a tribute to Madame C. J. Walker, America's first self-made female millionaire. The renovated theater now features theatrical productions, concerts and other cultural events. The center serves as an educational and cultural center for the city's African-American community. Tours are available by appointment.

See website for details.

MASS AVE

Massachusetts Avenue from City Market to 10th Street, Indianapolis; www.discovermassave.com

Massachusetts Avenue is a thriving art and theater district on the National Register of Historic Places. Five theaters are here, including the Theatre on the Square and Phoenix Theater, which both have year-round performance schedules, and the Murat Centre, which hosts national tours. Shops and restaurants—many independently owned—are also plentiful. Mass Ave is also home to the annual 10-day IndyFringe Festival, when local, national and international theater companies perform 60-minute shows in the district's theaters and outdoor performing spaces.

MONON TRAIL

Indianapolis; www.indygreenways.org

This busy urban greenway for cyclists, runners and walkers measures 10 ½ miles from 10th to 96th streets. It connects to the Fall Creek Trail, the Monon Greenway of suburban Carmel and the Central Canal Towpath.

NCAA HALL OF CHAMPIONS

700 W. Washington St., Indianapolis, 800-735-6222; www.ncaahallofchampions.org

Love college sports? This center celebrates intercollegiate athletics through photographs, video presentations and displays covering 23 men's and women's sports and all NCAA championships. The 25,000-square-foot area contains two levels of interactive displays and multimedia presentations.

Admission: adults $5, seniors and students $3, children 5 and under free. Tuesday-Saturday 10 a.m.-5 p.m., Sunday noon-5 p.m.

PRESIDENT BENJAMIN HARRISON HOME

1230 N. Delaware St., Indianapolis, 317-631-1888; www.presidentbenjaminharrison.org

Quick: Who was the 23rd president of the United States? Visit his former residence and find out. Benjamin Harrison served one term as president, from 1889 to 1893. Guided tours depart every 30 minutes and take visitors through

16 rooms with original furniture, paintings and the family's personal effects.
Admission: adults $8, seniors $6, students $3, children 4 and under free. Monday-Saturday 10 a.m.-3:30 p.m.; June-July, Monday-Saturday 10 a.m.-3:30 p.m., Sunday 12:30 p.m.-3:30 p.m. Closed January, Memorial Day weekend.

SUN KING BREWING COMPANY
135 N. College Ave., Indianapolis, 317-602-3702; www.sunkingbrewing.com
Indiana has a long history of brewing handcrafted beer. Get a taste for it at this craft brewery by sampling some suds in the onsite tasting room.
Thursday 4-7 p.m., Friday 1-7 p.m., Saturday 1-4 p.m.

USS INDIANAPOLIS MEMORIAL
1 Monument Circle, Indianapolis, 317-232-7615; www.in.gov/iwm
Part of the Indiana War Memorial Plaza Historic District, this memorial has engravings of the names of the ship's company and one passenger who made up the *USS Indianapolis'* crew when it sank during World War II. The outdoor site located at the north end of the Canal Walk.
Daily dawn-dusk.

WHOLESALE DISTRICT
Downtown Indianapolis; www.discoverwholesaledistrict.com
This historic downtown district is known for signature restaurants and entertainment, including the famous Slippery Noodle Jazz Club, St. Elmo's Steak House and Claddaugh's Irish Pub. It is also the locale of the Circle Centre shopping mall, many hotels, the Indiana Repertory Theatre, Conseco Fieldhouse, Lucas Oil Stadium and the Indianapolis Artsgarden. Events abound year-round, such as the Strawberry Festival and the Circle of Lights Holiday Celebration.

WHERE TO STAY

★★★CANTERBURY HOTEL
123 S. Illinois St., Indianapolis, 317-634-3000, 800-538-8186;
www.canterburyhotel.com
This European boutique-style hotel has been around since the 1850s. Mahogany furniture and traditional artwork decorate the guest rooms. The restaurant dishes up American and continental favorites for breakfast, lunch and dinner while the traditional afternoon tea is a local institution.
99 rooms. Restaurant, bar. Complimentary breakfast. Business center. Fitness center. $151-250

★★★CONRAD INDIANAPOLIS
50 W. Washington St., Indianapolis, 317-713-5000; www.conradindianapolis.com
Located in the heart of the city, the Conrad Indianapolis is an elegant spot: The lobby's crushed-glass chandelier is a replica of the one hanging in the New York Metropolitan Opera House. The Capital Grille serves culinary delights, and Spa Chakra offers exclusive Guerlain therapies. The Conrad's rooms, decked out in cozy golds, reds and greens, feature 500-thread-count Italian Anichini bed linens. If you must tear yourself away from all the amenities, a skybridge connects the hotel's meeting spaces with the Artsgarden, Circle Centre mall and the Indiana Convention Center.
241 rooms. Restaurant, bar. Business center. Fitness center. Pool. Spa. Pets accepted. $151-250

★★★CROWNE PLAZA HOTEL UNION STATION

123 W. Louisiana St., Indianapolis, 317-631-2221, 877-227-6963;
www.crowneplaza.com

Located in historic Union Station, this hotel offers 26 authentic Pullman sleeper train cars for overnight stays, each one named for a famous personality from the early 1900s. Full of Old World charm and modern convenience, this hotel is within walking distance of downtown restaurants and sports and cultural hot spots.

273 rooms. Restaurant, bar. Business center. Fitness center. Pool. $151-250

★★★HYATT REGENCY INDIANAPOLIS

1 S. Capitol Ave., Indianapolis, 317-632-1234; www.hyatt.com

This stylish downtown hotel is connected to the Indiana Convention Center and Lucus Oil Stadium by a skywalk. Rooms feature chrome accents, ultra-plush pillows and soft sheets. Bathrooms with granite-topped vanities boast Portico bath products.

497 rooms. Restaurant, bar. Business center. Fitness center. Pool. $251-350

★★★MARRIOTT INDIANAPOLIS DOWNTOWN

350 W. Maryland St., Indianapolis, 317-822-3500, 877-640-7666; www.marriott.com

Guest rooms at this downtown hotel are tastefully decorated with modern furnishings. The onsite Champions Sports Bar features more than 30 televisions, making it the perfect spot to watch a big race or game.

622 rooms. Restaurant, bar. Business center. Fitness center. Pool. $151-250

★★★OMNI SEVERIN HOTEL

40 W. Jackson Place, Indianapolis, 317-634-6664; www.omnihotels.com

This historic hotel is connected to the Circle Centre mall and located opposite Union Station. Rooms feature luxury linens and plush robes. An onsite martini bar is open for pre- or post-dinner libations.

424 rooms. Restaurant, bar. Business center. Fitness center. Pool. Pets accepted. $151-250

★★★SHERATON HOTEL AND SUITES

8787 Keystone Crossing, Indianapolis, 317-846-2700; www.sheraton.com

Connected to the city's most upscale shopping mall, the Fashion Mall at Keystone, this hotel is close to several restaurants and a nearby Bally's Health Club. The hotel has rooms and suites that feature spacious seating areas.

506 rooms. Restaurant, bar. Business center. Pool. Pets accepted. $61-150

★★★THE WESTIN INDIANAPOLIS

50 S. Capitol Ave., Indianapolis, 317-262-8100; www.westin.com

Connected to a shopping center, this hotel is convenient for business and leisure travelers. Rooms have plush, duvet-topped beds and spectacular views of the city.

573 rooms. Restaurant, bar. Business center. Fitness center. Pool. Pets accepted. $61-150

WHERE TO EAT

★★★THE OCEANAIRE SEAFOOD ROOM
30 S. Meridian St., Indianapolis, 317-955-2277; www.theoceanaire.com

This modern seafood house in downtown Indianapolis is a popular choice for power lunches. The menu changes daily and features fresh seafood, from ahi tuna to black bass. The oyster bar menu includes mollusks from both the Atlantic and Pacific oceans.

Seafood. Lunch, dinner. Reservations recommended. Bar. $36-85

★★★TURNER'S AT THE CANTERBURY
Canterbury Hotel, 123 S. Illinois St., Indianapolis, 317-634-3000, 800-538-8186; www.canterburyhotel.com

Located downtown in the Canterbury Hotel, this eatery is decorated more like an English club than a restaurant. American continental cuisine is the focus here, with classics like steak Diane and surf and turf served at dinner.

American, continental. Breakfast, lunch, dinner. Bar. Reservations recommended. $36-85

RECOMMENDED

ARISTOCRAT PUB & RESTAURANT
5212 N. College Ave., Indianapolis, 317-283-7388; www.aristocratpub.com

This favorite neighborhood bar has been around since 1933. Its specialties include traditional Irish fare like bangers and mash, fish and chips, and shepherd's pie.

American. Lunch, dinner, Sunday brunch. Outdoor seating. Children's menu. Bar. $16-35

BINKLEY'S KITCHEN & BAR
5902 N. College Ave., Indianapolis, 317-722-8888; www.binkleyskitchenandbar.com

This neighborhood eatery in Broad Ripple Village took the name of the beloved neighborhood drug store that stood in that spot for decades. The bacon and bleu cheese burger is a local favorite.

American. Lunch, dinner, Saturday-Sunday brunch. Outdoor seating. Children's menu. Bar. $16-35

CAFE PATACHOU
4901 N. Pennsylvania St., Indianapolis, 317-925-2823; 8697 River Crossing Blvd., Indianapolis, 317-815-0765; 225 W. Washington St., Indianapolis, 317-632-0765; www.cafepatachou.com

A self-proclaimed "Student Union for Adults," this restaurant features a menu of typical American fare at its locations. All chicken served is from Indiana, and is antibiotic, hormone and cage free. Crepes are the specialty, as well as the open-faced sandwiches.

American. Breakfast, lunch, Saturday-Sunday brunch. Outdoor seating. $15 and under

THE CAPITAL GRILLE
Conrad Indianapolis, 40 W. Washington St., Indianapolis, 317-423-8790; www.thecapitalgrille.com

Located inside the Conrad Indianapolis, this upscale chain restaurant is known for its juicy steaks and fresh seafood. Locals like to congregate at the bar for the signature Stoli Doli, made with pineapple-infused vodka.

American, French. Breakfast, lunch, dinner. Bar. $36-85

MCCORMICK AND SCHMICK'S SEAFOOD RESTAURANT
110 N. Illinois St., Indianapolis, 317-631-9500; www.mccormickandschmicks.com
This upscale chain is known for its fine seafood. Happy hour features a tasty $5 menu, which includes the restaurant's thick and juicy burger.
Seafood. Lunch, dinner. Bar. $36-85

PALOMINO
49 W. Maryland St., Indianapolis, 317-974-0400; www.palomino.com
This upscale chain has a varied menu, with options such as small plates (including truffle deviled eggs and pigs in a blanket with hot Italian sausage and smoky ketchup), flatbreads and pizzas, and specialties like steak frites with crisp herb fries.
Mediterranean. Lunch, dinner. Reservations recommended. Outdoor seating. Bar. $36-85

RICK'S CAFE BOATYARD
4050 Dandy Trail, Indianapolis, 317-290-9300; www.rickscafeboatyard.com
This waterfront restaurant offers a panoramic view of Eagle Creek Reservoir and has over 100 boat slips. It is known for its crab cakes and signature seafood dishes.
Seafood. Lunch, dinner, Sunday brunch. Outdoor seating. Bar. $36-85

ST. ELMO STEAK HOUSE
127 S. Illinois St., Indianapolis, 317-635-0636; www.stelmos.com
This steak restaurant—a landmark in downtown Indianapolis—is named for St. Elmo, the patron saint of sailors. Popular among the city's businesspeople, it is known for its award-winning wine cellar and the St. Elmo Shrimp Cocktail.
Steak. Dinner. Reservations recommended. Bar. $36-85

TASTE
5164 N. College Ave., Indianapolis, 317-925-2233; www.tastecafeandmarketplace.com
This popular breakfast and lunch spot near Broad Ripple Village and Butler University is a local favorite for gourmet sandwiches and the pommes frites. Dinner—Aftertaste—is limited to just two days a week. The grilled bacon chop with apple and horseradish slaw is a favorite. Delicious starters include truffle chick peas.
American. Breakfast, lunch daily, dinner Wednesday-Thursday. $16-35

YATS
5463 N. College Ave. Indianapolis, 317-253-8817; 659 Mass Ave, Indianapolis, 317-686-6380; www.yatscajuncreole.com
Hungry for Cajun cuisine, etouffee or jambalaya? Head to local favorite Yats, which has four locations.
Cajun-Creole. Lunch, dinner. Outdoor seating. $15 and under

NORTHERN INDIANA

This section of Indiana is most famous as home to Notre Dame University and the Fighting Irish, at least in the eyes of football fans. A visit to the South Bend campus, distinguished by the massive golden dome of the Administration Building, is surely worth the trip.

HIGHLIGHTS

WHAT ARE THE TOP THING TO DO IN NORTHERN INDIANA?

HEAD TO CAMPUS

You don't have to be a college student to appreciate the University of Notre Dame. Whether you take in a football game or see the gold dome of the Administration Building, a visit to South Bend is more than pleasant any time of year. Plus, who doesn't need a little luck of the Irish?

But the Fort Wayne area is one of the most historically significant in Indiana. The point where the St. Joseph and St. Mary's Rivers meet to form the Maumee was, for many years before and after the first European explorers came to Indiana, headquarters of the Miami Native Americans. Fur traders established a French fort here around 1690, and the settlement became known as Miami Town and Frenchtown. In 1760, English troops occupied the French fort but were driven out three years later by warriors led by Chief Pontiac. During the next 30 years, Miami Town became one of the most important trading centers in the West. President Washington sent out two armies in 1790 to establish a fort for the United States at the river junction, but both armies were defeated. A third American army, under General "Mad Anthony" Wayne, succeeded and set up a post called Fort Wayne across the river from Miami Town. Today, Fort Wayne is the second largest city in Indiana. The Midwest's largest flea market lures thousands of visitors to nearby Shipshewana, where vendors sell food to furniture.

WHAT TO SEE

FORT WAYNE

FOELLINGER-FREIMANN BOTANICAL CONSERVATORY

1100 S. Calhoun St., Fort Wayne, 260-427-6440; www.botanicalconservatory.org

Visit the showcase house with seasonally changing displays of colorful flowers, the tropical house with exotic plants, or the arid house with cacti and other desert flora native to Sonoran Desert. There is also a natural cascading waterfall. *Admission: $5 adults, $3 children, children 2 and under free. Tuesday-Wednesday, Friday-Saturday 10 a.m.-5 p.m., Thursday 10 a.m.-8 p.m., Sunday noon-4 p.m.*

FORT WAYNE CHILDREN'S ZOO

3411 Sherman Blvd., Fort Wayne, 260-427-6800; www.kidszoo.com

This museum is especially designed for children, with exotic animals, pony rides, a train and parent-child contact area. The 20-acre African veldt allows animals to roam free while visitors travel by miniature safari cars. Spend time in the tropical rain forest or the 5-acre Australian Outback area with dugout canoe ride and observe kangaroos and Tasmanian devils.

Admission: adults $13, seniors $10, children 2-14 $8, children 1 and under free. April-October, daily 9 a.m.-5 p.m.

HISTORY CENTER

302 E. Berry St., Fort Wayne, 260-426-2882; www.fwhistorycenter.com

This museum of the Allen County-Fort Wayne Historical Society has exhibits focusing on six themes: earliest times to the Civil War; 19th-century industrialization 1860s-1894; culture and society 1894-1920; 20th-century technology and industry 1920-present; old city jail and law enforcement 1820-1970; and ethnic heritage. There are also special temporary exhibits.

Monday-Friday 10 a.m.-5 p.m., Saturday, first Sunday of each month noon-5 p.m.

SHIPSHEWANA

SHIPSHEWANA FLEA MARKET

345 S. Van Buren St., Shipshewana, 260-768-4129; www.tradingplaceamerica.com

This Hoosier tradition features hundreds of vendors selling everything from fresh fruit to handcrafted furniture. The Auction Restaurant features home-style Amish cooking.

May-October, Tuesday-Wednesday 8 a.m.-5 p.m.

SOUTH BEND

NOTRE DAME STADIUM

Juniper and Edison streets, South Bend, 574-631-5267; www.und.com

Few sports arenas have as much history and tradition as Notre Dame Stadium. The stadium has hosted several national championship teams and some of the greatest players and coaches in collegiate history. It was expanded in 1997 to hold more than 80,000 fans and is well attended—if not sold out—for almost every regular-season game.

UNIVERSITY OF NOTRE DAME

112 Notre Dame Ave., South Bend, 574-631-5000; www.und.com

Founded in 1842, the University of Notre Dame is an independent, Catholic university. The 1,250-acre campus features two lakes and 138 buildings. Its football stadium, Basilica of the Sacred Heart, 14-story Hesburgh Library with a 132-feet-high mural of Christ the Teacher, and gold-domed Administration Building are known worldwide.

WHERE TO STAY

FORT WAYNE

★★★HILTON FORT WAYNE CONVENTION CENTER

1020 S. Calhoun St., Fort Wayne, 260-420-1100, 800-445-8667; www.hilton.com

Located in downtown Fort Wayne, this hotel and convention center has rooms decorated with contemporary furnishings. The hotel also has an onsite fitness center and indoor pool.

250 rooms. Restaurant, bar. Business center. Fitness center. Pool. Pets accepted. $61-150

★★★MARRIOTT FORT WAYNE

305 E. Washington Center Road, Fort Wayne, 260-484-0411, 800-228-9290;
www.marriott.com

Rooms at this Fort Wayne hotel have been updated with luxury linens and beds. Try Red River Steaks and BBQ Restaurant for a pleasurable dining experience.

222 rooms. Restaurant, bar. Fitness center. Pool. $151-250

SOUTH BEND

★★★MARRIOTT SOUTH BEND

123 N. St. Joseph St., South Bend, 574-234-2000, 800-328-7349; www.marriott.com

This downtown South Bend hotel has a nine-story atrium and lobby decorated in an Art Deco style. A skywalk connects the hotel to the Century Center Convention and Civic Complex, and the downtown location makes it accessible to local businesses, attractions and schools, including the University of Notre Dame.

298 rooms. Restaurant, bar. Business center. Fitness center. Pool. $61-150

RECOMMENDED

SOUTH BEND

INN AT SAINT MARY'S

53993 State Road 933, South Bend, 574-232-4000, 800-947-8627;
www.innatsaintmarys.com

This boutique hotel is on the campus of St. Mary's College, adjacent to the University of Notre Dame. Some suites feature private Jacuzzis and personalized concierge service.

150 rooms. Restaurant, bar. Complimentary breakfast. Business center. Fitness center. Pool. $61-150

THE MORRIS INN

Notre Dame Avenue, South Bend, 574-631-2000; www.morrisinn.com

This full-service hotel is on the campus of the University of Notre Dame, and is within walking distance to the football stadium.

92 rooms. Restaurant, bar. Complimentary breakfast. Business center. Fitness center. $61-150

WHERE TO EAT

SOUTH BEND

★★★THE CARRIAGE HOUSE DINING ROOM

24460 Adams Road, South Bend, 574-272-9220; www.carriagehousedining.com

A historic church is the setting for this South Bend gem, where an inventive American menu is complemented by professional, friendly service. All dishes, including signatures like hickory-smoked salmon, beef Wellington with Burgundian sauce, and steak Diane with dauphinoise potatoes, are prepared using classic French techniques as well as fresh, seasonal produce.

American, French. Dinner. Closed Sunday-Monday; also early January. Outdoor seating. Bar. $36-85

★★★LA SALLE GRILL
115 W. Colfax, South Bend, 574-288-1155; www.lasallegrill.com

This popular restaurant in downtown South Bend offers such creative American dishes as grilled Amish chicken with honey and raisin barbecue sauce and black pepper mashed potatoes. The dining room has high ceilings and tables topped with white linens and imported crystal. Its wine list includes nearly 350 selections.

American. Dinner. Closed Sunday. Bar. $35-85

★★★TIPPECANOE PLACE
620 W. Washington St., South Bend, 574-234-9077; www.tippe.com

This 1880s stone mansion once owned by the Studebaker family is now an elegant restaurant. The menu features classics like filet mignon or roasted salmon with mustard-basil glaze. The extensive wine list includes bottles from around the world, but spotlights winemakers from California.

American. Lunch, dinner, Sunday brunch. Closed Monday. Reservations recommended. Children's menu. Bar. $16-34

RECOMMENDED

FORT WAYNE
FLANAGAN'S
6525 Covington Road, Fort Wayne, 260-432-6666; www.eatatflanagans.com

Flanagan's Irish Pub has antique décor, a pleasant garden gazebo and a carousel. The countdown is on until St. Patrick's Day.

Irish, American. Lunch, dinner. Children's menu. Bar. $16-35

SOUTH BEND
SORIN'S RESTAURANT
The Morris Inn, Notre Dame Ave., South Bend, 574-631-2000; www.morrisinn.nd.edu

Located in the Morris Inn, this restaurant's menu changes with the season. Always save room for the signature carrot cake.

American, French. Breakfast, lunch, dinner, Sunday brunch. Closed mid-December-early January. Reservations recommended. Children's menu. Bar. $16-35

THE REGION

Hoosiers refer to northwest Indiana as simply "The Region." This area encompasses the counties of Lake, Porter, La Porte and Jasper, and two of its borders are the city of Chicago and Lake Michigan.

The largest cities you'll find here are industrial. Gary, located on Lake Michigan just outside Chicago, is probably best known for its steel mills and most famous offspring, Michael Jackson and the Jackson family. The business district of neighboring Hammond is just two blocks from the Indiana-Illinois state line, which separates the city from Calumet City, Illinois. Hammond is also adjacent to Chicago and is home to the popular Horseshoe Casino.

While La Porte is a busy manufacturing center, producing products such as

HIGHLIGHTS

WHAT ARE THE TOP THING TO DO IN THE REGION?

TAKE IN THE INDIANA DUNES

This area was protected and preserved in the early 1900s. Walk along the 15 miles of national lakeshore shoreline, hike up Mount Baldy or explore the moraines the Wisconsin glacier left behind.

industrial fans and plastic containers, it is also a popular resort area. City lakes border the city on the north and west, and offer fishing, snowmobiling and other recreational activities. Michigan City is another summer playground. Located in the famous Indiana sand dunes region, Michigan City offers miles of fine beaches. For fishermen, the lake has coho salmon from late March to November, as well as chinook salmon, lake trout and perch.

WHAT TO SEE

EAST CHICAGO

AMERISTAR CASINO
777 Ameristar Blvd., East Chicago, 866-667-3386; www.ameristar.com
This casino is adjacent to the East Chicago Marina. It features more than 1,900 slot machines, over 50 table games and high-limit table games.
Daily.

GARY

MAJESTIC STAR CASINO
1 Buffington Harbor Drive, Gary, 800-522-4700; www.majesticstarcasino.com
This casino offers over 2,400 slots and video poker games. You can also choose from 70 table games, and private rooms for poker and baccarat.
Daily.

U.S. STEEL YARD
One Stadium Plaza, Gary, 219-882-2255; www.railcatsbaseball.com
The U.S. Steel Yard is an extremely family friendly baseball stadium next to the Indiana Toll Road (I-90). It is home to the Gary SouthShore RailCats, a professional baseball team that is a member of the Northern League.
Admission: under $10. May-September. See website for details.

HAMMOND
HORSESHOE CASINO

777 Casino Center Drive, Hammond, 866-711-7463; www.horseshoehammond.com

This casino features over 3,000 slot machines, video poker and more than 100 tables for blackjack, craps, roulette and baccarat. The largest poker room in the Midwest has 34 tournament-caliber tables and "Benny's Back Room," a high-stakes area. The Venue, inside the casino, offers concert events and other entertainment and has brought in big names such as John Legend and BB King to perform. Reservations are recommended for fine dining at Jack Binion's Steak House.

Daily.

MICHIGAN CITY
BARKER MANSION

631 Washington St., Michigan City, 219-873-1520; www.emichigancity.com

This 38-room mansion (circa 1900) was built by one of the founding fathers of the rail car industry, John H. Baker, who was born in Michigan City in 1944. Tours are available.

Hours vary by season.

GREAT LAKES MUSEUM OF MILITARY HISTORY

360 Dunes Plaza, W. U.S. Highway 12, Michigan City, 800-726-5912; www.militaryhistorymuseum.org

This museum features military memorabilia from the Revolutionary War through present time.

Hours vary by the season.

LUBEZNIK CENTER FOR THE ARTS

101 W. Second St., Michigan City, 219-874-4900; www.lubeznikcenter.org

Three galleries and a studio feature paintings, sculptures and graphic art exhibits of regional, national and international origin.

Tuesday-Friday 10 a.m.-5 p.m., Saturday-Sunday 11 a.m.-4 p.m.

OLD LIGHTHOUSE MUSEUM

Heisman Harbor Road, Michigan City, 219-872-6133; www.oldlighthousemuseum.org

This is the oldest remaining lighthouse in Indiana, and the site of the launching of the first submarine on the Great Lakes in 1845.

Admission: adults $3, children 13-17 $1, children 5-12 $ .50, children 4 and under free. April-October, Tuesday-Sunday 1-4 p.m.

RAGTOPS MUSEUM

209 W. Highway 12, Michigan City, 219-878-1514; www.ragtopsmuseum.com

Car fanatics will want to make a pit stop here. The museum is housed in 70,000-square-foot former factory and features 60 cars, including a 1905 Smith, a 2001 Top Fuel New York Yankees dragster and the General Lee from the Dukes of Hazzard television show.

Admission: adults $6, seniors $5, children 4-17 $4, children 3 and under free. Tuesday-Saturday 10 a.m.-5 p.m., Sunday noon-4 p.m.

WASHINGTON PARK ZOO

115 Lakeshore Drive, Michigan City, 219-873-1510; www.washingtonparkzoo.com

Over 200 animals call this 15-acre zoo home, including mammals, reptiles, amphibians, birds and insects. The new Australian Avian Adventure exhibit allows visitors to hand-feed parakeets, which are found wild Down Under. There are picnic facilities and concessions.

Admission: adults $5.50, seniors and children 3-17 $4.50, children 2 and under free. April-October, daily 10 a.m.-5 p.m. Closed November-March.

WHERE TO STAY

LA PORTE

★★★ARBOR HILL INN AND THE GUEST HOUSE

263 W. Johnson Road, La Porte, 219-362-9200; www.arborhillinn.com

Built in 1910, this bed and breakfast inn welcomes guests with its fusion of old-world, turn-of-the-century charm. Nearby attractions include the Prime Outlet Mall, Notre Dame and Lake Michigan.

12 rooms. Complimentary breakfast. $61-150

RECOMMENDED

MERRILLVILLE

RADISSON HOTEL AT STAR PLAZA

800 E. 81st Ave., Merrillville, 219-769-6311, 800-333-3333; www.radisson.com

This hotel is only a 20-minute drive from the Indiana Dunes National Lakeshore. It is also home to a popular area venue, the Star Plaza Theatre, as well as two restaurants, the Star Cafe, and T.J. Maloney's Authentic Irish Pub and Restaurant.

343 rooms. Restaurant, bar. Business center. Fitness center. Pool. $151-250

MICHIGAN CITY

BLUE CHIP HOTEL AND CASINO

2 Easy St., Michigan City, 219-879-7711, 888-879-7711; www.bluechip-casino.com

The opening of the Spa Blue Tower added 300 new rooms to this casino hotel, many providing breathtaking views of Lake Michigan. All are upgraded with touches like marble-accented bathrooms.

486 rooms. Restaurant, bar. Business center. Fitness center. Pool. Casino. $151-250

WHERE TO EAT

GARY

★★★MILLER BAKERY CAFE

555 S. Lake St., Gary, 219-938-2229; www.millerbakerycafe.net

Located in the Miller Beach area, this charming restaurant's name comes from its setting in a renovated bakery building. The kitchen serves up mostly modern American fare, with specialties including pasta and seafood dishes.

International. Lunch, dinner. Closed Monday. Reservations recommended. $16-35

RECOMMENDED

MERRILLVILLE
GAMBA RISTORANTE
455 E. 84th Drive, Merrillville, 219-736-2203; www.gambaristorante.com

This restaurant features classic Italian cuisine, like spaghetti with veal meatballs, and has an expansive wine cellar.

Italian. Lunch, dinner. Closed Sunday. Reservations recommended. $36-85

MUNSTER
CAFE ELISE
435 Ridge Road, Munster, 219-836-2233

This local favorite is knows for its Cafe Elise crab cakes.

American. Lunch, dinner. Bar. $16-35

VALPARAISO
BISTRO 157
157 Lincolnway, Valparaiso, 219-462-0992; www.bistro157.net

Located in the historic downtown district, this bistro combines vintage wines with gourmet cuisine. Choose your steak and how you would like it (with a shitake mushroom cabernet sauce, herb butter or roasted garlic gorgonzola cream) or choose from one of the delicious entrees such as roasted chicken with apple butter grits.

Continental. Lunch, dinner. Closed Monday. Outdoor seating. $16-35

DISH
3907 Calumet Ave., Valparaiso, 219-465-9221; www.dishrestaurant.net

The tasty cuisine here uses local and regional ingredients. Try the whiskey barbecue baby back ribs or baked shrimp scampi. Save room for the cheesecake of the day. There's also a lengthy martini list and well-rounded wine list.

American. Lunch, dinner. Closed Sunday. Bar. $16-35

WHERE TO SHOP

MICHIGAN CITY
LIGHTHOUSE PLACE OUTLET CENTER
601 Wabash St., Michigan City, 219-879-6506; www.premiumoutlets.com/lighthouseplace

This center has 120 outlet stores, including Burberry, Brooks Brothers, Coach, J. Crew and Polo Ralph Lauren.

Monday-Saturday 9 a.m.-9 p.m., Sunday 10 a.m.-6 p.m.

SOUTHERN INDIANA

South of Indianapolis, the scenery quickly evolves from bland to beautiful as the pavement, at first level and unbending, begins to rise, fall and gently curve. On either side of the road, fields give way to dense forests.

Within an hour is the charming village of Nashville in Brown County. This area is also known as the art colony of the Midwest, a moniker earned in the early 1900s when the area was one of six art colonies established in the United States. The impressionist painter T. C. Steele moved here in 1907, and his homestead, the House of the Singing Winds, is now a state historic site. Many artists followed Steele's lead and moved to Brown County, and today Nashville is filled with shops and galleries featuring the works of local artists. Like the larger city of the same name, Nashville also has a vibrant country music scene.

The largest city in southern Indiana is Bloomington. Home to Indiana University, Bloomington is regarded as one of America's best college towns, thanks to its relaxed atmosphere, eclectic shops and restaurants, vast cultural offerings and scenic setting.

Bloomington's downtown, situated a couple of blocks west of the university, is anchored by the Monroe County Courthouse. The town has a vibrant arts scene, including the Indiana University Art Museum, which was designed by I. M. Pei and boasts a collection of more than 35,000 pieces, including paintings by Monet and Picasso. Each fall, Bloomington hosts the Lotus World Music and Arts Festival, a celebration of the world's diverse cultures.

Spring brings the annual Little 500 Bicycle Race, made famous by the 1979 film *Breaking Away*. Many avid cyclists live in Bloomington, and they can be seen pedaling on the streets and numerous riding trails in and around town. Basketball is popular throughout Indiana, and locals take pride in the fact that I.U.'s men's program has won five national championships.

Travel south to Bedford, the center of Indiana limestone quarrying, one of the state's top industries. Limestone quarried here was used in the construction of the World War II Memorial in Indianapolis, the Empire State Building in New York and the Federal Triangle in Washington, D.C. The headquarters of the Hoosier National Forest and Wayne National Forest are also in Bedford. Williams Dam, 11 miles southwest on Highway 450, offers fishing on the White River.

In the early 18th century, French Lick was the site of a French trading post. The post, and the existence of a nearby salt lick, influenced the pioneer founders of the later settlement to name it French Lick. Today, this small community is a well-known health and vacation resort centered around the French Lick springs and surrounding woodlands. The water contains a high concentration of minerals.

Southwest Indiana may be difficult to access, but is worth the journey. Separated from Kentucky by the Ohio River, Evansville has retained some of the atmosphere of the busy river town it once was, when steamboats cruised the Ohio and Mississippi Rivers. Evansville is the principal transportation, trade and industrial center of southwestern Indiana.

During the first half of the 19th century, New Harmony was the site of two social experiments in communal living. A town was founded here by religious leader George Rapp and members of the Harmony Society, who came from Germany and settled in Harmony, Pa. In 1814, the society moved to Indiana. The deeply religious members believed in equality, mutual protection and common ownership of property. They practiced celibacy and believed in the imminent return of Christ. In a 10-year period, they transformed 30,000 acres of dense forest and swampland into farms and a town that was the envy of the surrounding region. In 1825, the group returned to Pennsylvania and sold Harmony to Robert Owen, a Welsh social reformer and communal idealist. Owen, with his four sons and geologist William Maclure, attempted to organize a new social order, eliminating financial exploitation, poverty and competition. He tried to establish a model society in New Harmony, with equal opportunities for all, full cooperative effort and advanced educational facilities to develop the highest type of human beings. Within a short time, many of the world's most distinguished scientists, educators, scholars and writers came to New Harmony, which became a scientific center for America.

Though Owen's original experiment failed, mainly because of his absence from the community and rivalry among his followers, the scientists and educators stayed on. The first U.S. Geological Survey was done here, and the Smithsonian Institution has its origins in this community.

The town is in a rural area surrounded by rich farmland. Historic New Harmony and the New Harmony State Historic Sites are dedicated to the founders of this community. Many of the buildings and old homes still dominate New Harmony today.

WHAT TO SEE

BEDFORD
BLUESPRING CAVERNS
1459 Bluespring Caverns Road, Bedford, 812-279-9471; www.bluespringcaverns.com
One of the world's largest cavern systems, with more than 20 miles of explored passageways and 15 miles of underground streams join to form the large river upon which tour boats travel. Electric lighting reveals many unusual sights, including rare blind fish and crawfish living in darkness.
Admission: adults $14, children $17. June-late October, daily 9 a.m.-5 p.m.; April-May, Saturday-Sunday 9 a.m.-5 p.m.

HOOSIER NATIONAL FOREST
811 Constitution Ave., Bedford, 812-275-5987; www.fs.fed.us/r9/hoosier
This 200,000-acre forest is spread through nine counties. Recreation opportunities include swimming, boating, fishing, picnicking, hiking, mountain biking, horseback riding and hunting. Or you can simply take a scenic drive. There are campsites at Hardin Ridge Monroe County, German Ridge, Celina Lake, Tipson Lake, Indian Lake Perry Count and Springs Valley Orange County recreation areas. Campsites are available on a first-come, first-served basis. Fees are charged at recreation sites for camping; there is an entrance fee at Hardin Ridge.

EVANSVILLE
ANGEL MOUNDS STATE HISTORIC SITE
8215 Pollack Ave., Evansville, 812-853-3956; www.angelmounds.org
This 100-acre historic site is recognized as one of the best-preserved prehistoric

HIGHLIGHTS

WHAT ARE THE TOP THING TO DO IN SOUTHERN INDIANA?

HARMONIZE
Visit New Harmony, where two social experiments in communal living failed. The remnants are now a popular tourist destination. Start at the visitors center.

MOUNTAIN BIKE
Some of the best trails anywhere are in hilly Southern Indiana. Plan a day peddling at Hoosier National Forest or Brown County State Park.

Native American sites in the United States. From 1100 through 1450, several thousand people of the Middle Mississippi culture lived in a town on this site and, as was typical, built mounds. An interpretive center features films, exhibits and artifacts, as well as reconstructed dwellings.
Admission: adults $4, seniors $3.50, children $2. Tuesday-Saturday 9 a.m.-5 p.m., Sunday 1-5 p.m.

EVANSVILLE MUSEUM OF ARTS, HISTORY AND SCIENCE
411 S.E. Riverside Drive, Evansville, 812-425-2406; www.emuseum.org
This museum prides itself in its permanent art, history and science exhibits. The art is from the first century BC to today. There's also a sculpture garden, planetarium, and a re-creation of a turn-of-the-century village. Tours are available.
Admission: adults $4, children $2. Tuesday-Saturday 10 a.m.-5 p.m., Sunday noon-5 p.m.

NASHVILLE
BROWN COUNTY STATE PARK
Off Highway 46, Nashville; www.browncountystatepark.com
This is Indiana's largest state park and a Midwest mountain biking mecca with trails rated among the best on the continent. It includes over 20 miles of roads with scenic vistas, as well as a nature center, hiking trails, tennis courts, fishing, a swimming pool, bridle trails and saddle barn. Accommodations are available in a rustic lodge and at campgrounds.

NEW HARMONY
ATHENEUM/VISITORS CENTER
401 N. Arthur St., New Harmony, 800-231-2168; www.newharmony.org
Designed by Richard Meier, this award-winning building has a museum shop,

SPECIAL EVENT

LITTLE 500 BICYCLE RACE

Indiana University, 1606 N. Fee Lane, Bloomington, 812-855-9152; www.iusf.indiana.edu/little500
Check out the largest collegiate bike race in the United States. Riders compete in four-person teams in separate races for men and women around a quarter-mile track.
April 14-16.

exhibits on the communal history of New Harmony, and a large theater where an educational documentary film is shown. All tours begin here.
Daily 9:30 a.m.-5 p.m.

HARMONIST CEMETERY

West, Arthur and North streets, New Harmony, 800-231-2168
Buried here in unmarked graves dating from 1814 to 1824 are 230 members of the Harmony Society. The site also includes two Woodland Indian burial mounds and an apple orchard.
Daily dawn-dusk.

HARMONIST LABYRINTH

South Main Street, New Harmony, 800-231-2168
This circular maze of shrubbery was created to symbolize the twists and choices along life's pathway. A small temple is in the maze's center.
Daily dawn-dusk.

ROBERT HENRY FAUNTLEROY HOUSE

West and Church streets, New Harmony, 800-231-2168
This Harmonist family residence, known as Number 53, was enlarged and restyled by Robert and Jane Owen Fauntleroy. The house museum has been restored to its 1840 to 1860 appearance, the time period when the Fauntleroy family lived there.
Hours vary.

THRALL'S OPERA HOUSE

Church Street, New Harmony, 800-231-2168
Originally the Harmonist Dormitory Number 4, this building was later converted to a Victorian theater by Owen descendants in the late 19th century.
Showtimes vary.

ROOFLESS CHURCH

North and Main streets, New Harmony, 800-231-2168
This interdenominational church, designed by Philip Johnson and dedicated in 1960, commemorates New Harmony's religious heritage.

WHERE TO STAY

BELTERRA

★★★BELTERRA CASINO RESORT

777 Belterra Drive, Belterra, 812-427-7777, 888-235-8377; www.belterracasino.com

There's plenty to do at this resort, from a full-service spa and salon, to an outdoor pool, championship golf and plenty of restaurants. The 38,000-square-foot casino riverboat features 40 table games, a poker room and more than 1,600 slot machines. Rooms offer views of the Ohio River, the golf course or the hilly Indiana scenery.

600 rooms. Restaurant, bar. Business center. Fitness center. Pool. Spa. Golf. Casino. $151-250

FRENCH LICK

★★★FRENCH LICK SPRINGS HOTEL

8670 W. Highway 56, French Lick, 812-936-9300, 888-936-9360; www.frenchlick.com

This historic resort is set among gardens, mineral springs and blooming flowers, and features comfortable suites, golf, tennis and a spa. Rooms have plush mattresses with premium bedding and flat-screen TVs.

443 rooms. Restaurants, bar. Fitness center. Pool. Spa. Golf. Tennis. $151-250

★★★WEST BADEN SPRINGS HOTEL

8538 West Baden Ave., French Lick, 812-936-9300; www.frenchlick.com

This more than 100-year-old property—a National Historic Landmark—recently underwent a massive restoration. When built in 1902, it was considered one of the finest hotels in the country; its massive domed roof was deemed architecturally impossible to build at the time. The number of rooms has been reduced by half to create spacious retreats with plush beds topped with luxury bedding. The spa offers soothing treatments as well as the original Pluto mineral water baths, drawn from local springs.

243 rooms. Restaurant, bar. Fitness center. Pool. Spa. Pets accepted. Casino. Golf. Tennis. $151-250

RECOMMENDED

NASHVILLE

BROWN COUNTY INN

Highway 46, Nashville, 812-988-2291, 800-772-5249; www.browncountyinn.com

This inn within walking distance of downtown Nashville only appears rustic. Comfortable rooms are modern and up-to-date and all have a covered porch and balcony.

99 rooms. Restaurant, bar. Pool. Tennis. $61-150

THE SEASONS LODGE

560 Highway 46 E., Nashville, 812-988-2284, 800-365-7327; www.seasonslodge.com

This charming, rustic lodge has a view of the surrounding wooded hills. Some rooms have gas fireplaces, which complement the cabin-like feel.

80 rooms. Restaurant, bar. Pool. $151-250

NEW HARMONY

NEW HARMONY INN

504 North St., New Harmony, 812-682-4431, 800-782-8605; www.newharmonyinn.com

This inn on a bend of the Wabash River features a landscape of winding paths, labyrinth gardens, fountains, waterfalls and sculptures. On the property are four historical guesthouses with private gardens and one to four bedrooms.

90 rooms. Restaurant, bar. Fitness center. Pool. Tennis. $151-250

RISING SUN

GRAND VICTORIA CASINO & RESORT BY HYATT

600 Grand Victoria Drive, Rising Sun, 812-438-1234, 800-472-6311; www.grandvictoria.com

Rooms and suites are family friendly, with in room video game rentals, and some have scenic views of the riverboat casino or Links Golf Course. Historic Rising Sun is just a short walk or trolley ride away.

201 rooms. Restaurant. Business center. Fitness center. Pool. Tennis. $61-150

WHERE TO EAT

RECOMMENDED
BLOOMINGTON

LE PETIT CAFÉ

308 W. Sixth St., Bloomington, 812-334-9747

The menu changes daily at this French bistro run by the husband and wife team of chefs Patrick Fiore and Marina Ballor. Entrées are written on a whiteboard in front of the dining area. Thursday brings a lunch buffet and Sunday, a prix fixe brunch.

French. Lunch, dinner, Sunday brunch. Closed Monday. $16-35

NASHVILLE

THE ORDINARY

61 S. Van Buren St., Nashville, 812-988-6166; www.seasonslodge.com

In Colonial times, an "ordinary" was the tavern or restaurant where residents gathered. The Ordinary strives for the same, with a special menu that changes with the seasons.

American. Lunch, dinner. Closed Monday, except in October. Bar. $16-35

NEW HARMONY

RED GERANIUM RESTAURANT

504 North St., New Harmony, 812-682-4431, 800-782-8605; www.newharmonyinn.com

The menu at this local favorite features seasonal American cuisine, such as breaded pork loin and rack of lamb. Save room for the butterscotch bread putting with bourbon sauce.

American. Breakfast, lunch, dinner, Sunday brunch. Bar. $16-35

WELCOME TO OHIO

WITH ITS RENOWNED ART MUSEUMS AND ORCHESTRAS, quaint resorts and famous amusement parks, Ohio has plenty to offer.

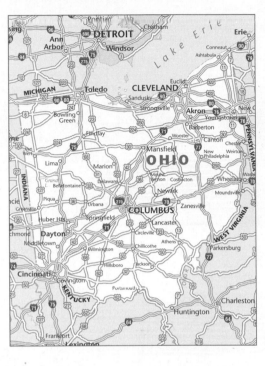

Between fishing on Lake Erie and the area's miles of hiking trails, Northeast Ohio is an ideal stop for nature lovers. For the ultimate outdoor adventure, visit Cuyahoga Valley National Park, covering 33,000 acres along the banks of the Cuyahoga River. Whether you hike steep backcountry slopes, cycle or take a stroll on the groomed Ohio and Erie Canal Towpath Trail, the park offers something for all outdoor enthusiasts. Because you're already in the neighborhood, and in a sporting mood, make a stop at the Pro Football Hall of Fame in nearby Canton and learn about the game's heroes.

Or continue on to Cleveland, where a rich arts scene, stellar sports teams and diverse neighborhoods make it one of the Midwest's most unique cities. Enjoy a night at the theater at Playhouse Square or experience University Circle, where you can see famed paintings at the Cleveland Museum of Art, explore 10 acres of landscaped gardens at the Cleveland Botanical Garden and hear the Cleveland Orchestra's symphonic sounds at Severance Hall.

Prefer rock to Ravel? No problem. Head to the Rock and Roll Hall of Fame and Museum. Perched on Cleveland's lakefront, it houses some of the world's most legendary rock 'n' roll memorabilia, including Janis Joplin's car and Jimi Hendrix's guitars.

If you'd rather feel the beat of feet stomping in a deafening stadium, don scarlet and gray and hasten to The Ohio State University in Columbus. The state's capital and largest city is home not only to the Columbus Museum of Art and a popular ethnic dining scene but also the Ohio State Buckeyes—and their storied football and basketball history.

BEST ATTRACTIONS

OHIO'S BEST ATTRACTIONS

CEDAR POINT
This Sandusky amusement park was deemed the world's best, as well as home to the "best roller coaster" at the 2010 Golden Ticket Awards. Cedar Point has 17 roller coasters, two water rides and four areas just for kids.

CUYAHOGA VALLEY NATIONAL PARK
The Southern Great Lakes' only national park offers 33,000 acres of unspoiled wilderness just a hop and a skip from Dayton and Cleveland. The Ohio and Erie Canal Towpath Trail allows you to travel the same historic route mules walked to tow canal boats. Explore the park by hike or bike, or climb aboard the Cuyahoga Valley Scenic Railroad.

NATIONAL MUSEUM OF THE UNITED STATES AIR FORCE
Dayton's Air Force base is home to the world's largest and oldest aviation museum. See more than 400 aerospace vehicles displayed on over 17 acres of indoor exhibit space.

ROCK AND ROLL HALL OF FAME AND MUSEUM
Head to Cleveland, on the shores of Lake Erie, if you love rock 'n' roll. An I. M. Pei-designed building is the permanent home of the Rock and Roll Hall of Fame and Museum, which features exhibits on rock's ongoing evolution and its impact on culture.

TOLEDO ART MUSEUM
Readers of *Modern Art Notes* voted it "America's Finest Art Museum." Stroll through the Toledo Art Museum's 50 galleries (for free!) and see if you agree.

For a fun family getaway, a trip to southern Ohio is a must. Take a white-water rafting trip down the Ohio River, learn about Ohio's integral role in the anti-slavery movement at Cincinnati's National Underground Railroad Freedom Center and get a thrill on one of 80 roller coasters, water rides and other attractions at nearby Kings Island.

Want even more amusement? Make your way to Cedar Point in Sandusky. The second oldest amusement park in North America boasts the most rides and some of the highest and fastest roller coasters in the world.

CENTRAL OHIO

The cities of Columbus and Dayton dominate Central Ohio. Columbus was created to be the capital of Ohio. But the broad and tree-lined streets are also the perfect setting for one of the nation's largest public universities, The Ohio State University. With its more than 55,000 students, Ohio State influences much of what happens in Columbus, as does the state government. It is no surprise that Columbus residents are civic-minded, sports-minded and cultured.

Dayton is located on a fork of the Miami River, which curves through the city from the northeast, uniting with the Stillwater River half a mile above the Main Street Bridge. The Mad River flows from the east and Wolf Creek from the west to join the others four blocks away. Dayton has 28 bridges crossing these rivers.

Though Dayton itself can seem like something of a ghost town these days, there is still plenty to see. Plus, plenty of famous residents have put the city on the map, including Orville and Wilbur Wright, inventors of the airplane.

WHAT TO SEE

COLUMBUS
COLUMBUS MUSEUM OF ART
480 E. Broad St., Columbus, 614-221-6801; www.columbusmuseum.org

This museum's collections focus on 19th- and 20th-century European and American paintings, sculptures, works on paper and decorative arts; contemporary sculpture; and 16th- and 17th-century Dutch and Flemish masters. Galleries are arranged chronologically.

Admission: adults $5, seniors and college students $4, students $3, children 5 and under free. Tuesday-Wednesday, Friday-Sunday 10 a.m.-5:30 p.m., Thursday 10 a.m.-8:30 p.m.

KELTON HOUSE MUSEUM AND GARDEN
586 E. Town St., Columbus, 614-464-2022; www.keltonhouse.com

Located in the East Town Street Historic District, the Kelton House provides a snapshot of 19th century life. Costumed docents serve as tour guides. The Kelton family supported the abolitionist movement, and the home is a historic Underground Railroad site.

Admission: $6 adults, $4 seniors, $2 students and children. Sunday 1-4 p.m.

OHIO STATEHOUSE
High and Broad streets, Columbus, 614-728-2695; www.ohiostatehouse.org

This 1861 Greek Revival-style capitol building has a group of bronze statues by Levi T. Scofield at its northwest corner depicting Ohio soldiers and statesmen under Roman matron Cornelia. Her words, "These are my jewels," refer to Grant, Sherman, Sheridan, Stanton, Garfield, Hayes and Chase, who stand below her. An interactive museum is located on the ground floor.

Monday-Friday 7 a.m.-6 p.m., Saturday-Sunday 11 a.m.-5 p.m.

HIGHLIGHT

WHAT ARE THE TOP THINGS TO DO IN CENTRAL OHIO?

GET YOUR FLIGHT ON

Love airplanes? More than 400 are on display at the National Museum of the United States Air Force, located on Wright-Patterson Air Force Base in Dayton.

CATCH A GAME

What's better than an autumn Saturday spent tailgating and watching the Ohio State University Buckeyes at the Big Ten school's famed Horseshoe-shaped stadium? Most Ohioans would say: nothing.

THE OHIO STATE UNIVERSITY

124 W. 12th Ave., Columbus, 614-292-6446; www.osu.edu

Established in 1870, this Big Ten conference member has over 55,000 students on its 1,762-acre campus. Fourteen colleges offer 160 undergraduate majors and 240 master's, doctoral and professional degree programs.

DAYTON

AMERICA'S PACKARD MUSEUM

420 S. Ludlow St., Dayton, 937-226-1710; www.americaspackardmuseum.org

Fascinated by the infamous luxury Packard? America's Packard Museum is the world's only restored Packard dealership operating as a museum.

Admission: adults $6, seniors $5, students $4. Monday-Friday noon-5p.m., Saturday-Sunday 1-5 p.m.

DAYTON ART INSTITUTE

456 Belmonte Park North, Dayton, 937-223-5277; www.daytonartinstitute.org

Housed in a historic 1930 Italian Renaissance-inspired building overlooking the Great Miami River, the Dayton Art Institute features wings of European, American and Asian art. The collection includes Claude Monet's *Waterlilies,* Edgar Degas' *The Bath*, Mary Cassatt's *Portrait of a Woman* and Georgia O'Keeffe's *Purple Leaves.*

Admission: free. Tuesday-Wednesday, Friday-Saturday 10 a.m.-5 p.m., Thursday 10 a.m.-8 p.m., Sunday noon-5 p.m.

NATIONAL MUSEUM OF THE UNITED STATES AIR FORCE

1100 Spaatz St., Wright-Patterson Air Force Base, Dayton, 937-255-3286; www.nationalmuseum.af.mil

The world's largest and oldest aviation museum features more than 400 aerospace vehicles and over 17 acres of indoor exhibit space. The history of the U.S. Air Force is told through thousands of personal artifacts, photographs and documents. The National Aviation Hall of Fame is adjacent.

Admission: free. Daily 9 a.m.-5p.m.

OREGONIA
FORT ANCIENT STATE MEMORIAL

6123 State Route 350, Oregonia, 513-932-4421; www.ohiohistory.org

Fort Ancient is one of the largest and most impressive prehistoric earthworks of its kind in the United States. The Fort Ancient earthworks were built by the Hopewell people between 100 B.C. and A.D. 500. This site occupies an elevated plateau overlooking the Little Miami River Valley. Its 18,000 feet of massive earthen walls, more than 23 feet high in places, enclose an area of 100 acres. Within this area are earth mounds once used as calendar markers and other archaeological features. Relics from the site and the nearby prehistoric Native American village are displayed in Fort Ancient Museum. The site includes hiking trails and picnic facilities.

Admission: adults $6, seniors $5, children $4, children 5 and under free. Hours vary by season.

WHERE TO STAY

COLUMBUS
★★★THE BLACKWELL

2110 Tuttle Park Place, Columbus, 614-247-4000, 866-247-4003; www.theblackwell.com

You can't get any closer to the action on football Saturdays. Located right on the Ohio State campus, The Blackwell features simply decorated, comfortable rooms with pillow-top mattresses and thick comforters and spacious bathrooms. The hotel also houses a conference center.

151 rooms. Restaurant, bar. Business center. Fitness Center. $151-250

★★★CROWNE PLAZA

33 E. Nationwide Blvd., Columbus, 614-461-4100, 800-227-6963; www.crowneplaza.com

This hotel is just steps from the convention center and within walking distance to Nationwide Arena and LC Pavilion. With a convenient shuttle service, guests are only minutes away from downtown.

375 rooms. Restaurant, bar. Business center. Fitness center. Pool. $61-150

★★★HYATT ON CAPITOL SQUARE

75 E. State St., Columbus, 614-228-1234, 800-233-1234; www.capitolsquare.hyatt.com

This hotel is in the downtown area across from Capitol Park and connected to the Columbus City Center shopping and historic Ohio Theater. The health club overlooks the state capitol.

400 rooms. Restaurant, bar. Business center. Fitness center. $61-150

★★★HYATT REGENCY COLUMBUS

350 N. High St., Columbus, 614-463-1234, 800-233-1234; www.hyatt.com

Connected to the Columbus Convention Center, this hotel is conveniently located for both business and leisure travel. The comfortable guest suites are

SPECIAL EVENT

THE ARNOLD SPORTS FESTIVAL

www.arnoldsportsfestival.com

The largest multi-sport festival in the nation takes place in Columbus each spring. In 2011, more than 17,000 athletes will compete in 44 sports and events, including 12 Olympic sports, at six venues. A sports film festival debuts this year, along with a hockey challenge.

March 3-6.

spacious. The hotel also houses a deli, café and 63,000 square feet of meeting space.

631 rooms. Restaurant, bar. Business center. Fitness center. Pool. $151-250

★★★THE LOFTS

55 E. Nationwide Blvd., Columbus, 614-461-2663, 800-735-6387; www.55lofts.com

Located in downtown Columbus, the 100-year-old warehouse that houses this hotel has been energized with contemporary design. Clean, simple lines and furnishings create an uncluttered look in the guest rooms, while pillow-top mattresses, Frette Italian linens and Aveda bath products make everything more comfortable.

44 rooms. Restaurant, bar. Business center. Fitness center. Pool. $151-250

DANVILLE

★★★WHITE OAK INN

29683 Walhonding Road, Danville, 740-599-6107, 877-908-5923; www.whiteoakinn.com

Enjoy the peace and quiet at this inn, a turn-of-the-century farmhouse situated on 14 acres in the heart of Ohio Amish country. The inn features original white oak woodwork and beckoning front porch swings.

10 rooms. Restaurant. Complimentary breakfast. Pets accepted. No children under 12. $151-250

DAYTON

★★★CROWNE PLAZA

33 E. Fifth St., Dayton, 937-224-0800, 800-227-6963; www.crowneplaza.com

Located in the downtown business district, this hotel is adjacent to the convention center and near many local attractions. The rooftop restaurant offers spectacular views of the city, and serves breakfast and dinner.

291 rooms. Restaurant, bar. Business center. Fitness center. Pool. $151-250

★★★MARRIOTT DAYTON

1414 S. Patterson Blvd., Dayton, 937-223-1000, 800-450-8625; www.marriott.com

Rooms at this hotel, located just outside downtown next to the University of Dayton, have been updated with plush new beds, feather duvets and luxury linens. Fitness and business centers are just a few of the amenities.

399 rooms. Restaurant, bar. Business center. Fitness center. Pool. Pets accepted. $61-150

DUBLIN

★★★MARRIOTT COLUMBUS NORTHWEST

5605 Paul G. Blazer Memorial Parkway, Dublin, 614-791-1000, 800-228-9290;
www.marriott.com

This hotel is located in one of Columbus' upscale suburbs. Nearby attractions include the Columbus Zoo, Murfield Village and Golf Club and Anheuser Busch Brewery. Rooms feature luxury bedding and large work areas.

303 rooms. Restaurant, bar. Business center. Fitness center. Pool. $61-150

ROCKBRIDGE

GLENLAUREL

14940 Mount Olive Road, Rockbridge, 740-385-4070, 800-809-7378;
www.glenlaurel.com

This Scottish country inn is located on a 140-acre estate in the Hocking Hills. Accommodations are available at the inn or in the property's cottages and crofts. Hiking the grounds reveals a series of waterfalls, a private gorge and 50-foot rock cliffs.

19 rooms. Restaurant. Complimentary breakfast. Spa. No children under 13. $251-350

RECOMMENDED

COLUMBUS

EMBASSY SUITES

2700 Corporate Exchange Drive, Columbus, 614-890-8600, 800-362-2779;
www.embassysuites.com

This hotel, with a beautiful atrium setting, is perfect for guests who want extra space and comfort. Two-room suites offer sofas and work desks with ergonomic chairs. Guests can unwind at the nightly manager's reception.

221 rooms. Restaurant, bar. Complimentary breakfast. Business center. Fitness center. Pool. $61-150

GRANVILLE

BUXTON INN

313 E. Broadway, Granville, 740-587-0001; www.buxtoninn.com

This 1812 inn has antique-filled rooms. The four-building restored complex features gardens, a restaurant with seven dining rooms, and a tavern.

25 rooms. Restaurant, bar. $61-150

WHERE TO EAT

COLUMBUS

★★★L'ANTIBES

772 N. High St., Columbus, 614-291-1666; www.lantibes.com

Sophisticated French fare served in an unpretentious atmosphere defines dining at this small restaurant. The sweetbreads are the talk of the town.

French. Dinner. Closed Sunday-Monday; also last week in January and one week in July. Reservations recommended. $36-85

HIGHLIGHT

WHAT ARE OHIO'S EARTHWORKS?

One of Central Ohio's greatest attractions is not new. In fact, it's ancient. The Newark Earthworks State Memorial is the largest system of connected geometric earthworks built in the world. Built by the Hopewell culture about 2,000 years ago and used for social, religious and ceremonial purposes, these earthworks once covered an area of 4 square miles. Today, only three remain. The Ohio Historical Society owns and operates the Newark Earthworks State Memorial and is committed to preserving and improving public access to the sites.

GREAT CIRCLE EARTHWORKS

65 Messimer Drive, Newark, 740-344-1920, 800-600-7174; www.ohiohistory.org
Formerly known as the Moundbuilders State Memorial, the Great Circle is nearly 1,200 feet in diameter with walls ranging from 8- to 14-feet high, and with burial mounds in the center. The Great Circle Museum contains a timeline of Ohio's ancient cultures, Hopewell artifacts of pottery, beadwork, copper, bone and shell, and an interactive video.
Park: daily. Museum: Hours vary by season.

OCTAGON EARTHWORKS

North 30th Street, Newark, 740-344-1920, 800-600-7178
These octagon-shaped earthworks enclose 50 acres, and are joined by parallel walls to a circular embankment enclosing 20 acres. Small mounds can be found within the octagon. Now on the site of the Moundbuilders Country Club golf course, the Octagon Earthworks can be viewed from a platform near the parking lot.

WRIGHT EARTHWORKS

James and Waldo streets, Newark, 740-344-1920, 800-600-7174
The Wright Earthworks is a 50-foot long segment that is one side of a large square enclosure. It was an important feature of the original Newark Earthwork.
Admission: free. Daily.

★★★REFECTORY
1092 Bethel Road, Columbus, 614-451-9774; www.therefectoryrestaurant.com

Housed in a historic church, this fine French restaurant is known as one of the area's most romantic. For a great deal, try chef Richard Blondin's three-course bistro menu served Monday through Thursday in the lounge or on the outdoor patio.

French. Dinner. Closed Sunday. Reservations recommended. Outdoor seating. Bar. $36-85

DAYTON
★★★L'AUBERGE
4120 Far Hills Ave., Dayton, 937-299-5536; www.laubergedayton.com

For more than 20 years, serious lovers of classic French fare have dined at L'Auberge. Owner Josef Reif has succeeded in creating an elegant restaurant filled with flowers. The food spotlights seasonal ingredients of the region, prepared with a light, classic French hand.

French, seafood. Lunch, dinner. Closed Sunday. Outdoor seating. Jacket required. Bar. $36-85

GRANVILLE
★★★BUXTON INN DINING ROOM
313 E. Broadway, Granville, 740-587-0001; www.buxtoninn.com

Choose one of seven dining rooms for classic dishes like porterhouse steaks or salmon with lemon caper sauce. The tavern serves a more casual menu of bar favorites like burgers or French onion soup.

American. Lunch, dinner, Sunday brunch. Closed Monday. Children's menu. Bar. $16-35

LANCASTER
★★★SHAW'S
123 N. Broad St., Lancaster, 740-654-1842, 800-654-2477; www.shawsinn.com

This charming restaurant is located in an inn in historic Lancaster. The menu features regional specials from southwestern to country French. Fresh fish is flown in from Boston, and tangy ribs and steaks are cooked to perfection.

Continental. Breakfast, lunch, dinner. Outdoor seating. Bar. $36-85

RECOMMENDED

COLUMBUS
ALEX'S BISTRO
4681 Reed Road, Columbus, 614-457-8887; www.alexsbistro.com

Since 1985, chef Alex Gosetto has offered a taste of French and Italian food at this cozy bistro. House specialties include sweetbreads, seafood crepes and beef burgundy.

French, Italian. Lunch, dinner. Closed Sunday. Reservations recommended. Bar. $16-35

CAP CITY FINE DINER & BAR
1299 Olentangy River Road, Columbus, 614-291-3663; www.capcityfinediner.com

Diner favorites are given upscale touches at this "fine diner." Meatloaf is sided with buttermilk-chive mashed potatoes; salmon is glazed with a pineapple ginger sauce; the All-American cheeseburger has a bleu cheese option.

American. Lunch, dinner, Saturday-Sunday brunch. Outdoor seating. Children's menu. Bar. $16-35

KATZINGER'S DELICATESSEN

475 S. Third St., Columbus, 614-228-3354; www.katzingers.com

Sandwiches can be ordered in two sizes at this deli: big or huge. The corned beef is cooked onsite and the pastrami imported from Brooklyn.

Deli. Breakfast, lunch, dinner. Outdoor seating. Children's menu. $15 and under

LINDEY'S

169 E. Beck St., Columbus, 614-228-4343; www.lindeys.com

This German Village staple serves American bistro fare atop white tablecloths. Specialties include lobster and shrimp risotto and rack of lamb.

American. Lunch, dinner, Saturday-Sunday brunch. Reservations recommended. Outdoor seating. Children's menu. Bar. $16-35

RIGSBY'S KITCHEN

698 N. High St., Columbus, 614-461-7888; www.rigsbyskitchen.com

For delicious Italian in an unfussy atmosphere, look no further than Rigsby's Kitchen. Local ingredients are used whenever possible, influencing the daily specials, like local sweet potato agnolotti and cauliflower-truffle purée.

Italian. Lunch, dinner. Closed Sunday. Reservations recommended. Bar. $16-35

SCHMIDT'S SAUSAGE HAUS

240 E. Kossuth St., Columbus, 614-444-6808; www.schmidthaus.com

This has been a local German Village favorite since 1886. Traditional German dinners include hoffbrau schnitzel, weiner schnitzel and gravy and alpine chicken spatzel.

German. Lunch, dinner. Children's menu. Bar. $16-35

TONY'S ITALIAN RISTORANTE

16 W. Beck St., Columbus, 614-224-8669; www.tonysitalian.net

Signature homemade pastas and hand-cut meats dominate the menu of this restaurant in Columbus' historic Brewery District. Be sure to try a house pasta specialty, such as capellini pomodore or Tony's own fettuccini.

Italian. Lunch, dinner. Closed Sunday. Reservations recommended. Outdoor seating. Bar. $16-35

DAYTON

THE BARNSIDER

5202 N. Main St., Dayton, 937-277-1332; www.barnsider-restaurant.com

Hand-carved steaks are the favorites here, with prime rib slow roasted daily, filet mignon covered with bleu cheese crumbles, and the New York strip served with the escargot's garlic herb butter. The signature onion soup is complemented with Parmesan croutons.

Steak. Lunch, dinner, Saturday-Sunday brunch. Children's menu. Bar. $16-35

JAY'S SEAFOOD

225 E. Sixth St., Dayton, 937-222-2892; www.jays.com

Located in the historic Oregon District, this premier seafood restaurant was once an 1862 Grist Mill. Fresh fish arrives at Jay's four times weekly from the coasts and Lake Erie. Specialties include sautéed walleye and salmon wrapped in puffed pastry and served with lobster sauce.

Seafood. Dinner. Bar. $16-35

HIGHLIGHT

WHAT ARE OHIO'S SPORT TEAMS?

CINCINNATI BENGALS
One of two National Football League teams in Ohio, the Cincinnati Bengals are a member of the North Division of the American Football Conference. Games are played at Paul Brown Stadium in downtown Cincinnati.

CINCINNATI REDS
Baseball's first professional franchise—they were once known as the Cincinnati Red Stockings—is a member of Major League Baseball's Central Division of the National League. The Reds have won five World Series titles over the past 120-some years. The team's home, the Great American Ballpark, is located on the banks of the Ohio River in downtown Cincinnati.

CLEVELAND BROWNS
Cleveland Browns Stadium is home to this NFL franchise, which is part of the North Division of the American Football Conference.

CLEVELAND CAVALIERS
This National Basketball Association team plays games at downtown Cleveland's Quicken Loans Arena, or "the Q".

CLEVELAND INDIANS
This two-time World Series championship team is in the Central Division of MLB's American League. Games are played in Progressive Field, rated best ballpark in 2008 by a *Sports Illustrated* fan poll.

COLUMBUS CREW
One of Major League Soccer's first teams and the 2008 MLS Cup Champions, the Columbus Crew plays in Crew Stadium, the first American stadium built specifically for soccer.

COLUMBUS BLUE JACKETS
This National Hockey League team plays in Nationwide Arena. The Columbus Blue Jackets were founded in 2000 and are members of the Central Division of the Western Conference.

THE OHIO STATE UNIVERSITY BUCKEYES
Ohioans take college football very seriously. And the Buckeyes give them reason to—the football team claims seven national championship titles. The home field, Ohio Stadium on the Big Ten school's Columbus campus, is known as "The Horseshoe."

CLEVELAND

Out-of-towners who know Cleveland only as a Rust-Belt manufacturing town with losing sports teams and bad winters may be surprised to a find that the city is home to a thriving arts scene. It is also a virtual fairyland of old-growth forest, thanks to the Cuyahoga Valley National Recreation Area and the extensive "Emerald Necklace" Metroparks system.

Affordable housing (and space in empty warehouses) makes Cleveland especially friendly to visual artists who need lots of studio space; several gallery districts in Cleveland's Tremont, Murray Hill, and Collinwood neighborhoods keep their work in circulation.

Theater districts include Playhouse Square just east of downtown for Broadway shows and repertory theater in restored Art Deco-era opulence, and Gordon Square on the city's West Side for experimental and community theater.

With the I.M. Pei-designed Rock and Roll Hall of Fame sparkling on the lakefront, and the city's tour-bus-refueling-friendly location in between Chicago and New York, Cleveland's music scene is rich and varied for a mid-sized city. For classical fans, the world-renowned Cleveland Orchestra—performing at Blossom Music Center in summer and Severance Hall the rest of the year—needs no introduction. The Beachland Ballroom, a former Croatian dance hall—its walls still adorned with the original murals of rural Slavic scenes—is a favorite performance stop for alt-country and indie-rock bands. Nearby, Kent State University hosts a nationally acclaimed Folk Festival each fall and Oberlin College's Conservatory is a hot spot for experimental, world and chamber music.

The city has experienced a dining renaissance in recent years. Tremont, downtown's East Fourth Street, Shaker Square and University Circle are especially rewarding neighborhoods for the food-centered.

In this sports town, dinner is only a prelude to a bigger event: the game, whether it be the Cavs at the Quicken Loans Arena ("the Q"), the Indians at old-meets-new ballpark Progressive Field, or fending off frostbite in the windswept Cleveland Browns Stadium.

WHAT TO SEE

CLEVELAND BOTANICAL GARDEN
11030 E. Blvd., Cleveland, 216-721-1600; www.cbgarden.org

Meander through these aromatic herb, rose, perennial, wildflower, Japanese and reading gardens. The 10-acre garden in University Circle also features the Eleanor Armstrong Smith Glasshouse, a conservatory featuring more than 350 species of exotic plants and over 50 species of butterflies, insects, birds, reptiles and amphibians.

Admission: adults $8.50, seniors $5.50 (Tuesday only), children $3, children 3 and under free. Hours vary by season.

HIGHLIGHT

WHAT ARE THE TOP THINGS TO DO IN CLEVELAND?

CHECK OUT ARTWORK
Head to the Cleveland Museum of Art where you can take in their contemporary collection including work from Andy Warhol, Anselm Kiefer, Louise Nevelson and Lee Krasner. Check out the new wing by Uruguayan architect Rafael Vinoly.

ROCK 'N' ROLL, BABY
Commune with the glittered shards of rock gods at the Rock and Roll Hall of Fame and Museum. This building is impressive—both inside and out.

SHOP AT THE WEST SIDE MARKET
Head to this Old World market where you can pick up fresh fruits and vegetables and also find falafel stands, Hungarian bakers, coffee microroasters, and pierogi purveyors.

CLEVELAND METROPARKS
4101 Fulton Parkway, Cleveland, 216-635-3200; www.clemetparks.com
Established in 1917, this park system circles the city with more than 20,000 acres of land in 14 reservations, their connecting parkways and the Cleveland Metroparks Zoo. Bike paths lace throughout the park, and driving through the heavily wooded areas is a favorite fall pastime. Also available are swimming, boating and fishing, picnic areas and play fields; hiking; bridle trails and stables; golf courses; and tobogganing, sledding, skating and cross-country skiing areas. Eight outdoor education facilities offer nature exhibits and programs.

CLEVELAND METROPARKS ZOO
3900 Wildlife Way, Cleveland, 216-661-6500; www.clemetzoo.com
The seventh-oldest zoo in the country, this zoo has more than 3,300 mammals, land and water birds. Animals are displayed in naturalized settings. More than 600 animals and 7,000 plants are featured in the 2-acre Rainforest exhibit.
Admission: adults $10 ($7 November-March), children $7 ($5 November-March), children 2 and under free. Daily 10 a.m.-5 p.m.

CLEVELAND MUSEUM OF ART
11150 E. Blvd., Cleveland, 216-421-7340; www.clemusart.com
Democratic in its admission fee—free for all but special exhibits—but sometimes rather stuffy and aristocratic in its acquisitions over the years, the museum just opened a heralded new wing by Uruguayan architect Rafael Vinoly, and has plans for further expansion. Much of its acclaimed Asian

collection is in storage right now, as the construction continues. But a good bit of the contemporary collection is on display, including Andy Warhol's Marilyn Diptych and major works by Anselm Kiefer, Louise Nevelson and Lee Krasner. A breathtaking intersection: 12 Rodin sculptures fill a glass-box gallery that looks out on the cascading metal backdrop of the Frank Gehry-designed building nearby.

Admission: free. Tuesday, Thursday, Saturday-Sunday 10 a.m.-5 p.m., Wednesday, Friday 10 a.m.-9 p.m.

CLEVELAND MUSEUM OF NATURAL HISTORY

1 Wade Oval, Cleveland, 216-231-4600, 800-317-9155; www.cmnh.org

Discover dinosaurs, mammals, birds, geological specimens and historic gems at one of North America's finest natural history museums. Popular permanent exhibits include the 3-million-year-old Australopithecus afarensis, known as "Lucy," and the 150-million-year-old Haplocanthosaurus delfsi, one of the most complete mounted sauropods on display in the world. There are also exhibits on prehistoric Ohio, North American native cultures and ecology, and a planetarium and observatory. The Wildlife Center and Woods Garden on the grounds feature native plants and animals.

Admission: adults $10, seniors, youths and college students $8, children $7, children 2 and under free. Monday-Tuesday, Thursday-Saturday 10 a.m.-5 p.m., Wednesday 10 a.m.-10 p.m., Sunday noon-5 p.m.

CLEVELAND ORCHESTRA

Severance Hall, 11001 Euclid Ave., Cleveland, 216-231-1111; www.clevelandorchestra.com

The Cleveland Orchestra is one of the world's finest performing ensembles. International soloists and guest conductors are featured each season. Its home is Severance Hall but during the summer months, the orchestra performs at Blossom Music Center, approximately 28 miles south of the ciy via Interstate 71.

Mid-September-mid-May, Tuesday, Thursday-Sunday. Check website for details.

FREDERICK C. CRAWFORD AUTO-AVIATION MUSEUM

Magnolia Drive and East 108th, Cleveland, 216-721-5722; www.wrhs.org

This museum has an extensive collection of antique and modern-day cars as well as aircraft.

Admission: adults $8.50, seniors $7.50, veterans $6.50, youths $5. Tuesday-Saturday 10 a.m.-5 p.m.

GREAT LAKES SCIENCE CENTER

601 Erieside Ave., Cleveland, 216-694-2000; www.greatscience.com

Demonstrations and more than 400 hands-on exhibits explain scientific principles and topics specifically relating to the Great Lakes region. The center also features an Omnimax domed theater.

Admission: adults $9.95, seniors, students and military $8.95, youths $7.95. Daily 10 a.m.-5 p.m.

PLAYHOUSE SQUARE CENTER

1501 Euclid Ave., Cleveland, 216-771-4444, 800-766-6048; www.playhousesquare.org

Five restored theaters form the nation's second-largest performing arts and entertainment center. Performances include theater, Broadway productions, popular and classical music, ballet, opera, children's theater and concerts.

Show times vary; check website for details.

ROCK AND ROLL HALL OF FAME AND MUSEUM

1 Key Plaza, Cleveland, 216-781-7625, 888-764-7625; www.rockhall.com

Keith Richards' jacket, the Everly Brothers' tap shoes, Les Paul's first electric guitar—there's room after room of satisfaction here. But the Rock Hall is not just a dust-controlled shrine to a dying art form. Live music, interactive stations and lively rotating exhibits on everything from Jimi Hendrix to the Warped Tour keep the I.M. Pei-designed glass rafters rattling.

Admission: adults $22, seniors $17, children $13, children 8 and under free with adult admission. Daily 10 a.m.-5:30 p.m.

WEST SIDE MARKET

1979 West 25th Street, Cleveland, 216-664-3386; www.westsidemarket.org

The setup at this Old World market, built in 1912, is much like it was 98 years ago—except a bit better in the winter months since the city outfitted the open-air produce arcade with heat and a glass enclosure in 2004. The building's façade hints at the bounty within, featuring sculptural adornments of livestock heads and fruits and vegetables. In the arcade, vendors of all nations shill cantaloupes, strawberries, jimica and bok choy, some at amazingly low prices. Inside, beneath the massive vaulted ceiling, falafel stands, Hungarian bakers, coffee microroasters and pierogi purveyors beckon. You need not have a yen for a whole goat to make the market a destination—though if you're in search of one for your next backyard barbecue, one of the meat vendors will surely provide.

Monday, Wednesday 7 a.m.-4 p.m., Friday-Saturday 7 a.m.-6 p.m.

WHERE TO STAY

★★★CLEVELAND AIRPORT MARRIOTT

4277 W. 150th St., Cleveland, 216-252-5333, 800-228-9290; www.marriott.com

This hotel is located near Cleveland Hopkins Airport and only 10 miles from downtown. Its newly opened chef Dean James Max destination restaurant, Amp 150, offers eclectic cuisine for breakfast, lunch and dinner.

372 rooms. Restaurant, bar. Business center. Fitness center. Pool. $61-150

★★★GLIDDEN HOUSE INN

1901 Ford Drive, Cleveland, 216-231-8900, 800-759-8358; www.gliddenhouse.com

Located on the campus of Case Western Reserve University, this charming boutique hotel is close to the medical centers—including the Cleveland Clinic—and attractions of the school. The contemporary guest rooms have flat-screen TVs and luxury bedding.

60 rooms. Restaurant, bar. Business center. Fitness center. $61-150

★★★HYATT REGENCY CLEVELAND AT THE ARCADE

420 Superior Ave., Cleveland, 216-575-1234, 800-233-1234; www.cleveland.hyatt.com

Attached to the 1890 Cleveland Arcade, one of America's first indoor shopping malls, this hotel has updated rooms featuring Portico bath products and luxury linens. The onsite spa offers a complete menu of services.

293 rooms. Restaurant, bar. Business center. Fitness center. Spa. $61-150

★★★INTERCONTINENTAL HOTEL & CONFERENCE CENTER

9801 Carnegie Ave., Cleveland, 216-707-4100, 888-424-6835;
www.intercontinental.com

Spacious guest rooms (the largest in Cleveland) with tasteful, soothing décor and high-end linens make this a destination for Cleveland Clinic visitors. Located on the Clinic campus, the hotel is accessible to most hospital buildings by a short walk on the glass-enclosed skyway. It's also a stone's throw from University Circle, home to the Cleveland Museum of Art, the Botanical Garden, the Natural History Museum, and Case Western Reserve University. Guests from all over the world sit and linger in the hotel's welcoming lobby, where works by prominent contemporary artists make the environment intellectually interesting. Two restaurants, the eclectic Table 45 and the more casual North Coast Café, offer a variety of dining options. Executive suites include a large workspace and complimentary in-room breakfast and cocktails. Note: The guest rooms were slated for remodeling in late 2010, with an estimated completion date of winter 2011.

299 rooms. Restaurant, bar. Business center. Fitness center. $151-250

★★★THE RITZ-CARLTON, CLEVELAND

1515 W. Third St., Cleveland, 216-623-1300, 866-372-7868; www.ritzcarlton.com

The Ritz-Carlton's warm, knowledgeable staff and showstopping views of downtown are unparalleled in the city. Sparkling marble bathrooms, flat-screen TVs, a skylit swimming pool, and a well-appointed fitness center with massage rooms add to the luxury. Business travelers will feel pampered here, yet so will families and four-legged friends. Upon check in, small children can choose a toy from the Red Wagon, while the front desk has Nintendo ready for the teens. Rover, meanwhile, is treated to a room-service menu all his own. Muse restaurant features excellent farm-to-table cuisine, and the Lobby Lounge on 6 offers martinis designed by local celebrities.

205 rooms. Restaurant, bar. Business center. Fitness center. Pool. Spa. Pets accepted. $251-350

★★★WYNDHAM CLEVELAND AT PLAYHOUSE SQUARE

1260 Euclid Ave., Cleveland, 216-615-7500, 800-996-3426; www.wyndhamcleveland.com

The Wyndham's main appeal is its location: it's situated in the footlights of Playhouse Square—the country's second-largest theater complex and home to five restored movie/vaudeville palaces from the 1920s. Guest rooms are spacious and clean, with crisp linens. An unfortunate orange-brown paint job makes the pool area seem drab and uninviting (the pool water actually looks green). The staff is friendly and upbeat, despite the loud print carpeting in the public areas. Complimentary coffee is served from 7:30 to 9 a.m. in the lobby, and the theater-themed Encore restaurant offers hearty breakfasts as well as fine dining that draws the pre-show crowd.

205 rooms. Restaurant, bar. Business center. Fitness center. Pool. $61-150

RECOMMENDED

INTERCONTINENTAL SUITES HOTEL CLEVELAND

8800 Euclid Ave., 216-707-4300, Cleveland; www.ichotelsgroup.com

Located on the Cleveland Clinic campus and designed for longer stays by hospital patients and their families, this homier cousin of the Intercontinental Hotel is distinguished by its room layouts that maximize privacy. In the standard suite, a large bathroom with two entrances separates bedroom and living room, so a recuperating patient can rest quietly while, say, a caregiver has the TV on in the other room (the suites were slated for remodeling in late 2010). The living area also features a convertible couch and kitchenette with sink and microwave. The Citrus dining room serves breakfast, lunch and dinner; during the warmer months, Rumbar pours tropical drinks al fresco. Shuttle service is available to Cleveland Clinic buildings as well as University Circle attractions.

304 rooms. Restaurant, bar. Business center. Fitness center. $61-150.

WHERE TO EAT

★★★BARICELLI INN

2203 Cornell Road, Cleveland, 216-791-6500; www.baricelli.com

Located in University Circle's Little Italy neighborhood, this inn and Italian restaurant are perched on a bluff in a large, turn-of-the-century brownstone mansion. The Little Italy location delivers romantic, old-world charm, and the seasonal menu features thoughtful preparations of local ingredients.

Continental. Dinner. Closed Sunday. Outdoor seating. $16-35

★★★JOHNNY'S BAR

3164 Fulton Road, Cleveland, 216-281-0055; www.johnnyscleveland.com

One of the most popular restaurants in the city, Johnny's Bar offers fine dining and an excellent wine list. Patrons can expect large portions, a variety of dishes and a selection of over 850 fine wines.

Italian. Lunch, dinner. Closed Sunday. Reservations recommended. Bar. $36-85

★★★MORTON'S, THE STEAKHOUSE

1600 W. Second St., Cleveland, 216-621-6200; www.mortons.com

This branch of the national steakhouse chain offers more than 10 different cuts of perfectly prepared steaks and plenty of classics from Caesar salad to creamed spinach to go with them. Traditional desserts such as thick, creamy cheesecake and warm apple pie complete the experience.

Steak. Dinner. Bar. $36-85

★★★RISTORANTE GIOVANNI

25550 Chagrin Blvd., Cleveland, 216-831-8625; www.giovanniscleveland.com

Dine in a romantic setting at this restaurant, which serves fine classic Italian dishes and pastas. Enjoy a good cigar with dessert.

Italian. Lunch, dinner. Closed Sunday. Reservations recommended. Jacket required. Bar. $36-85

★★★SANS SOUCI

24 Public Square, Cleveland, 216-696-5600; www.sanssouicleveland.com

Fine cuisine is served in this comfortable dining room, which has exposed beams and a stone hearth. This Renaissance hotel space is sectioned into intimate rooms where classic cooking is served.

Mediterranean. Dinner. Bar. $36-85

RECOMMENDED

CROP BISTRO

1400 W. Sixth St., Cleveland, 216-696-2767; www.cropbistro.com.

Although its egg-salad sandwiches are truffled and its fried chicken and waffles gilded in a maple demi glace, there is nothing fussy about this farm-to-table oasis in downtown Cleveland's Warehouse District. The spacious surroundings, punctuated with bare-wood cabinetry and copper pans hanging decoratively over the bar, generate the feel of a high-end lodge. Chef Steve Schimoler, an avid customer of family farms in the area, pays proper homage to the pork god with the Pig Mac sandwich—braised pork, pork loin, bacon and special sauce on a sesame-seed challah bun. The inventive libations menu seamlessly incorporates nature's bounty, with cocktails that include the Slanted Cuke—cucumber, lime and Shochu—and a zippy Hibiscus Margarita that blends the hummingbird's favorite nectar with lime and tequila.

American. Lunch, dinner. Bar. $36-85

GREENHOUSE TAVERN

2038 E. Fourth St., Cleveland, 216-443-0511; www.thegreenhousetavern.com

Unabashed carnivores and committed vegetarians alike will feel welcome in this loftlike space, where most of the furnishings are made of reclaimed or recycled materials and where chef Jonathon Sawyer lovingly elevates both raw beef (in a lusty beef tartare) and root vegetables (in a simple but elegant salad of French breakfast radishes) to gourmet heights. The decadent foie gras steamed clams and a lyrical spring spaghetti with hen of the woods mushrooms and wild Ohio ramps are especially memorable.

French. Lunch, dinner. Reservations recommended. $36-85

TABLE 45

InterContinental Hotel and Conference Center, 9801 Carnegie Ave., Cleveland, 216-707-4045; www.tbl45.com

Street-cart fare goes high end in Chef Zac Bruell's newly revamped menu, which fits in nicely with the international staff and clientele populating the Intercontinental Hotel and the Cleveland Clinic's main campus. Here, the naan of the day shares menu real estate with ceviche, marinated hangar steak with plantains and a sushi bar's worth of sashimi and futomaki. The zenlike décor, featuring low lighting and modernist leather chairs, encourages both intimate conversation and convalescing in style after heart surgery—though the place does get a little boisterous during happy hour, when residents and other hospital types indulge in after-work camaraderie.

International. Lunch, dinner. Reservations recommended. $36-85

WHERE TO SHOP

BANYAN TREE

2242 Professor Ave., Cleveland, 216-241-1209; www.shopbanyantree.com

Tasteful, edgy and spirited, Banyan Tree offers a sprinkling of well-known boutique names, like Free People, mixed with lesser known ones, such as local label Figwood (high-quality cotton basics in happy colors) and Atlanta party girl Judith March (cherry-print mini-skirts). Jewelry by Tremont designer Modern Pixie, among the store's treasure trove of stylin' accessories, features vintage materials reworked into fun, current pieces that announce themselves with a wink rather than a clank. The store's second half includes stylish housewares, gifts for fashion-forward babies, and a few racks of mod men's clothing. *Monday-Wednesday 11 a.m.-7 p.m., Thursday-Saturday 11 a.m.-9 p.m., Sunday 11 a.m.-4 p.m.*

BEACHWOOD PLACE

26300 Cedar Road, Beachwood, 216-464-9460

This pleasant mall is located about 25-minutes away from downtown Cleveland. You'll find Norstrom, Dillard's and Saks Fifth Avenue here along with stores such as Lacoste, Ann Taylor, Arden B, Nine West, H&M, BCBGMaxazria, Sephora and many others. Restaurants include Maggiano's Little Italy, McCormick & Schmick's along with your typical food court. *Monday-Saturday 10 a.m.-9 p.m., Sunday noon-6 p.m.*

BOOM

2218 Lee Road, Cleveland Heights. 216-320-1784; www.boommodern.com

Mid-century modernists of all economic situations can go home happy at Boom, where the owner has not only a curator's eye but also an appreciation that good taste is not just the provenance of the wealthy. Plenty of items can be had here for under $100, especially in the vintage jewelry (Bakelite beaded bracelet for $48, anyone?), dishware (a 1960s Scandinavian saffron-colored bowl for $30) and tchotcke departments (including an assortment of 1950s-era dog-themed knickknacks). It only goes up from there—all the way up to vintage furniture by Eames and Knoll. *Call for hours.*

BIG FUN TOY STORE

11512 Clifton Blvd., Cleveland, 216-631-4386; 1814 Coventry Road, Cleveland Heights, 216-371-4386; www.bigfunbigfun.com

This is a one-stop shop for flowers that squirt, hot-pepper gum and whoopee cushions. If the names "G.I. Joe," "Howdy Doody," and "Pee Wee Herman" are uttered with reverence in your home, there will be much authentic to peruse here. Amid the $100 superhero lunchboxes, small (and big) fry will delight in yanking open the card-catalog drawers stuffed full of bubble-gum-machine charms and plastic parachute men. *Cleveland: Monday-Thursday 11 a.m.-8 p.m., Friday-Saturday 11 a.m.-10 p.m., Sunday 11 a.m.-7 p.m. Cleveland Heights: Tuesday-Thursday 11 a.m.-8p.m., Friday-Saturday 11 a.m.-9 p.m., Sunday 11 a.m.-6 p.m.*

CROCKER PARK

25 Main St., Westlake, 440-871-6880; www.crockerpark.com

This "lifestyle center" about a 30-minutes' drive from downtown Cleveland, features a plethora of upscale mall names including Banana Republic, J. Crew, the Apple Store, L'Occitane en Provence, plus an H&M and a Trader Joe's. A splash pad, grassy courtyard with colorful chairs, and an outdoor promenade outfitted with sandboxes and chess tables help make the shopping experience family-friendly.

Monday-Saturday 10 a.m.-9 p.m., Sunday 11 a.m.-6 p.m.

NORTHEAST OHIO

Northeast Ohio is probably most famous for the Ohio and Erie Canal. But the area also offers the cities of Cleveland, Canton and Akron, as well as the state's only national park.

Once called the "rubber capital of the world," Akron is the headquarters for four major rubber companies, including Goodyear and Firestone. Akron owes its start to the Ohio and Erie Canal, which was opened in 1827. The town was already thriving when Dr. Benjamin Franklin Goodrich launched the first rubber plant there in 1870. When automobiles were invented, Akron became a boomtown. Though industry isn't quite what it once was, the signs of the city's past affluence can still be seen.

Canton is a large steel-processing city, important a century ago for farm machinery. It is in the middle of rich farmland on the edge of "steel valley" where the three branches of Nimishillen Creek come together. It is also home to the Pro Football Hall of Fame.

In 1867, president-to-be William McKinley opened a law office in Canton and later conducted his "front porch campaign" for the presidency here. After his assassination, his body was brought back to Canton for burial. Because of his love for the red carnation, it was made the state flower. A visit to the McKinley Presidential Library and Museum should include a run up the steps of the McKinley Monument, which is a Canton landmark and President McKinley's final resting place.

To experience Northeast Ohio in its pure state, head just a short distance outside Akron to Cuyahoga Valley National Park. Any time of year is the perfect time to experience the beauty of the 33,000 preserved acres along 22 miles of the Cuyahoga River.

WHAT TO SEE

AKRON

AKRON ART MUSEUM

1 S. High, Akron, 330-376-9185; www.akronartmuseum.org

Collections of the Akron Art Museum focus on art produced since 1850. Permanent collections and rotating exhibitions are displayed in over 12,000

HIGHLIGHT

WHAT ARE THE TOP THINGS TO DO IN NORTHEAST OHIO?

GET READY FOR SOME FOOTBALL

Head to the Pro Football Hall of Fame in Canton, a five-building museum dedicated to the game and its players. It houses memorabilia, a research library, a movie theater and a museum store.

GO FOR A HIKE

No worries: You don't need to cover all 33,000 acres of Cuyahoga Valley National Park to experience its beauty. And you don't even need to exert energy if you don't want to—simply board the Cuyahoga Valley Scenic Railroad.

GET WET

Geauga Lake's Wildwater Kingdom in Aurora offers plenty of ways to cool off in summer.

square feet of gallery space.

Admission: adults $7, seniors and students $5, children 12 and under free. Free first Sunday of the month. Wednesday, Friday-Sunday 11 a.m.-5 p.m., Thursday 11 a.m.-9 p.m.

AKRON ZOO

500 Edgewood Ave., Akron, 330-375-2550; www.akronzoo.org

This nearly 50-acred zoo features more than 700 animals from around the world, including endangered Humboldt penguins, Sumatran tigers and Malayan sun bears. Stroller rentals are available.

Admission: May-October, adults $10, seniors $7.50, children 2-14 $6; November-April, adults, seniors and children $6. May-October, daily 10 a.m.-5 p.m.; November-April, daily 11 a.m.-4 p.m.

STAN HYWET HALL AND GARDENS

714 N. Portage Path, Akron, 330-836-5533; www.stanhywet.org

This Tudor Revival manor house built by F. A. Seiberling, co-founder of Goodyear Tire & Rubber, contains 65 rooms with antiques and art. Some pieces date from the 14th century. The 70 acres of grounds include English and Japanese gardens. Tours are available.

Admission: adults $12, students $6. Tuesday-Sunday 10 a.m.-6 p.m.

AURORA
GEAUGA LAKE'S WILDWATER KINGDOM
1100 Squires Road, Aurora, 330-562-8303; www.wildwaterfun.com

The family water park has something for everyone, from an activity pool to a 60-foot-tall, 253-foot-long funnel with a spiral finale. Private cabanas, with lounge chairs and a dining table with umbrella, offer between-fun respite. *Admission varies by height. May-September.*

BATH
HALE FARM AND VILLAGE
2686 Oak Hill Road, Bath, 330-666-3711, 800-589-9703; www.wrhs.org

A living history museum, Hale Farm and Village provides a slice of 19th century life. An authentic Western Reserve house circa 1825 and other authentic buildings in the village setting depict northeastern Ohio's rural life in the mid-1800s. Period crafts are made on the premises, with artisans demonstrating blacksmithing, spinning, weaving, and candle and basket making. *Admission: adults $10, children $5. Hours vary by season.*

BRECKSVILLE
CUYAHOGA VALLEY NATIONAL PARK
15610 Vaughn Road, Brecksville, 800-445-9667; www.nps.gov/cuva

Ohio's only national park preserves 33,000 acres along 22 miles of the Cuyahoga River in northeastern Ohio, between Cleveland and Akron. It is home to native Ohio wildlife, including deer, coyotes, foxes, otters and beavers, as well as over 200 species of birds. Recreation activities include EarthCaching and questing, fishing, hiking, bicycling, canoeing and kayaking, and primitive camping. The Cuyahoga Valley Scenic Railroad offers excursions year-round from three stations. *Admission: free. Daily.*

CANTON
MCKINLEY PRESIDENTIAL LIBRARY AND MUSEUM
800 McKinley Monument Drive N.W., Canton, 330-455-7043; www.mckinleymuseum.org

The 25th president of the United States is Canton's favorite son. The museum contains McKinley artifacts and chronicles the life of William McKinley, from his birth to assassination. The McKinley Monument is a Canton landmark and the final resting place for President McKinley. *Admission: adults $8, seniors $7, children $6, children 2 and under free. Monday-Saturday 9 a.m.-4 p.m., Sunday noon-4 p.m.*

NATIONAL FIRST LADIES' LIBRARY AND RESEARCH CENTER
205 S. Market Ave., Canton, 330-452-0876; www.firstladieslibrary.org

Learn more about our nation's First Ladies and other important women in history at this museum. The library includes the Ida Saxton McKinley Historic Home, located a block north. Tours are available. *Admission: adults $7, seniors $6, children $5. Closed Monday, hours vary by season.*

PRO FOOTBALL HALL OF FAME
2121 George Halas Drive N.W., Canton, 330-456-8207; www.profootballhof.com

Are you ready for some football? This museum, a five-building complex, is dedicated to the game and its players. It houses memorabilia, a research library, a movie theater and a museum store. Annual inductees are celebrated with an event-filled Enshrinement Festival.

Admission: adults $20, seniors $16, children $14, children 5 and under free. June-August, daily 9 a.m.-8 p.m.; September-May, daily 9 a.m.-5 p.m.

MENTOR

LAWNFIELD JAMES A. GARFIELD NATIONAL HISTORIC SITE

8095 Mentor Ave., Mentor, 440-255-8722; www.nps.gov/jaga

This was the 20th president's last house before the White House, and the site of the first successful front porch campaign. After his assassination, his wife added the memorial library wing—the first presidential library. The restored home features original furnishings, including his books and desk in the library. The visitor center, in the 1893 carriage house on the grounds, has exhibits about President Garfield's life. Tours are available, including a behind-the-scenes tour of areas not accessible during regular tours.

Admission: adults $5, children 15 and under free. May-October, Monday-Saturday 10 a.m.-5 p.m., Sunday noon-5 p.m.; November-April, Saturday-Sunday noon-5 p.m.

YOUNGSTOWN

BUTLER INSTITUTE OF AMERICAN ART

524 Wick Ave., Youngstown, 330-743-1107; www.butlerart.com

The Butler is the first museum of American art, with holdings exceeding 20,000 individual works. The collection includes works from four centuries and tells the history of America.

Admission: free. Tuesday-Saturday 11 a.m.-4 p.m., Sunday noon-4 p.m.

LANTERMAN'S MILL

980 Canfield Road, Youngstown, 330-740-7115; www.millcreekmetroparks.com

One of Mahoning County's most historic landmarks, Lanterman's Mill was built in the mid-1800s to grind corn, wheat and buckwheat. It was restored in the 1980s and still operates today. Visitors can step into the past and observe the process, and buy the goods in the gift shop. The site is part of Mill Creek Park and includes an observation deck overlooking Lanterman's Falls, a covered bridge upstream and hiking trails.

Admission: adults $1, seniors and students $ .50, children 6 and under free. May-October, Tuesday-Friday 10 a.m. 5 p.m., Saturday-Sunday 11 a.m.-6 p.m.; April, November, Saturday-Sunday noon-4 p.m.

WHERE TO STAY

AKRON

★★★HILTON AKRON-FAIRLAWN

3180 W. Market St., Akron, 330-867-5000, 800-445-8667; www.akronfairlawn.hilton.com

This hotel is near Summit Mall and Cuyahoga Valley National Park. Large rooms feature marble bathrooms and Crabtree and Evelyn La Source bath products.*203 rooms. Restaurant, bar. Business center. Fitness center. Pool. Pets accepted. $61-150*

★★★QUAKER SQUARE INN AT THE UNIVERSITY OF AKRON

135 S. Broadway St., Akron, 330-253-5970; www.quakersquareakron.com

There is nothing square about these guest rooms—they are perfectly round. This historic hotel is constructed from 19th-century silos that once stored 1.5 million grain bushels for the Quaker Oats Company, and is an Akron landmark.

65 rooms. Restaurant, bar. Complimentary breakfast. Business center. Fitness center. Pool. $61-150

AURORA

★★★THE BERTRAM INN AND CONFERENCE CENTER

600 N. Aurora Road, Aurora, 330-995-0200, 877-995-0200; www.thebertraminn.com

This sprawling resort attracts large conferences. Spacious rooms are decorated with traditional furnishings. The onsite Leopard restaurant is acclaimed for its creative cooking—the menu includes everything from veal Milanese to bouillabaisse with clams, lobster, shrimp and salmon.

162 rooms. Restaurant, bar. Business center. Fitness center. Pool. $61-150

INDEPENDENCE

★★★DOUBLETREE HOTEL CLEVELAND SOUTH

6200 Quarry Lane, Independence, 216-447-1300; www.doubletree1.hilton.com

A contemporary stay in a suburban setting, this hotel is located in a suburb just south of Cleveland. The onsite restaurant is a sports-themed Shula's 2 steakhouse, known for its exclusive cuts of meats. Local attractions, such as Progressive Field, are just a short drive away.

193 rooms. Restaurant, bar. Business center. Fitness center. Pool. $61-150

PAINSVILLE

★★★RENAISSANCE QUAIL HOLLOW RESORT

11080 Concord-Hambden Road, Painesville, 440-497-1100, 800-468-3571; www.quailhollowresort.com

This hotel is nestled on 700 wooded acres outside of Cleveland. The property includes two golf courses, three lakes and creeks. The restaurant, CK's Steakhouse, features classic selections along with its signature dish, medallions of tenderloin.

176 rooms. Restaurant, bar. Business center. Fitness center. Pool. Golf. $61-150

WARREN

★★★AVALON INN RESORT AND CONFERENCE CENTER

9519 E. Market St., Warren, 330-856-1900, 800-828-2566; www.avaloninn.com

This inn is situated between two golf courses, but offers plenty of other activities with a junior Olympic-sized pool and tennis, racquetball and volleyball courts. Well-appointed rooms offer golf course views and are decorated in a colonial style.

140 rooms. Restaurant, bar. Complimentary breakfast. Fitness center. Pool. Golf. Tennis. Pets accepted. $61-150

WHERE TO EAT

AKRON

★★★LANNING'S

826 N. Cleveland-Massillon Road, Akron, 330-666-1159; www.lannings-restaurant.com

On the banks of Yellow Creek, this fine dining room has offered fresh fish and hand-cut steaks since 1967. Everything is made in-house, including salad dressings, sauces, soups, breads and desserts.

American. Dinner. Closed Sunday. Reservations recommended. Bar. $36-85

★★★TANGIER

532 W. Market St., Akron, 330-376-7171, 800-826-4437; www.thetangier.com

This local gem is considered one of Ohio's top spots for live music, from jazz to light rock. Listen to the entertainment while sampling the eclectic Middle Eastern cuisine.

American, Middle Eastern. Lunch, dinner. Closed Sunday. Reservations recommended. Outdoor seating. Children's menu. Bar. $36-85

NILES

★★★ALBERINI'S

1201 Youngstown-Warren Road, Niles, 330-652-5895; www.alberinis.com

Husband-wife team Richard and Gilda Alberini preside over this popular Italian restaurant that boasts the "original" spaghetti and meatballs. Alberini's has a cigar room and a pleasant, glass patio.

Italian. Dinner. Closed Sunday-Monday. Reservations recommended. Bar. $16-35

RECOMMENDED

CANTON

JOHN'S GRILLE

2749 Cleveland Ave. N.W., Canton, 330-454-1259; www.johnsgrille.com

This family owned restaurant has been a local favorite since 1945. Try the Grecian grouper or the tender and juicy lamb chops.

American. Breakfast, lunch, dinner. Closed Sunday. Children's menu. Bar. $15 and under

KENT

THE PUFFERBELLY LTD.

152 Franklin Ave., Kent, 330-673-1771; www.pufferbellyltd.com

Located in a former railway depot, this restaurant serves a variety of tastes. Swiss steak can be found on the menu alongside a bourbon apple pork porterhouse; save room for the Pufferbelly ice cream cake.

American. Lunch, dinner, Sunday brunch. Reservations recommended. Children's menu. Bar. $16-35

LAKEWOOD

PLAYERS ON MADISON

14523 Madison Ave., Lakewood, 216-226-5200; www.playersonmadison.com

Start by choosing a bottle from the impressive wine list at this restaurant, then decide whether to start with Tuscan pizzettes or panko-encrusted crab cakes.

Entrées include a delicious macaroni and cheese with herb grilled chicken, apple wood-smoked bacon and three-cheese sauce.

Italian. Dinner. Outdoor seating. Bar. $36-85

MENTOR
MOLINARI'S

8900 Mentor Ave., Mentor, 440-974-2750; www.molinaris.com

More than 200 wines are available in the wine shop to accompany a stone-oven pizza or a four-course meal. Menu standards include fresh fish, veal specialties and risotto.

Italian. Lunch, dinner. Closed Sunday-Monday. Bar. $16-35

WOOSTER
TJ'S

359 W. Liberty St., Wooster, 330-264-6263; www.tjsrestaurants.com

This Wooster favorite for over 35 years is known for its prime rib, which is available only Friday and Saturday. On other days of the week, check out specialties like martini chicken pasta, coconut shrimp and sweet chili shrimp bruschetta.

American. Lunch, dinner. Closed Sunday. Reservations recommended. Children's menu. $16-35

NORTHWEST OHIO

When most people think of Northwest Ohio, Toledo comes to mind. Because of the city's large, natural harbor, it is an important port on the Great Lakes.

Edward Libbey introduced the glass industry to Toledo in 1888, with high-grade crystal and lamp globes. Michael Owens, a glassblower, joined him and invented a machine that turned molten glass into bottles by the thousands. Today, a number of companies manufacture a variety of glass products. The city boasts a world-class art museum, a botanical gardens and symphony. And if you follow the shoreline to the east, you will find a ferry at Port Clinton that will take you to Put-in-Bay, a village on South Bass Island in Lake Erie. This all-year resort area claims the best smallmouth black bass fishing in America in spring and walleye and perch fishing at other times of the year. In summer, the area teams with boaters who come here to party at the many bars and restaurants near the town's marina.

Sandusky lies further east. On a flat slope facing 18-mile-long Sandusky Bay, this town stretches for more than six miles along the waterfront. Originally explored by the French, the town was named by the Wyandot "Sandouske," meaning "at the cold water." When the amusement park Cedar Point opened here in 1870, Sandusky became a center for summertime tourism—and roller coasters.

HIGHLIGHT

WHAT ARE THE TOP THINGS TO DO IN NORTHWEST OHIO?

SEE PRETTY PAINTINGS

The Toledo Museum of Art is one of the top art museums in the world. The Glass Pavilion is a work of art alone.

GET TO THE POINT

Cedar Point in Sandusky has roller coasters, a water park and corn dogs. No one should need more convincing that that.

WHAT TO SEE

PUT-IN-BAY

PERRY'S CAVE

979 Catawba Ave., Put-in-Bay, 419-285-2283; www.perryscave.com

Commodore Perry is rumored to have stored supplies here before the Battle of Lake Erie in 1813; later, prisoners were kept here for a short time. The cave is 52 feet below the surface and measures 208 feet long by 165 feet wide; the temperature is 50 F year-round. It has an underground lake that rises and falls with the level of Lake Erie. Private, after-hours guided lantern tours are available.

Admission: adults $7.50, children $4.50, children 6 and under free. Lantern tours $20. May-September, daily 10 a.m.-6 p.m.; April, October, Saturday-Sunday 11 a.m.-5 p.m.

PERRY'S VICTORY AND INTERNATIONAL PEACE MEMORIAL

2 Bay View Ave., Put-in-Bay, 419-285-2184; www.nps.gov/pev

This Greek Doric granite column is 352 feet tall and commemorates Commodore Oliver Hazard Perry's 1813 victory over the British naval squadron at the Battle of Lake Erie, near Put-in-Bay. The United States gained control of the lake, preventing a British invasion. The 3,986-mile U.S.-Canadian boundary, which passes near here through the lake, is the longest unfortified border in the world.

Admission: adults $3, children 16 and under free with adult. Hours vary by season.

SANDUSKY

CEDAR POINT

1 Cedar Point Drive, Sandusky, 419-627-2350; www.cedarpoint.com

The second oldest amusement park in North America, Cedar Point consistently wins awards for its roller coasters. The park currently has 17, including the

310-foot-tall steel Millennium Force and record-breaking Magnum XL-200. Other diversions include water rides, live shows, restaurants, Soak City Water Park, Challenge Golf miniature golf course, Challenge Park and the Cedar Point Grand Prix go-cart racetrack (additional fee). Price includes unlimited rides and attractions, but not Challenge Park or Soak City Water Park.

Admission: adults $45.99 (48" and taller), seniors and children (under 48") $19.99 (and under 48"), military personnel $35.99. Hours vary by season.

TOLEDO

TOLEDO BOTANICAL GARDEN

5403 Elmer Drive, Toledo, 419-936-2986; www.toledogarden.org

This garden has over 60 acres of display gardens and plant collections, including seasonal floral displays, herb, rhododendron and azalea gardens, a perennial garden, a rose garden, and a fragrance garden for the visually and physically impaired. Original sculptures found throughout will please art lovers, as well as the annual Crosby Festival of the Arts. A summer concert series features local jazz musicians.

Admission: free. Daily dawn-dusk. Visitor center: Monday-Friday 9 a.m.-5 p.m.; and May-October, Saturday-Sunday 11 a.m.-4 p.m.

TOLEDO MUSEUM OF ART

2445 Monroe St., Toledo, 419-255-8000; www.toledomuseum.com

Voted "America's Finest Art Museum" by readers of Modern Art Notes, the Toledo Art Museum boasts more than 30,000 works in collections from ancient Egypt, Greece and Rome through the Middle Ages and the Renaissance to European and American arts of the present. Included in the museum's galleries, sculpture garden and glass pavilion are a renowned glass collection and paintings and sculptures by Calder, Degas, El Greco, Matisse, Monet and Picasso.

Admission: free. Tuesday-Thursday, 10 a.m.-4 p.m., Friday 10 a.m.-10 p.m., Saturday 10 a.m.-6 p.m., Sunday noon-6 p.m.

TOLEDO SYMPHONY

1838 Parkwood Ave., Toledo, 419-246-8000, 800-348-1253; www.toledosymphony.com

Each season, this symphony presents hundreds of classical, pop, casual, chamber and all-Mozart concerts. Performances are at various locations in northwest Ohio and southeast Michigan.

Mid-September-May.

TOLEDO ZOO

2700 Broadway, Toledo, 419-385-5721; www.toledozoo.org

The Toledo Zoo is home to over 9,000 mammals, fish, reptiles, amphibians, birds and invertebrates, representing over 800 species. Favorites include polar bears in the Arctic Encounter and the massive yet graceful floating hippos in the Hippoquarium. Wagon and stroller rentals are available.

Admission: adults $11, children $8, children 2 and under free. Labor Day-Memorial Day, Daily 10 a.m.-4 p.m.; Memorial Day-Labor Day, Daily 10 a.m.-5 p.m.; May and September, Monday-Friday 10 a.m.-4 p.m., Saturday-Sunday 10 a.m.-5 p.m.

WHERE TO STAY

TOLEDO

★★★HILTON TOLEDO

3100 Glendale Ave., Toledo, 419-381-6800, 800-445-8667; www.hilton.com

Situated on the University of Toledo Health Science Campus, this hotel offers easy access to nearby attractions. Fitness options are plentiful, with a jogging and walking track and basketball, squash, racquetball and tennis courts on the property, along with the standard fitness center and pool.

212 rooms. Restaurant, bar. Business center. Fitness center. Pool. Tennis. $61-150

RECOMMENDED

PUT-IN-BAY

BAYSHORE RESORT

328 Toledo Ave., Put-In-Bay, 866-422-9746; www.bayshoreresortpib.com

The only lakefront hotel in Put-in-Bay covers almost 3 acres of waterfront property. Take in the views in one of two heated lakefront swimming pools, the 30-person hot tub or at the pool-side tiki bar. Golf carts to tool around town are available for rent.

60 rooms. Restaurant, bar. Pool. $251-350.

SANDUSKY

GREAT WOLF LODGE

4600 Milan Road, Sandusky, 866-257-5627; www.greatwolf.com

Although this all-suites hotel is near Cedar Point, kids may not want to venture far from this indoor water park resort. Two upgraded suites are kid-oriented, with either a wolf den—a cave-themed area with a bunk bed—or a log cabin area.

271 rooms. Restaurant, bar. Business center. Fitness center. Pool. $151-250

HOTEL BREAKERS

1 Cedar Point Drive, Cedar Point, Sandusky, 419-627-2106; www.cedarpoint.com

Unwind after a day at Cedar Point, or take an afternoon break, at the hotel closest to the amusement park. Guests can purchase discounted tickets at the front desk plus enter the park early—one hour before the general public arrives.

650 rooms. Restaurant, bar. Pool. $151-250

SANDCASTLE SUITES

1 Cedar Point Drive, Cedar Point, Sandusky, 419-627-2106; www.cedarpoint.com

This all-suite hotel is on the property of Cedar Point, and has rooms large enough to house families partaking of the amusement park fun. Guest rooms feature remodeled bathrooms, flat-screen TVs and the décor is all new in this all-suite hotel. Guests can purchase discounted tickets at the front desk plus enter the park one hour early.

187 rooms. Restaurant, bar. Pool. Tennis. $251-350

WHERE TO EAT

TOLEDO

★★★FIFI'S

1423 Bernath Parkway, Toledo, 419-866-6777; www.fifisrestaurant.com

Fifi's offers a wide array of regional and traditional dishes prepared with a creative flair. House specialties are soups, such as traditional vichyssoise or gourmet fruit soups served as dessert. Entrées include red wine braised duck breast, rack of lamb, and a variety of steaks.

French. Dinner. Closed Sunday. Bar. $36-85

VERMILION

★★★CHEZ FRANÇOIS

555 Main St., Vermilion, 440-967-0630; www.chezfrancois.com

Located in a small Lake Erie harbor town, this French restaurant has a formal dining room and a more casual, outdoor dining area with a view of the Vermilion River. The menu changes with the seasons.

French. Dinner. Closed Monday; also January-mid-March. Outdoor seating. Jacket required. $36-85

RECOMMENDED

SANDUSKY

BAY HARBOR AT THE CEDAR POINT MARINA

1 Cedar Point Drive, Sandusky, 419-625-6373; www.cedarpoint.com

Although this restaurant is part of Cedar Point, park fare is not on the menu. The house specialties include prime rib, New York strip and chicken stuffed with crabmeat.

Seafood. Dinner. Closed Monday-Tuesday. Bar. $35-86

TOLEDO

MANCY'S STEAK HOUSE

953 Phillips Ave., Toledo, 419-476-4154; www.mancys.com

Mancy's has been a Toledo staple since 1921. The restaurant delivers quality meats cooked to perfection, and is famous for its surf and turf.

Seafood, steak. Lunch, dinner. Closed Sunday. Bar. $16-35

TONY PACKO'S CAFE

1902 Front St., Toledo, 419-691-6054; www.tonypackos.com

Tony Packo's has been serving authentic Hungarian food since 1932. Don't leave without trying the restaurant's signature sweet hot pickles, homemade Hungarian noodles or chili hot dog.

Hungarian. Lunch, dinner. Children's menu. Bar. $16-35

SOUTHERN OHIO

Cincinnati is by far the largest city in Southern Ohio. At one point, it was a busy frontier riverboat town and one of the largest cities in the nation when poet Henry Wadsworth Longfellow called it the "queen city of the West." Although other cities farther west have since outstripped it in size, Cincinnati is still the Queen City to its inhabitants and to the many visitors who rediscover it. With a wealth of fine restaurants, a redeveloped downtown with a Skywalk, its own Montmartre in Mount Adams and the beautiful Ohio River, Cincinnati has a cosmopolitan flavor uniquely its own.

Cincinnati is the home of two universities and several other institutions of higher education and has its own symphony orchestra, opera and ballet. Major hotels, stores, office complexes, restaurants, entertainment centers and the Cincinnati Convention Center are now connected by a skywalk system, making the city easy to walk, even in winter.

Other visitors to Southern Ohio are likely looking for thrills. They will find them easily at two popular amusement parks: Kings Island, with its legendary Beast roller coaster, and The Beach Waterpark, which features the largest wave pool in Ohio.

WHAT TO SEE

CINCINNATI

CINCINNATI ART MUSEUM

953 Eden Park Drive, Cincinnati, 513-639-2995, 877-472-4226; www.cincinnatiartmuseum.org

Founded in 1881, this museum features 88 galleries and a permanent collection of over 60,000 works of international art spanning 6,000 years. Its most notable gems include the only collection of ancient Nabataean art outside of Jordan, the renowned Herbert Greer French collection of old master prints, and a fine collection of European and American portrait miniatures.

Admission: free. Tuesday-Sunday 11 a.m.-5 p.m.

CINCINNATI BALLET

Aronoff Center, 1555 Central Parkway, Cincinnati, 513-621-5219; www.cballet.org

This professional ballet company, founded in 1963, performs a five-series program at the Aronoff Center of both contemporary and classical, full-length works. Live orchestras regularly accompany performances.

September-April. See website for details.

CINCINNATI MUSEUM CENTER AT UNION TERMINAL

1301 Western Ave., Cincinnati, 513-287-7000, 800-733-2077; www.cincymuseum.org

The Cincinnati Museum Center at Union Terminal is home to the Cincinnati History Museum, Duke Energy Children's Museum, the Museum of Natural History & Science, the Cincinnati Historical Society Library and an Omnimax theater.

Admission: adults $12.50, seniors $11.50, children $8.50, toddlers $4.50, children 1 and under free. Monday-Saturday 10 a.m.-5 p.m., Sunday 11 a.m.-6 p.m.

CINCINNATI OPERA

Cincinnati Music Hall, 1241 Elm St., Cincinnati, 513-241-2742; www.cincinnatiopera.com

The nation's second oldest opera company offers a four-performance summer season at the Cincinnati Music Hall. Capsulized English translations are projected above the stage for all operas.

June-July. See website for details.

CINCINNATI SYMPHONY ORCHESTRA

Cincinnati Music Hall, 1241 Elm St., Cincinnati, 513-381-3300; www.cincinnatisymphony.org

The fifth-oldest orchestra in the United States presents symphony and pops programs year-round at the Cincinnati Music Hall and other area venues.

See website for details.

CINCINNATI ZOO AND BOTANICAL GARDEN

3400 Vine St., Cincinnati, 513-281-4700, 800-944-4776; www.cincyzoo.org

More than 500 animal species can be seen in a variety of naturalistic habitats, including the world-famous gorillas and white Bengal tigers. The Cat House features 16 species of cats; the Jungle Trails exhibit is an indoor-outdoor rain forest. Rare okapi, walrus, Komodo dragons and giant eland also are on display. Enjoy the participatory children's zoo, animal shows, elephant and camel rides. There are also picnic areas and an onsite restaurant.

Admission: adults $25, seniors and children $20, children 2 and under free. Daily 9 a.m.-5 p.m.

EDEN PARK

1501 Eden Park Drive, Cincinnati, 513-421-4086; www.cincinnatiparks.com

One of the most popular Cincinnati parks, Eden Park is more than 185 acres initially called "the Garden of Eden." It is home to the Cincinnati Art Museum, Cincinnati Playhouse in the Park and the Krohn Conservatory. Popular landmarks are Mirror Lake, the Bettman Fountain and the Hinkle Magnolia Garden, which has a picturesque gazebo, memorial tree groves and paths. Four overlooks offer scenic views of the Ohio River, the city and Kentucky hillsides.

Daily.

HARRIET BEECHER STOWE HOUSE

224 W. Liberty St., Cincinnati, 513-632-5120; www.harrietbeecherstowecenter.org

The author of *Uncle Tom's Cabin* lived in this charming Victorian Gothic Revival home from 1873 to 1896. It has been completely restored with some original furnishings and contains a collection of books, manuscripts and memorabilia.

Admission: adults $9, seniors and students $8, children $6, children 5 and under free. Closed Monday. Hours vary by season.

NATIONAL UNDERGROUND RAILROAD FREEDOM CENTER

50 E. Freedom Way, Cincinnati, 513-333-7500, 877-648-4838; www.freedomcenter.org

This museum is dedicated to telling freedom stories, from the Underground Railroad era to modern times. Permanent exhibits include The Underground Railroad, the 19th century movement that aided more than 100,000 enslaved people seeking freedom, and Invisible: Slavery Today, about slavery and human trafficking that occurs today. The FamilySearch Center allows visitors to research their family tree, using free family history resources with assistance from volunteers.

Admission: adults $12, seniors and students $10, children $8, children 5 and under free. Tuesday-Saturday 11 a.m.-5 p.m.

WILLIAM HOWARD TAFT NATIONAL HISTORIC SITE

2038 Auburn Ave., Cincinnati, 513-684-3262; www.nps.gov/wiho

This is the birthplace and boyhood home of the 27th president and 10th chief justice of the United States. Four rooms on the first floor are decorated with period furnishings; second floor rooms contain exhibits on Taft's life and careers.

Admission: free. Daily 8 a.m.-4 p.m.

MASON

THE BEACH WATERPARK

2590 Waterpark Drive, Mason, 513-398-7946, 800-886-7946; www.thebeachwaterpark.com

This water park has over 50 rides and attractions, including the largest wave pool in Ohio, a heated spa pool and the only water coaster in the Midwest. Winter brings a 7,500-square-foot ice rink.

Admission: adults $27.99, military personnel $15.50, seniors and children (48" and under) $10.50. Hours vary by season.

KINGS ISLAND

6300 Kings Island Drive, Mason, 513-754-5700, 800-288-0808; www.pki.com

This 350-acre seasonal family theme park has over 100 rides and attractions, such as the legendary Beast, the longest wooden roller coaster in the world, the Planet Snoopy kid's area, water adventures and family rides, and live entertainment.

Admission: varies by day. Hours vary by season.

WHERE TO STAY

CINCINATTI

★★★★CINCINNATIAN HOTEL

601 Vine St., Cincinnati, 513-381-3000, 800-942-9000; www.cincinnatianhotel.com

Open since 1882, the Cincinnatian Hotel was one of the first hotels in the world to have elevators and incandescent lighting; it is now listed on the National Register of Historic Places. In 1987, the hotel underwent a $25 million renovation and the original 300 rooms were reduced to 146 rooms, including seven luxurious suites. The hotel's old-world charm was retained, though—evidenced largely by the marble and walnut grand staircase that continues to impress those who enter the lobby. The accommodations are lovingly maintained and incorporate modern technology. Furnishings lean toward the contemporary, while some rooms feature balconies and fireplaces. The eight-story atrium of the Cricket Lounge serves afternoon tea and evening cocktails. The fine dining and impeccable service at the Palace Restaurant make it one of the top tables in town.

146 rooms. Restaurant, bar. Fitness center. Pets accepted. $151-250

WHAT IS THE MOST LUXURIOUS HOTEL IN SOUTHERN OHIO?

Cincinnatian Hotel:
Built in 1882 as a "Grand Hotel" of the 19th century, this Cincinnati landmark remains the finest hotel in the city.

★★★HILTON CINCINNATI NETHERLAND PLAZA

35 W. Fifth St., Cincinnati, 513-421-9100, 800-445-8667; www.hilton.com

The Hilton Cincinnati Netherland Plaza is a showpiece of Art Deco design in the heart of the city, across from the city's Fountain Square. Listed on the National Register of Historic Places, this elegant hotel marries historic character with modern amenities. The Orchids at Palm Court restaurant is one of the city's most fashionable dining rooms.

561 rooms. Restaurant, bar. Business center. Fitness center. Pool. $151-250

★★★HYATT REGENCY CINCINNATI

151 W. Fifth St., Cincinnati, 513-579-1234, 800-233-1234; www.cincinnati.hyatt.com

This well-appointed hotel is located across from the convention center and connected to the business district and a shopping mall by an enclosed skywalk. The bright and airy atrium lobby has a huge skylight and fountain. One restaurant serves breakfast and lunch buffets, while a sports bar offers pool tables and traditional bar food.

486 rooms. Restaurant, bar. Business center. Fitness center. Pool. $151-250

★★★MILLENNIUM HOTEL CINCINNATI

150 W. Fifth St., Cincinnati, 513-352-2100, 866-866-8086; www.millenniumhotels.com

Business travelers choose this downtown hotel for amenities like an onsite car rental desk and the enclosed skywalk leading to the Duke Energy Convention Center. Rooms are decorated with natural wood and glass furnishings and have ergonomic desk chairs. A poolside bar and grill livens warmer months.

872 rooms. Restaurant, bar. Business center. Fitness center. Pool. Pets accepted. $61-150

★★★THE WESTIN CINCINNATI

21 E. Fifth Street, Cincinnati, 513-621-7700, 800-937-8461; www.westin.com

Overlooking the city's Fountain Square and within steps of restaurants, museums and other cultural attractions, this stylish hotel is connected to a shopping center and the convention center by an enclosed skywalk. Guest rooms feature subdued contemporary furnishings. The onsite restaurant serves American fare and the lounge offers pub food in a sports bar setting.

456 rooms. Restaurant, bar. Business center. Fitness center. Pool. Pets accepted. $151-250

LEBANON
★★★GOLDEN LAMB
27 S. Broadway, Lebanon, 513-932-5065; www.goldenlamb.com

This national historic inn, built in 1803, has an outstanding collection of shaker antiques, many of which are used daily in the dining room. Rooms have antique furnishings and are named after a famous guest of the inn, from John Quincy Adams to Charles Dickens.

18 rooms. Restaurant, bar. Complimentary breakfast. $61-150

MASON
★★★KINGS ISLAND RESORT & CONFERENCE CENTER
5691 Kings Island Drive, Mason, 513-398-0115, 800-727-3050; www.kingsislandresort.com

Located across the street from Kings Island theme park, this resort offers 13,000 square feet of meeting space and various recreational facilities. Visit the Main Street Grill for the weekend prime rib buffet. Guests can purchase discounted tickets to Kings Island and The Beach Waterpark and take advantage of the free shuttle.

284 rooms. Restaurant, bar. Business center. Fitness center. Pool. Tennis. $61-150

★★★MARRIOTT CINCINNATI NORTHEAST
9664 Mason Montgomery Road, Mason, 513-459-9800, 800-228-9290; www.marriott.com

This hotel is ideal for both business travelers and visitors to nearby Kings Island and The Beach Waterpark. Sixteen meeting rooms provide nearly 13,000 square feet of meeting space.

295 rooms. Restaurant, bar. Business center. Fitness center. Pool. $61-150

WEST CHESTER
★★★MARRIOTT CINCINNATI NORTH
6189 Muhlhauser Road, West Chester, 513-874-7335, 800-228-9290; www.marriott.com

Located near Interstate 75 between Cincinnati and Dayton, this hotel is ideal for business travelers. Guest rooms and suites have traditional furniture and luxury bedding. Fifteen meeting rooms provide nearly 14,000 square feet of meeting space.

295 rooms. Restaurant, bar. Business center. Fitness center. Pool. $151-250

WHERE TO EAT

CINCINATTI
★★★CELESTIAL
1071 Celestial St., Cincinnati, 513-241-4455; www.thecelestial.com

This restaurant's name could just as easily refer to its stunning view of the Ohio River and city as to its street address. Dining takes place in a clubby atmosphere of carved wood, and aged, hand-cut steak are the specialty. Stop at the Incline Lounge to sip a cocktail and watch the sunset, or for live music and dancing on Friday and Saturday.

Steak. Dinner. Reservations recommended. Outdoor seating. Bar. $16-35

★★★ORCHIDS AT PALM COURT

Hilton Cincinnati Netherland Plaza, 35 W. Fifth St., Cincinnati, 513-421-9100; www.orchidsatpalmcourt.com

The Orchids at Palm Court, located in the Hilton Cincinnati Netherland Plaza, has an elegant dining room with friendly, accommodating service. Menu standouts include the phyllo venison wrapped in bacon. On Friday and Saturday, a jazz trio and pianist perform.

American. Dinner, Sunday brunch. Reservations recommended. Children's menu. Bar. $36-85

★★★THE PALACE

Cincinnatian Hotel, 601 Vine St., Cincinnati, 513-381-3000, 800-942-9000; www.palacecincinnati.com

This elegant restaurant inside the Cincinnatian hotel is now under the direction of chef Jose Salazar. The menu features traditional dishes such as rack of lamb with crushed chickpeas, tomato and eggplant tarte-tatin, or angus rib-eye with corn and mascarpone flan.

American. Breakfast, lunch, dinner. Closed Sunday. Reservations recommended. Children's menu. Bar. $36-85

★★★PRECINCT

311 Delta Ave., Cincinnati, 513-321-5454, 877-321-5454; www.jeffruby.com

This restaurant, housed in a former police precinct that was used from the 1900s to the 1940s, offers steakhouse classics—from aged Angus beef to the perfect rib eye broiled to perfection and seasoned with a secret spice mix. At night, the exterior of this historic building is bathed in neon light. Bananas Foster is prepared tableside.

Steak. Dinner. Reservations recommended. Bar. $86 and up

★★★PRIMAVISTA

810 Matson Place, Cincinnati, 513-251-6467; www.pvista.com

The view of Cincinnati from its floor-to-ceiling windows is one reason to dine at Primavista, but it is not the only one. A menu of creative but classic Italian fare including fresh seafood, meat and veal specialties as well as pizzas and pasta dishes are featured. Dishes include pine nut crusted salmon over fettuccine with pesto cream sauce and roasted tomatoes, filet mignon broiled and served with calamari, and risotto with porcini and exotic mushrooms.

Italian. Dinner. Reservations recommended. Bar. $36-85

RECOMMENDED

CINCINATTI
THE BISTRO

413 Vine St., Cincinnati, 513-621-1465; www.bistrojeanro.com

The Bistro's menu lists dishes as well as the local farms it patronizes. Dishes include mussels with local tomatoes and garlic, herb crusted rack of lamb with local succotash and side dishes such as duck fat fries. The chocolate pot de crème is the perfect finish.

American. Lunch, dinner. Reservations recommended. Bar. $16-35

MECKLENBURG GARDENS

302 E. University, Cincinnati, 513-221-5353; www.mecklenburgs.net

Inside this 19th century building on the National Registry of Historic Places is Cincinnati favorite. Traditional German dishes like wiener schnitezel and sauerbraten are served alongside American favorites.

German, American. Lunch, dinner. Closed Sunday. Reservations recommended. Outdoor seating. Children's menu. Bar. $16-35

MONTGOMERY INN AT THE BOATHOUSE

925 Riverside Drive, Cincinnati, 513-721-7427; www.montgomeryinn.com

Get ready to get messy—ribs and other barbecued fare are world-famous here. For dessert, choose another Cincinnati tradition: Graeter's black raspberry chip ice cream.

American. Lunch, dinner. Outdoor seating. Children's menu. Bar. $16-35

NICOLA'S

1420 Sycamore St., Cincinnati, 513-721-6200; www.nicolasrestaurant.com

Italian fine dining can be found at Nicola's, consistently rated a top Cincinnati restaurant. The menu features handmade house pastas, such as tagliolini with blue crab, San Marzano tomatoes and navy beans, and entrees of duck breast, braised prime beef short ribs and monk fish.

Italian. Dinner. Closed Sunday. Reservations recommended. Outdoor seating. Bar. $36-85

GLENDALE

GRAND FINALE

3 E. Sharon Road, Glendale, 513-771-5925; www.grandfinale.info

American food with a French flair is on tap at this Glendale staple. While this restaurant is known for its ginger chicken, the crepes are hard to skip.

American. Lunch, dinner, Sunday brunch. Closed Monday. Reservations recommended. Outdoor seating. Children's menu. Bar. $16-35

IRON HORSE

40 Village Square, Glendale, 513-772-3333; www.ironhorseinn.com

This restaurant in the heart of historic Glendale features finer dining on the main floor and a casual bar area upstairs. Entrées include small or large plates, as well as a few likely to be kept to oneself, like the rack of lamb marinated in local honey and herbs.

American. Lunch, dinner. Closed Sunday-Monday. Outdoor seating. Children's menu. Bar. $16-35

MONTGOMERY

MONTGOMERY INN

9440 Montgomery Road, Montgomery, 513-791-3482; www.montgomeryinn.com

The original location of this Cincinnati chain is now a local institution. More than five generations of diners have feasted on ribs and other barbecue specialties.

American. Lunch, dinner. Children's menu. Bar. $16-35

INDEX

I

ILLINOIS

CHICAGO OVERVIEW

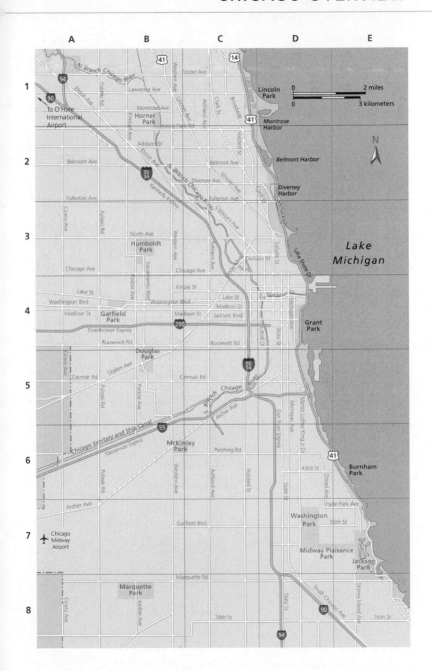

CHICAGO: NORTH SIDE

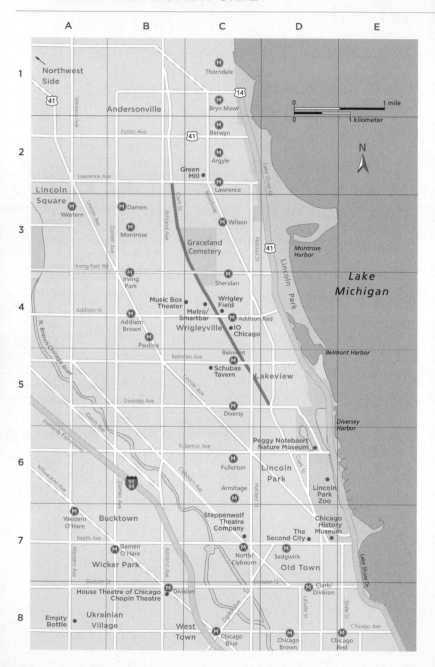

CHICAGO: DOWNTOWN

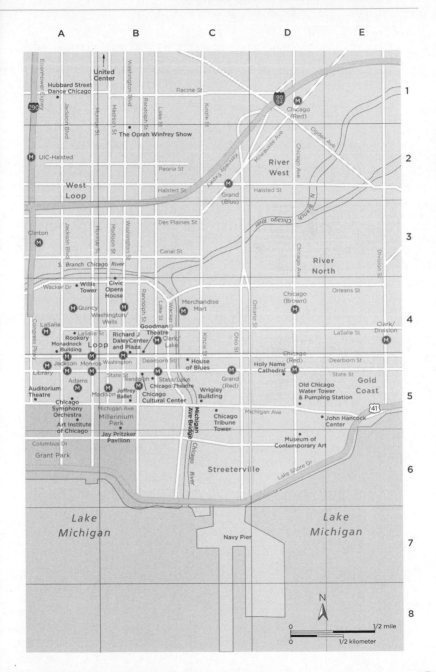

CHICAGO: SOUTH SIDE

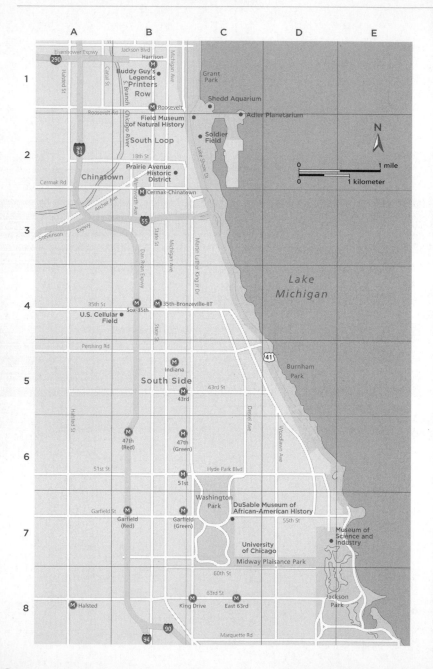

A   B   C   D   E

Eisenhower Expwy
Jackson Blvd
Harrison
Buddy Guy's
Legends
1 Printers
Row
Grant
Park
Roosevelt
Shedd Aquarium
Field Museum
of Natural History
Adler Planetarium
Soldier
Field
2 South Loop
Halsted St
Canal St
S. Branch
Michigan Ave
Chicago River
Roosevelt Rd
18th St
Prairie Avenue
Historic
District
Chinatown
Cermak Rd
Cermak-Chinatown
Wentworth Ave
Archer Ave
3 55
Stevenson Expwy
State St
Michigan Ave
Martin Luther King Jr Dr
Lake Shore Dr
Dan Ryan Expwy

Lake
Michigan

35th St
U.S. Cellular
Field
Sox-35th
35th-Bronzeville-IIT
4
State St
Pershing Rd
41
Burnham
Park
Indiana
5 South Side
43rd St
43rd
47th
(Red)
47th
(Green)
Drexel Ave
Woodlawn Ave
6 51st St
Hyde Park Blvd
51st
Garfield St
Washington
Park
DuSable Museum of
African-American History
Garfield
(Red)
Garfield
(Green)
55th St
Museum of
Science and
Industry
7
University
of Chicago
Midway Plaisance Park
Halsted St
60th St
63rd St
Halsted
King Drive
East 63rd
Jackson
Park
8
90
94
Marquette Rd

N

0   1 mile
0   1 kilometer

CHICAGO: PUBLIC ART WALKING TOUR

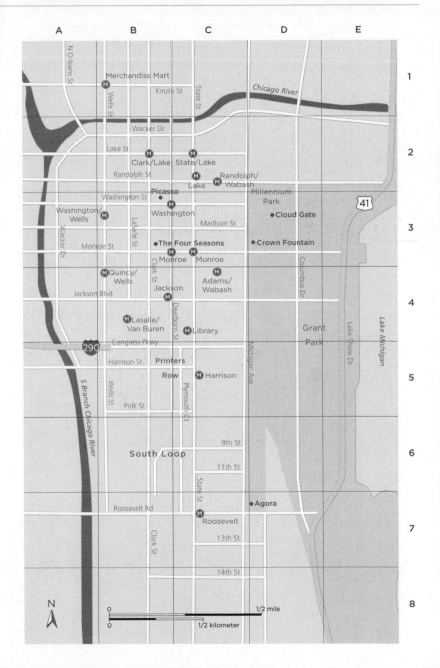

CHICAGO PUBLIC TRANSIT SYSTEM

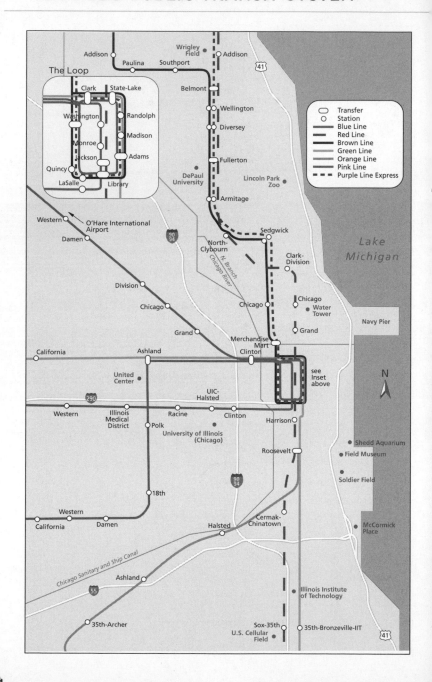

The Loop

Transfer
Station
Blue Line
Red Line
Brown Line
Green Line
Orange Line
Pink Line
Purple Line Express

Lake Michigan

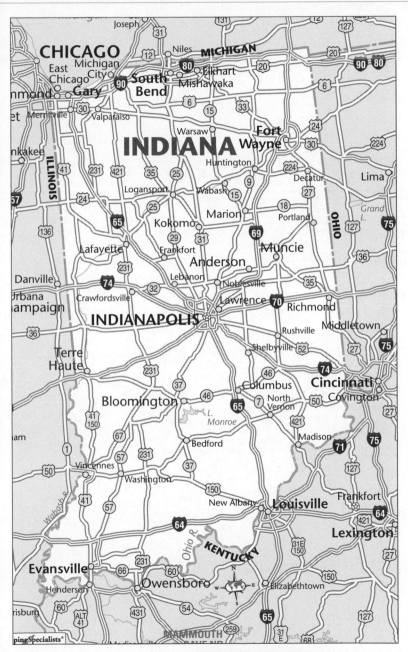

OHIO

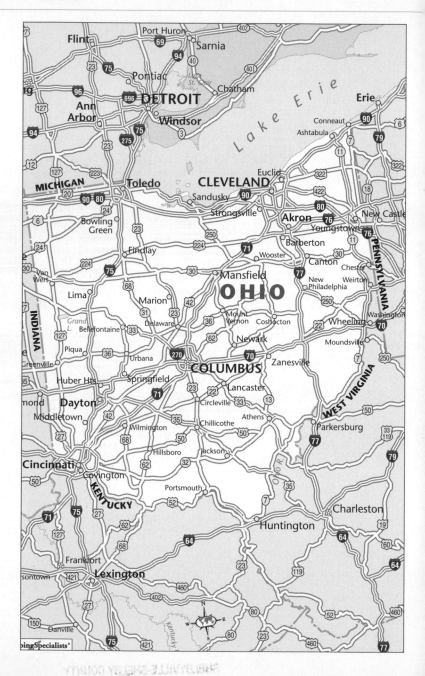